THINKING ABOUT RACE

Second Edition

Naomi Zack
University of Oregon

THOMSON

WADSWORTH

Australia • Canada • Mexico • Singapore • Spain
United Kingdom • United States

Publisher: Holly J. Allen
Philosophy Editor: Steve Wainwright
Assistant Editors: Lee McCracken,
　Anna Lustig
Editorial Assistant: Barbara Hillaker
Technology Project Manager: Julie Aguilar
Marketing Manager: Worth Hawes
Marketing Assistant: Andrew Keay
Advertising Project Manager: Laurel Anderson
Art Director: Maria Epes
Composition Buyer: Ben Schroeter

Print/Media Buyer: Rebecca Cross
Permissions Editor: Kiely Sexton
Production Service: Matrix Productions
Text Designer: Adrian Bosworth
Copy Editor: Patricia Herbst
Cover Designer: Yvo Riezebos
Compositor: International Typesetting
　and Composition
Text and Cover Printer: Malloy
　Lithographing, Inc.

For more information about our products, contact us at:
Thomson Learning Academic Resource Center
1-800-423-0563

For permission to use material from this text or product, submit a request online at
http://www.thomsonrights.com.
Any additional questions about permissions can be submitted by email to thomsonrights@thomson.com

Library of Congress Control Number: 2004110110

ISBN 0-534-53564-X

Thomson Wadsworth
10 Davis Drive
Belmont, CA 94002-3098
USA

Asia
Thomson Learning
5 Shenton Way #01-01
UIC Building
Singapore 068808

Australia/New Zealand
Thomson Learning
102 Dodds Street
Southbank, Victoria 3006
Australia

Canada
Nelson
1120 Birchmount Road
Toronto, Ontario M1K 5G4
Canada

Europe/Middle East/Africa
Thomson Learning
High Holborn House
50/51 Bedford Row
London WC1R 4LR
United Kingdom

Latin America
Thomson Learning
Seneca, 53
Colonia Polanco
11560 Mexico D.F.
Mexico

Spain/Portugal
Paraninfo
Calle Magallanes, 25
28015 Madrid, Spain

To my sons, Alexander Linden Erdmann and Bradford Zack Mahon

WHEN MICHEL FOUCAULT WAS ASKED WHAT WAS HIS CONCEPTION OF A BOOK, HE REPLIED: A TOOL BOX.

—GILLES DELEUZE AND FELIX GUATTARI

CONTENTS

PREFACES AND ACKNOWLEDGMENTS

TO THE SECOND EDITION

It is rare for a philosophy textbook to survive a decade in print these days, especially if the subject is socially relevant. So I am very grateful to Wadsworth for publishing this second edition seven years after the first, and I particularly want to thank my editor, Anna Lustig, for her careful and knowledgeable attention to the project. I am again grateful to Matrix Productions for getting the book through press, particularly to Aaron Downey for expert oversight and to Patricia Herbst for superb copyediting. This update is necessary because much has happened concerning race in the United States since 1997, and as a result, both racial identities and race relations have become more subtle and complicated.

Since the first edition of *Thinking About Race,* I have continued with my scholarly work in the topics that support this textbook. In *Philosophy of Science and Race* I wrote an extensive analysis of the ways in which the contemporary biological sciences fail to support a division of human beings into distinct races. My edited anthology *Women of Color and Philosophy* provided a series of inquiries about philosophy, gender, and race by the field's smallest minority. My anthology edited with Laurie Shrage and Crispin Sartwell, *Race, Class, Gender, and Sexuality: The Big Questions,* provided a comprehensive examination of major questions in contemporary social issues. I have just finished a manuscript titled *Inclusive Feminism: A Third Wave Theory of Women's Commonality,* which attempts to reunite women across differences in race, class, and nationality. I have also participated in numerous conferences throughout the United States, and I have published several more articles about mixed race, anthropological theory, racial categories, and racism.

My family life has also progressed since 1997. Alex, my older son, has begun a career in graphic design; Bradford, my younger son, graduated from Harvard University and is going to begin graduate school in the Psychology Department there this fall. There has also been a big change in my professional life through a move to the Department of Philosophy at the University of Oregon. Race feels different here than in the Northeast. There is less demographic diversity, both on campus and in the surrounding community, and those who work in the fields of race and ethnicity have a sharper sense of urgency.

I continue to learn from my students. As I began final revisions on this book, I used it as introductory material for a graduate seminar on race, PHIL 607. All of the students approached the material with a wealth of experience and mature perspectives, and I thank them for their participation and insights: Tomas J. Hulick Baiza, "Zelda" Teresa Lopez Haro, Maria Cecilia R. Hwang, Diane L. Teeman.

The most specific and direct influences for updating have come from Wadsworth's external reviewers. I am able to thank them all collectively by name (although I do not know who wrote which report, since the reports themselves were anonymous): Elliott R. Barkan, California State University, San Bernardino; J. Angelo Corlett, San Diego State University; Douglas Davidson, Western Michigan University; Sandra L. Dwyer, Georgia State University; Jo-Ann Pilardi, Towson University, Maryland; John Santiago, University of Illinois at Chicago; and Louis E. Schubert, City College of San Francisco.

These reviewers' suggestions, criticism, and underlying support for the book were invaluable to me, and I hope that each will see how I have taken the major portion of their comments to heart.

I have made many, many detailed changes in going over the manuscript, although its length remains about the same. The major changes can be found as follows:

■   Introduction: A more thorough examination of critical thinking at the end of Section B.

■   Chapter 1: Contemporary genetic and biological data on race added to Section B.

■   Year 2000 census data added to statistical discussions throughout the book but especially in the Introduction and Chapters 1, 2, and 3.

■   Chapter 6: Discussion of U.S. Supreme Court rulings in 2003 Michigan cases added.

■   Chapters 9 and 10 updated with references to recent social events and more contemporary media portrayals, as well as consideration of same-sex unions.

■   Updated sources added to the bibliography to reflect recent scholarship (and expanded index reflecting all changes).

There are as well many small stylistic changes and shifts in tone to accommodate the ways in which national and local discourses of race have moved into another century. As before, readers will be my best critics.

NZ
Eugene, OR
June 2004
nzack@uoregon.edu

To the First Edition

This book is meant to be a toolbox for thinking rationally and reasonably about race. It is designed for the college classroom but I hope it will also be useful for high school seniors and juniors and anyone else who wants to calmly reflect, talk, and write about the topics and problems concerning race that confront us at the close of the twentieth century in the United States. The conceptual approach might also serve as a warmup or overview for graduate students and other scholars new to the subject matter.

Peter Adams, philosophy and religion editor at Wadsworth, suggested I write a short textbook on race when he stopped at my office during the fall of 1995. By that time I had already written and edited theoretical books and articles about race, and it was a new idea that some of this scholarship could be a foundation for introductory course material. I had designed a course called *Philosophy and Race* for the Department of Philosophy at the University at Albany but had not yet taught it. So my initial reaction to Peter's suggestion was tentative.

During the spring 1996 semester, my *philosophy and Race* course was scheduled for the following fall. I decided to compile a course reader of reprints, which would be framed by a series of topic analyses. It occurred to me that those analyses could be put together as a book proposal for Wadsworth, and that if the proposal were accepted I could use my lecture notes for the course, as well as my experience in the classroom, to write the book. And that is basically what happened. Wadsworth's external reviewers reacted favorably to the proposal, and the material for the chapters of the book emerged from lectures and class discussions. I told my students that the general idea was to apply philosophical methods of investigation and argument to issues concerning race, and that I intended to learn from their opinions and reflections. My students of PHI 328, *Philosophy and Race,* fall, 1996, helped me understand how to apply basic philosophical tools to race in ways that addressed their present concerns, and I hereby thank them, very warmly, albeit alphabetically: Constance Aker, Cynthia L. Asmus, Eleni D. Athanasiou, Jordan H. Bennett, Michael H. Berendt, Craig A. Bergen, Rachel B. Blatter, Jean-Jacques Cadet, Greg K. Campbell, Hyacinth Chu, Jereme B. Corrado, Jessica M. Costosa, Rebecca A. Curry, Christophe D'Arconte, Charles S. Dixon, Jeremy W. Fibiger, Michael A. Furgang, Joseph A. Gallagher, Mark T. Gorthey, Denis M. Kaye, Kathleen B. Keough, Roland J. Lavigne, Jr., Hwanhee "Mark" Lee, Miamah Jo Richards, Dorey A. Roland, Elizabeth A. Rudolph, Michael C. Schoenbach, Kevin V. Sheehan, Niels Ter Meulen, John P. Urcioli, Frederic K. Vanstrander, Nisse Varghese, Brian M. Vicari, Wendy L. Weidman, and Michael G. Wood.

I have been writing and speaking about many of the subjects addressed in this book since 1991. Faculty and student audience responses to my talks on aspects of the subjects presented in chapters here were an important background contribution as I wrote the manuscript. I am grateful for comments and discussion following my presentations at the University at Albany, Brown University, University of California at Berkeley, Carleton University (Ottawa), Dickinson College, University of Helsinki, Nazareth College, University of Pittsburgh, Rutgers University, Trinity College, Vassar College, and Eastern and Western Division meetings of the American Philosophical Association from 1994 to 1997.

I am very grateful to Laurie Shrage for the care she took in reading the entire prepublication manuscript and in writing comments and suggestions on many, many pages. This close reading for stylistic presentation, scholarship, and conceptual clarity was a supportive and much needed collegial gift, rarely received by academic writers in these times of general overwork. I followed most of her suggestions and the book is better for Laurie being a friend to it, and to me.

I am also grateful to Crispin Sartwell, my valued e-mail friend and colleague, for ongoing discussion about the topics in the book as well as an encouraging reading of Chapter 7.

As always, I have been empowered by the support of my colleagues in the Department of Philosophy at the University at Albany, especially Bob Howell, who while he was Chair expressed his goodwill, and that of other members of the Department, toward me in ways too numerous to document. Thanks, also, in particular, to Tony Ungar for confirming the contradictory logical structure of black and white racial categories, as discussed in Chapter 1.

Wadsworth's four external anonymous reviewers of the penultimate manuscript provided much detailed constructive criticism and suggestions for fine-tuning. The final work is more clear and comprehensive than it would have been without their influence on the last revision. Their comments from feminist, legal, critical thinking, and African American philosophy perspectives led to additional bibliographic sources, additions to the glossary, qualifications in some places, wider claims in others, and altogether more precision.

Thanks also to Merrill Peterson and Terri Froemel at Matrix Productions for getting the manuscript to press. Deborah Meyers made sure that the glossary was complete and references were accurate during copyediting.

My friend Helena Jia Hershel provided ongoing e-mail encouragement and company which made the project much easier to complete on a daily basis.

I want to express appreciation to my older son, Alex, who was always positive about the project during our telephone conversations. Alex and I have had many informative and reinforcing discussions about race over the past five or six years. He is an artist and a writer, now studying film at U.C.L.A., who has lived through many problems concerning racial identity and racism while growing up in Los Angeles.

I am deeply indebted to my younger son, Bradford, who made time out of an overwhelming junior year schedule as a student at the Albany Academy to read and offer suggestions on the penultimate copy of the manuscript. Bradford and I are mutually unsparing when it comes to criticism so when something has his stamp of approval, I know it's okay.

My students and my sons are part of the generation that will have well-formed memories of the twentieth century as they reach full adulthood in the twenty-first. W. E. B. Du Bois' prediction that the main American social problem in the twentieth century would involve race has proved true. It may also hold for the twenty-first century. But it will not hold for the next millennium. This generation of my sons and students is destined to span two millennia. They have the right stuff to do that: speed, strength, skill, talent, ambition, and desire for all of the good things this earth still has to offer. The complaint of some members of my generation that they are not humanitarians and scholars obscures the ease with which these young adults learn what they need to know. As they come into their full powers, their compassion will flower. Some of them will love truth or beauty for its own sake. They will honor us.

A book like this emerges through a social process, as mention of the contributions above indicates. Still, I know it has flaws, gaps, blind spots—those are mine.

Naomi Zack
Albany, NY
October 1997

INTRODUCTION

A. TO THE INSTRUCTOR

This book develops conceptual tools for addressing race in American life and scholarship. It can be used by itself or supplemented with further readings from sources selected by the instructor, chosen by the student, or recommended here. The general ideas presented arise from and are inspired by the vast, multidisciplinary, existing literature on race. For this reason, footnotes keyed into the text would be arbitrary and distracting to the flow of thought the reader is invited to develop. The aim is to enable a forum in which ideas about race are addressed analytically and critically, with dialogue, emphasis, and content provided by the particular thinking context. The general context assumed for this forum is the United States at the beginning of the twenty-first century, though many of the issues may apply to other cultural and national situations, and some are useful for the history of race.

B. TO THE STUDENT

Background

During the 1980s and 1990s, many Americans came to see themselves as "a society divided by race." There are complex political, economic, and social reasons for this image, even though racial divisions are accepted as a natural part of everyday life. The causes of many of these divisions can be found in recent historical changes. American demographics of race, as recorded in the U.S. census, changed dramatically between 1950 and 1990: the percentage of the population listed as *white*[1] decreased from 89 to 80 percent; the percentage listed as *black* increased from 11 to 12 percent; *Native Americans,* Eskimos, and Aleut increased to 1 percent; the category of *"other"* increased from 1 to 4 percent; Asian Americans increased in population from

---

[1] See the glossary for words and phrases in *boldface italic.*

about 1 million to 7 million; 9 percent of Americans were listed as Hispanic (an ethnic category that overlapped with the racial categories). Also between 1950 and 1990, the percentage of women in the workforce increased from 27 to 57. According to the 2000 census, between 1990 and 2000, whites decreased again, to 75 percent, blacks increased to 12.3 percent, Native Americans remained at 1 percent, Asians increased to 10 million or 3.6 percent, and Hispanics or Latinos increased to 12.5 percent. In addition to these increases, over 15 million or 5.5 percent indicated that they were "some other race," and 6.8 million or 2.4 percent identified themselves as members of "two or more races." Also between 1990 and 2000, the percentage of women in the workforce increased to 58, a somewhat misleading figure because at the same time the percentage of men in the workforce decreased from 65 to 64 and the percentage of the total population in the workforce decreased from 74 to 71.

A politically significant part of the white middle class has recently returned to *traditional values* that are not shared by all members of a racially *pluralistic society*. The U.S. economy no longer expands evenly in all sectors. This results in more competition for desirable jobs and educational opportunities. Fiscal *conservatism* in government has led to budget cuts in human services, public education, and other forms of institutional assistance to minority racial groups, women, and the poor. There is an increased awareness of racial differences because most people of color now affirm their distinct racial identities as positive aspects of themselves and their culture. Many whites come in contact with people of color for the first time in schools and workplaces.

The ways in which the United States is divided by race vary according to the race and politics of those concerned. Thus, a difference in race may result in a distinct *perspective* or point of view on racial problems. Examples of contemporary racial divisions include the following. Housing remains segregated. African Americans are disproportionately poor, unemployed, and "in" the criminal justice system. Middle-class African Americans do not think that their status or opportunities are equal to those of middle-class whites. *Neoconservative* intellectuals and academics have claimed that poor African Americans are the cause of their own problems because they are less intelligent than whites or do not value family and work as much. Many Hispanic and Asian immigrants are employed at subsistence wages in industry and agriculture. Native Americans claim that their culture, as well as their land, has been appropriated by the white majority. Many whites believe that *affirmative action* is a form of *reverse discrimination* that unjustly deprives them of opportunities for education and employment. American social life and housing remain segregated by race, and new forms of apparently voluntary segregation have developed in places that it was once assumed would be models of integration, such as college campuses. Many parents, students, teachers, and college professors insist that educational curricula are biased against nonwhites because they perpetuate intellectual traditions that have always been dominated by white men. Others claim that *multiculturalism* undermines standards that must be met for anyone to get an education. Members of *mixed-race* movements are demanding recognition in new racial categories. Old ideologies of *white supremacy* have revived on the fringes of society, and racial hate crimes still occur. The field of *whiteness studies* addresses whiteness as an identity that people create, while a tongue-in-cheek backlash affirms *white-trash* identities. New immigrants must learn this system to survive in American society.

Aims of This Book

Perhaps Americans are not so much divided by race as splintered by it. Race is a topic that few are able to discuss in depth without frustration and anger. The first job of this book is to introduce neutral concepts to racial topics to assist *thinking critically* about race. Thinking critically about race is the same as thinking critically about any other topic. One uses *basic rules of logic* and requires *good evidence* for factual claims. These rules of *logic* largely mirror ordinary intuitions about whether conclusions are justified by their premises. Critical thinking does not require special training but simply an avoidance of contradiction and an awareness of when one statement follows from another and when it does not. In constructing logical arguments or making a persuasive case for an opinion, all of the gaps in reasoning ought to be filled in. The same logical rules one follows in stating one's own views should be used in evaluating what others claim.

What counts as good evidence for factual claims is often a matter of common sense. Scientific claims that have withstood examination and duplication by other scientists, or commonsense claims that are supported by a wide range of ordinary experience, are examples of good evidence. Speculations, personal opinions, emotional reactions, and generalizations drawn from a few examples are not good evidence for claims made about racial groups—or about anything else. Subjective experience and feelings are good evidence only when presented as the view of the person they belong to.

Because race is often an emotionally charged subject, learning to think critically about race is difficult. Sometimes we have to detach from our own perspective and revise cherished beliefs. We need to give reasons for opinions and be prepared to define even ordinary words. Even our identities may be revised. But once such difficulties have been faced, the same critical thinking skills can be applied to other subjects. All critical thinking skills are learned and developed through thinking, reading, writing, and conversation.

Although thinking critically about race does not directly solve racial problems, it can enlarge the area in which people agree to disagree in orderly ways. Of course, race is more than an academic subject. Race is an important part of personal and public daily life. The second job of this book is to encourage the student to bring his or her own racial experience to bear on the academic subject of race. Some readers will want to share their particular experience in discussion and writing; others will want to retain their privacy. Both choices deserve the same degree of respect.

The combination of thinking critically about race as an academic subject, and relating one's own experience to that work, should result in greater understanding of treatments of race in the news media, popular culture, and art. It should also make it easier to understand the opinions of those with different experiences of race. Personal attitudes and opinions may also change in ways that are difficult to predict. Therefore, the third job of this book is to assist the student in developing *principles,* or general moral rules for behavior, and *strategies,* or ways of achieving goals, for dealing with race in daily life.

Structure of the Book

The book is divided into eleven chapters and a conclusion, which represent areas of current scholarly and practical concern about race. At the opening of each chapter is a thought exercise. The chapters progress cumulatively and discussions in later chapters rely on earlier analyses. Each chapter begins with an introduction and overview of the topics covered. Then the topics are *analyzed*—that is, they are broken down into their simplest concepts and those concepts are related to one another. The chapters conclude with questions for discussion, reflection, and essay writing, and recommendations for further reading. The recommended readings are meant to provide content for the issues raised in the chapter sections, but the reader is also expected to find and apply additional or alternative material from other study and life experiences. There is a vast array of scholarly publication about race in philosophy, history, literature, sociology, psychology, anthropology, feminism, fields of specific racial and ethnic studies, and other sources including print media, theater, art, movies, music, TV, and pop fiction. It is hoped that the tools developed while working with this book will help the reader sort out the parts of that material that interest him or her.

A Personal Note

As your author, I should tell you that I am a philosopher, a woman, and a mixed-race American, probably in that order. While I've tried to present aspects of race here with as much ordinary logic and good evidence as I can muster, the reader should rely on his or her own careful judgment and be encouraged to disagree with the text as necessary.

Because black-white race relations and black *liberation* have been the most problematic aspects of race in American history, there is often more in this book about African American perspectives than about white, Asian, or Native American. However, I have tried to address American racial differences broadly and inclusively. I hope that students who feel that their racial or ethnic group and its unique problems have not been satisfactorily represented will make their views known in class assignments and discussion. I also hope that such underrepresented students will take the time to e-mail me so that I can take your concerns into account in the next edition.

Naomi Zack
Professor of Philosophy
Philosophy Department
1295 University of Oregon
Eugene, OR 97403
e-mail:nzack@uoregon.edu

C. DISCUSSION QUESTIONS

1. Make as long a list as you can of additional current problems with race.

2. Choose one or two positions on race, state why you agree with them, or argue against them.

3. Describe the last time you felt angry or frustrated about a racial issue. Explain what you were thinking and what you think the other party was thinking.

4. Describe several ordinary rules of logic that are important for thoughtful discussion. Explain how they apply to discussions about racial issues.

5. Give examples of good evidence in several racial contexts.

D. RECOMMENDED READING[2]

Statistical information on race can be found in varied U.S. Census Bureau reports at www.census.gov. Cornel West, in *Race Matters*, considers black-white racial divisions from the position of being black. Contemporary philosophers discuss the situations of poor urban blacks in Bill E. Lawson, ed., *The Underclass Questions*. Glenn C. Loury offers an economic analysis of black disadvantage in *The Anatomy of Racial Inequality*. Dinesh D'Souza argues that American black cultural values are the source of black problems in *The End of Racism*. In *Blood in the Face*, James Ridgeway chronicles recent white supremacist ideology. For analysis of racial whiteness as a social and political identity, see Michael Omi and Howard Winant, *Racial Formation in the United States: From the 1960s to the 1980s*. The debate about affirmative action is closely analyzed by Gertrude Ezorsky in *Racism and Justice*. For a recent debate, see Carl Cohen and James P. Sterba, *Affirmative Action and Racial Preferences: A Debate*. M. A. Jaimes, ed., presents a range of Native American political positions in *The State of Native America*. See also Anne Schulherr Waters, ed., *American Indian Thought*. Problems faced by contemporary Asian Americans are described and discussed in separate contributions from Karen Hossfeld, Bonnie Thornton Dill, and Nazli Kibria in Maxine Baca Zinn and Bonnie Thornton Dill, eds., *Women of Color in U.S. Society*. Issues of American mixed-race identities are explored in Naomi Zack, ed., *American Mixed Race: The Culture of Microdiversity*. The basic rules of logic and the importance of evidence in critical thinking can be found in introductory logic textbooks, such as Irving M. Copi's *Introduction to Logic,* as well as in textbooks on informal logic, such as *Understanding Arguments* by Robert J. Fogelin. See also Patrick J. Hurley and Joseph P. DeMarco, *Learning Fallacies and Arguments*.

---

[2] Sources listed in the Recommended Reading sections of chapters are fully cited in the bibliography at the end of the book.

CHAPTER 1

WHAT IS RACE?

Y ou are a college freshman assigned to a dorm. When you meet your roommate for the first time, there is a half-second pause before you introduce yourselves. In that half-second, each of you perceives that the other is a different race. How did you both know that? What does it mean to say that someone belongs to this or that race?

INTRODUCTION

We take *race* for granted in the United States, and someone's race may be the first thing you notice about a stranger. We know that there are serious "racial tensions" and "racial problems" in our society. If pressed, what most of us understand by those expressions is that people of different races react to one another with hostility and that members of each race have problems that are the result of being members of their race. We do not usually think that there is anything wrong with the ways in which people are sorted into races—that is, with the *criteria* for membership in different races—because we think that a person's race is obvious from looking at him or her. We do not question the *naturalness* of racial differences or the very existence of races. We go on about our business as though there always have been human races and there always will be. We assume that the physical differences that make up the different races have always been the same and will never change. We believe that races are a fact of human life and that all of the problems with race concern *race relations.*

The truth is that the word *race* and the idea the word stands for have meant very different things throughout Western European and American history. Section A is an analysis of some of those different historical meanings. The core meaning of race at present would seem to be distinctive biological types of human beings that can be studied by scientists. This suggests that scientists must have an idea of race that could give our ordinary thinking about race a factual basis. But the biological sciences do not have useful or verified concepts of race at this time, and there is no reason to believe that they ever will. In Section B, the problems with race in the biological sciences are analyzed. Despite the lack of a physical, scientific foundation, categories of race remain deeply embedded in common sense and social reality. Section C analyzes the definitions of black, white, Indian, and Asian race that have been in use in American society since about 1900, and then offers some observations about broad cultural ideas of race.

A. THE HISTORY OF THE CONCEPT OF RACE

A *word* is a sign or sound that stands for something else, such as a thing that exists outside of the mind, an image in the mind, or a *concept.* A concept is an idea or the meaning of a word. Concepts change over time and these changes depend on changes in the world. Words may be spelled and pronounced the same from one century to the next, or they may look and sound different. In either case, the same concepts can sometimes be traced. In translations from different languages, a word may look and sound the same yet stand for a different concept, or look and sound different but stand for the same concept. Throughout European history, until the eighteenth and nineteenth centuries, the word *race* (and its synonyms and the words meaning "race" in different languages) meant family or national group. In ancient Greece and Rome, a person's race was the group to which he or she belonged, associated with an ancestral place and culture. During the Middle Ages, a person's race was literally his or her family and ancestors, in the sense of a *line,* which was an English synonym for *race.* By the seventeenth century, the start of the modern period in which nation-states began to emerge, the word *race* was associated with cultures and civilizations in particular geographic areas. Through the eighteenth century, although physical differences such as the darker skin hues of Africans were associated with race, racial divisions were based on differences in religion and cultural tradition rather than on human biology. Anthropology was the first biological science of race, and nineteenth-century anthropologists assumed that there were human races. Authorities for that early assumption were the philosophers David Hume (1711–1776), and Immanuel Kant (1724–1804), who thought that the existence of human races was self-evident. The modern science of biology, with systematic methods for dividing living things into genus, species, and subspecies, was not developed until the late eighteenth and early nineteenth centuries.

By the second half of the nineteenth century, *race* came to mean a distinct biological group of human beings who were not all members of the same family but shared inherited physical and cultural traits that were different from those shared within other races. This meaning of *race* was constructed by American anthropologists during slavery and segregation. The claims of these scientists of race were used as justifications for black chattel slavery and white social and economic dominance over Negroes. Based on reports of *empirical* findings that were often incomplete or even falsified, hierarchies of human races were postulated. Always, the black race was on the bottom and the white race on the top, with

Asians and Indians in the middle. Inherited *racial essences* were posited as the cause of superior or inferior intellectual, aesthetic, spiritual, and moral qualities. This concept of race was more *abstract* than the older family line concept, because race was believed to be the cause of characteristics that were inherited through family descent. It was also more *general* because each of the main racial groups included many family lines within them. The notion of essence did not allow for mixed essences; in cases of racial mixture it was assumed that offspring inherited the essence of the hierarchically "inferior" race. During the early twentieth century, social scientists began to realize that differences in human culture, behavior, intellect, morality, and spirituality were the result of environment, education, and history rather than biology. The anthropologist Franz Boas and his students Claude Lévi-Strauss, Margaret Mead, Ruth Benedict, Melville Herskovitz, and Alfred Kroeber established the importance of history and culture as the source of human differences. As a result, the concept of race shrank to mean biological differences only. To this day, as a factual basis for individual and group identification, *race* means inheritable physical characteristics only.

B. THE PROBLEMS WITH RACE IN SCIENCE

If you ask adult Americans what race is, you might be told that races are different *breeds* of human beings and that there are three of them: Negro, Caucasian, and Mongoloid, or black, white, and Asian. The U.S. census and most public institutions gather information and keep records based on the racial categories of black, white, Asian or Pacific Islander and American Indian or Alaska Native. In recent decades, everyone who has applied to be a student or an employee in a large institution has been required to indicate his or her race and whether he or she is of *Hispanic* or non-Hispanic *ethnicity.*

The Hispanic ethnic category first appeared in the 1980 U.S. census. In the 2000 census, it became "Spanish/Hispanic/Latino," a category that cuts across all of the racial categories. People who are *biracial* or *multiracial* were frustrated by the bureaucratic system of racial classification that required checking one race only or *identifying* as *"other."* The 2000 U.S. census allowed respondents to check all races that applied to them, and some institutions permit respondents to write in their racial self-identifications.

Most Americans believe that the information requested on such forms has a factual basis apart from its interest to officials. The 1990 U.S. census recorded the following data for a population of 249 million: 200 million whites; 30 million blacks; 7 million Asians and Pacific Islanders; 2 million Native Americans, Eskimos, and Aleut; 10 million "other." Additionally, there were 22 million Hispanics. In the 2000 census, for a population of 281 million, these were the figures: 211 million whites; 35 million blacks; 10 million Asians and Pacific Islanders; 2 million Native Americans and Alaska Natives; 15 million who were "some other race"; 7 million who were two or more races. Also, there were 35 million Hispanics in 2000. These figures are important. They are used by government for *entitlement* programs for nonwhite minority groups and for information about the population by business and educational institutions. They are also a source for national, group, and individual self-images. Individuals believe that their types of skin color, hair texture, facial features, and bone structure are the results of the race to which they belong. And the race to which you belong, even if it is that cryptic category of "other," has a place on the national map of races.

If it were true that being black, white, Asian, or Indian caused human beings to have the types of physical traits they do, then there ought to be some physical marker for race, apart from those traits, that scientists could identify. Otherwise, there is nothing general about a race that could cause specific physical traits in individuals. However, neither biologists, nor anthropologists, nor physiologists, nor geneticists, nor any of the other scientists who have studied physical race have ever identified any general racial characteristics shared by all members of any particular race. No genes or other hereditary factors are shared by every member of any of the main racial groups. In this sense, race provides an interesting contrast to biological sex. There are chromosomal markers, *XY* and *XX*, for male and female biological sex. Given the presence of XY(male) or XX (female), the presence of specific sexual traits, such as having testicles or ovaries, can be predicted. But there is nothing analogous for race. When scientists study physical traits or diseases that are more prevalent in people of some races, they depend on social definitions of race in order to pick out the members of the race they are studying. And even if an individual belongs to a race with a high incidence of a certain disease, that person must be tested, diagnosed, and treated on a physical basis that has nothing to do with race—because there is no general race factor for any race.

The colloquial association of "blood" with race, as in the expressions "She has black blood" or "He has some Indian blood," is no more than a metaphor left over from the nineteenth-century pseudosciences of race. The four major human blood groups were identified in the early 1900s, and it has been known since then that these blood types do not correspond to membership in races. There is some correspondence over the surface of the globe between geographical areas and blood types, but this is no more than a loose statistical association. There are thirty-two human blood-type systems (including the ABO typology used for transfusions), and they are all inherited in complex ways that do not correspond to races. We do think about the main racial groups as having originated in specific continental areas, such as Caucasians from northern Europe, Negroes from Africa, Asians from Asia, and Indians from the Americas. When existing populations are tracked back to their ancestral locations, the genetic material that is compared is mitochondrial DNA. Mt DNA is inherited from mothers only, and it has no connection with physical traits of any kind because it does not "code for," or produce, proteins. Therefore, tracing racial origins through Mt DNA does not trace the traits that society considers to be racial. Some anthropologists even believe that the original African population of modern humans that existed from 100,000 to 150,000 years ago had what we would call white skin and was hirsute. Also, human populations have been in constant movement all over the globe for millions of years. And the ordinary idea of race purports to tell us something about people as they are now, not about where their ancestors may have lived at some time in the past. Most anthropologists now believe that modern human beings originated in Africa; a smaller number think that modern humans originated on every continent but then interbred. Neither hypothesis supports a taxonomy of human races.

Racial membership has been culturally associated with some inherited physical characteristics, such as skin color and types of facial features, but these traits are no different in principle from other physical traits that have no racial significance, such as height. Moreover, the traits that are considered racial traits do not all get inherited together for any race but are subject to dispersal and recombination each time a child is conceived. Children resemble their parents if their parents resemble each other, but there are always exceptions.

Not only is there no general characteristic that determines racial membership, but the specific traits of skin color, hair texture, and bone structure vary more within any of the main racial groups than they do between any two racial groups. Indeed, scientists now speak of *populations* when referring to groups that the layperson would call races. Such populations may share more of some inherited physical traits than other populations. But the distribution of these traits within the membership of a population changes over generations, and the human physical trait boundaries between populations cannot be sharply drawn. Furthermore, there is no consensus on how many human populations exist, and figures have varied from five to several to hundreds of thousands. Even when the physical traits that are considered racial traits are compared within the general human population, they represent very small variations in genetic material, on the order of one ten-thousandth of all human genetic material. The scientists who mapped the first sequences of the human genome (all 30,000–40,000 genes in our species) did not once mention "race" in their reports. Indeed, several authorities remarked that despite an existing population of over 6 billion, human beings have the genetic variation of a population of 10,000.

In short, in 2004–2005 there is no scientific basis for our idea of race as a taxonomy of human biological difference. Race as something general about a person or a group is a social overlay on actual physical traits. This is not to deny that people perceive what they think are racial traits or that race has a powerful social reality. But it means that what we think of as race is solely a matter of convention and imagination. We follow a convention of imagining the existence of races and sorting people into these imaginary divisions. Once this realization of the imaginary nature of race sinks in, the human differences that are attributed to race have to be explained and understood in other terms. The physical differences of skin, hair, and bone that have been associated with race are of course inherited like other physical traits, although they are not otherwise important in terms of biological functions. However, many of the intellectual and moral differences that have been attributed to race are very important in terms of social status and individual well-being, and it is those alleged differences that require careful study.

C. THE CULTURAL MEANINGS OF RACE

Even though race does not have the biological foundation it is assumed to have in common sense, not only is race very important in the United States but most adult Americans know what race they are and how to sort other people into their appropriate races. The question is, how do they—we—do that if there is greater physical variation within races than between races? Generally, people rely on the race of their close family members as a source of their own racial identity. And they rely on physical appearance for classifying others. This asymmetry between subjective and external racial identity is problematic when the two do not coincide. Still, we have fairly distinct images, in our minds and presented to us through the mass media, of how blacks, whites, Asians, and Indians are "supposed" to look. We expect people of our own and different races to conform to these images, and most of the time they seem to do so. However, the images or stereotypes of racial appearance have varied historically and geographically in the United States, and they do not work for classifying people who do not look "typical."

When physical appearance is ambiguous or atypical, the race of kin, of parents and other forebears, is the determining factor for racial classification. This family-inheritance aspect of race is also at work in determining the race of people whose appearance is racially "clear." It's just that if someone looks black and has black kin, or looks white and has white kin, there need be no explicit reference to the race of his or her ancestors. The ambiguous cases draw out the formal basis that underlines all racial classification. The formal basis for black and white racial identity amounts to this:

> **Black:** Λ person is black if he or she has a black ancestor anywhere in family history. This is known as the ***one-drop rule*** of black classification because it is based on a myth that one drop of "black blood" is sufficient to determine racial blackness. The one-drop rule is a legacy of nineteenth-century ideas of racial essences that results in ***hypodescent*** for racial mixture. A social system of hypodescent for racial mixture requires that offspring have the race of the parent with the lower racial status. Thus, Americans with both white and black ancestry are officially classified as black and often encouraged to identify as black in personal and social contexts.

> **White:** A person is white if he or she has no black ancestry anywhere in family history. This means that in order to be white, a person has to be purely white. This is a condition impossible to prove because it would be ***proving a negative,*** in this case the absence of black ancestors. Before about 1900, definitions of whiteness were less restricted in some states because definitions of blackness rested on having one black grandparent, great-grandparent, or great-great-grandparent. This meant that someone could be white if he or she had a black ancestor one generation back from the generation in which a black ancestor would result in being black. (In Virginia, where one black grandparent determined blackness, someone with one black great-grandparent and no known black ancestry more recent than that would have been classified as white.) However, social practices were often more strict about white purity.

The formal one-drop rule definitions of black and white race posit those two races as ***logical contradictories*** of one another. This entails that everyone is either black or white and that no one is both. However, it has been acknowledged since at least the beginning of the nineteenth century that other races besides black and white exist, so black and white cannot be logical contradictories. Therefore, the formal definitions are misleading, if not actually false.

Like the definitions of black and white, American cultural definitions of Asian and Indian rely on physical appearance and the race of ancestors. Indigenous American Indian cultures did not have biological concepts of race, and rules for tribal membership allowed for adoption into tribes other than those to which one or both biological parents belonged. However, because American Indians have entitlements based on treaty law, the U.S. federal government has sometimes imposed requirements for *blood quanta* of at least 50 percent ancestry from one tribe in order to be classified as an Indian. As a result of this policy, and due to loyalty to traditional cultural identities, many American Indian tribes have developed their own criteria for *full bloods,* some more strict than the government's, some less. Indian identity is further constrained for those descended from tribes never recognized by the U.S. government, tribes classified as "terminated," or tribes from Canada or Latin America.

Asian Americans have been present in the United States since the mid-nineteenth century. Since that time, new immigrants have been sources of cheap labor, and those born here have met with varied barriers to success. However, Asian Americans have not been as visible as American blacks or American Indians in *liberatory* literary and activist traditions that resist dominance by the white majority. At this time, Asian American groups include Cambodian, Chinese, Japanese, Filipino, Hmong and Laotian, East Indian, Korean, Pacific Islander, Thai, and Vietnamese. The differences in appearance, culture, language, and ancestral origins among Asian American groups often make it difficult for their members to accept a common racial designation.

Despite the formal one-drop rule definitions of American blackness and whiteness, in reality there is considerable racial mixture in this country. Only a minority of American Indians can prove they are full bloods; half of all Asian Americans marry non-Asians; approximately 6 percent of all whites have some black ancestry; approximately 90 percent of American blacks have nonblack ancestry; and the Hispanic population has included wide racial variations of black, white, and Indian for hundreds of years. Still, few Americans choose to identify as mixed race, and the idea of mixed race as a positive identity is relatively new. That Americans still use a system of three or four main races despite these commonly known facts about mixed race suggests that the false nineteenth-century biological theory of racial essences is deeply embedded in "*folk* wisdom," or that Americans suspend their rational disbeliefs about this theory for *pragmatic* reasons, or both.

Where the false nineteenth-century biological theory of racial essences is still believed, it is appropriate to refer to the scientific evidence against it, or rather to the lack of scientific evidence for it. Many people continue to believe that there is a scientific basis for racial divisions, and the lack of this basis in itself makes their ideas about race false.

Pragmatic reasons for believing in racial categories have always been fairly obvious from the standpoint of the dominant group. Black slavery was accepted by the framers of the U.S. Constitution at a time when it was believed that all human beings had natural rights to freedom. It was written into the Constitution that three-fifths of the slave population would be included in the headcount that determined how many representatives each state would send to the House of Representatives. In effect, each black slave was counted as three-fifths of a person. One way to justify slavery was to insist that blacks were inferior or incomplete human beings. Slavery, segregation, and other forms of injustice against blacks benefited whites economically, politically, and socially at the expense of blacks. Beliefs in natural human differences based on race were used to *rationalize* unjust treatment from motives of self-interest that could not otherwise be admitted or defended. The systematic theft of American Indian land and the destruction of native cultures, as well as the exploitation of the cheap labor of Asian immigrants, were similarly rationalized by myths of white racial superiority.

However, there is another side to this crude pragmatic coin of racial categorization. Nonwhite Americans who have been categorized in biological racial terms have found it useful to use their categories as *identities* from which to protest and resist injustice based on race. Nineteenth-century pseudoscience falsely connected unsubstantiated ideas of biological race with ideas of less advanced or degenerate inherited cultural traits and practices. Speculation was substituted for empirical methodology, and connections were made between biology and culture that had no empirical or logical justification. There was no biological foundation even for ideas of biological race. But the groups thus racialized have included positive and valued aspects of their cultures as part of their racial identities. Indeed, what black Americans often mean by the word *race* is a shared history of survival and struggle. American Indians, when they identify as *full bloods,* often use the racial classification to indicate loyalty to traditional Indian religious beliefs and ways of living, although identities based on *indigenism* are independent of Euro-American classifications. Asian Americans also have group and individual interests in preserving traditional lifestyles and religions, although they have less often presented themselves as racially distinct on that basis.

The pragmatic importance of racial identification, for all groups, also derives from an association of racial identity with family relations. Almost all human beings claim to value their family members and their family relationships. The false biological concept of race was attached to real, physical, inherited traits. These physical inherited traits are anchored in family descent, which is also real.

The real and fulfilling, political, cultural, and familial associations with racial classification and belonging suggest that not all the connotations and associations of race are ungrounded or humanly diminishing. Therefore, care and skill must be used in dissolving the ignorant and unjust aspects of racial classification. The important question to consider and reconsider is this: do differences among human groups require a *taxonomy* or classification scheme that creates the kind of strong divisions associated with the idea of race in the false biological sense?

D. DISCUSSION QUESTIONS

1. What are the scientific problems with race, and how are they surprising?

2. What difference, if any, does the lack of a scientific foundation for race make in how you think about race?

3. Suppose that next year, all redheaded people will be defined as a separate race and there will be laws against their intermarriage with those of different hair color. Could redheads eventually become a race?

4. Do the folk definitions of black and white make sense to you? Why or why not?

5. Given the varied history of race and the problems with race in the biological sciences, how would you explain what race is to a seven-year-old?

E. RECOMMENDED READING

For an account of the meaning of the word *race* in the ancient world, see M. I. Finley, *Ancient Slavery and Modern Ideology*. A discussion of early modern philosophic ideas of race can be found in Naomi Zack, *Bachelors of Science: Seventeenth Century Identity, Then and Now*, chapter 12. Mark Twain's *The Tragedy of Pudd'nhead Wilson* depicts a clash between the idea of race as biological and the experience of race as cultural in nineteenth-century America. Stephen Jay Gould, in *The Mismeasure of Man*, documents the errors and fraud in nineteenth-century scientific studies of race. On Franz Boas's pivotal work that disproved white superiority in science, see Claudia Roth Pierpont's "The Measure of America." Nancy Leys Stepan compares the mismeasure of race to false ideas of female gender in "Race and Gender: The Role of Analogy in Science," in David Theo Goldberg, ed., *Anatomy of Racism*. See also Stepan's *The Idea of Race in Science: Great Britain, 1800–1950*. Nineteenth-century myths of race are further discussed in William Stanton's *The Leopard's Spots: Scientific Attitudes Toward Race in America, 1819–59*. See Derrick Bell's *And We Are Not Saved: The Elusive Quest for Racial Justice*, chapter 1, for discussion of the "three-fifths person" status of black slaves in the U.S. Constitution as it was originally framed.

Analyses of the scientific emptiness of race are offered in K. Anthony Appiah, *In My Father's House*, and "Race, Culture, Identity," in K. Anthony Appiah and Amy Gutman, *Color Consciousness: The Political Morality of Race;* Nancy Holmstrom, "Race, Gender and Human Nature," in Naomi Zack, ed., *RACE/SEX: Their Sameness, Difference and Interplay;* Richard C. Lewontin, Steven Rose, and Leon J. Kamin, *Not in Our Genes;* and Naomi Zack, *Race and Mixed Race*, chapter 2, and "Race and Philosophic Meaning," in Naomi Zack, ed., *RACE/SEX*. See also Naomi Zack, *Philosophy of Science and Race*; Daniel G. Blackburn, "Why Race Is Not a Biological Concept"; and Joseph L. Graves, *The Emperor's New Clothes*. There are classic articles on the separation of ideas of biological race from ideas of culture in *Race, Science and Society*, edited by Leo Kuper. On the skin color of the original African population, see Nina Jablonski and George Chaplin, "The Evolution of Human Skin Coloration." On the human genome, see International Human Genome Sequencing Consortium, "Initial Sequencing and Analysis of the Human Genome," and Natalie Angier, "Do Races Really Matter?" As well, view the 2003 PBS documentary *Race: The Power of an Illusion, Part I* (2003).

R. Fred Wacker documents the changing meaning of race in American social science in *Ethnicity, Pluralism and Race*. The history of the American one-drop rule is presented in Joel Williamson's *New People* and F. James Davis's *Who Is Black?*

Terry P. Wilson documents American Indian racial criteria in "Blood Quantum: Native American Mixed Bloods," in Maria P. P. Root, ed., *Racially Mixed People in America.* The role of appearance for racial classification is discussed by J. Angelo Corlett in "Parallels of Ethnicity and Gender," in Naomi Zack, ed., *RACE/SEX.* Mariella Squire-Hakey examines American Indian experience of the importance of appearance for American Indian classification in "Yankee Imperialism and Imperialist Nostalgia," in Naomi Zack, ed., *American Mixed Race: The Culture of Microdiversity.* Carlos Fernández compares North and South American concepts of race based on European Protestant versus Roman Catholic attitudes toward foreigners, in "La Raza and the Melting Pot," in Maria P. P. Root, ed., *Racially Mixed People in America.*

Positive constructions of racial identity occupy most of the liberatory literature on race. In particular, see Leonard Harris, ed., *The Philosophy of Alain Locke,* and John Langston Gwaltney's documentation of core black identities in *Drylongso: A Self-Portrait of Black America.* Primary sources of writings in black liberation are presented in Joanne Grant's *Black Protest: History, Documents and Analyses, 1619–Present.* See also Tommy Lott, *The Invention of Race.*

Literary reflections on Asian and American Indian experiences of difference are Maxine Hong Kingston's memoir of Chinese American identity in *Woman Warrior,* and the collected stories of Native American cultural identities in Craig Lesley, ed., *Talking Leaves: Contemporary Native American Short Stories.* On contemporary Native American liberation philosophies and activism, see Ward Churchill, *Indians Are Us?* and Ward Churchill, ed., *From a Native Son: Selected Essays on Indigenism, 1985–1995,* and Ernest L. Schusky, *The Right to Be Indian.* See also the essays in Anne Schulherr Walters, ed., *American Indian Thought: Philosophical Essays.* The possibility of united Asian American identity is explored by Yen Le Espiritu in *Asian American Panethnicity: Bridging Institutions and Identities.* The relatively recent focus on political empowerment among Asian Americans is presented in a microcosm by the Illinois Advisory Committee to the United States Commission on Civil Rights in *Civil Rights Issues Facing Asian Americans in Metropolitan Chicago.* See also the PBS documentary *Searching for Asian America* (2004).

On racial integration among the U.S. professoriate, see Robin Wilson, "A Kinder Less Ambitious Professoriate." On the history of ideas of race, see Emmanvel Eze, ed., *Race and the Enlightenment* and Charles Mills, *The Racial Contract.*

CHAPTER 2

THE SOCIAL REALITY OF RACE

Y ou know the stereotypes and insulting names associated with members of the race to which you belong. When someone of your race jokingly applies them to you, you may not like it but you don't get angry. The effect is different if the source is someone of a different race. Why is that?

INTRODUCTION

We've seen in Chapter 1 that the notion of human races has no foundation in physical science. In contemporary society, especially in educated or "enlightened" subcultures, there is broad agreement that the findings of the physical sciences are the most reliable source of information about physical reality. To the extent that the word *race* means something proved to exist by science, the word has no meaning.

However, if you told most people that race is not real, you would get a blank stare. Most Americans believe that race is biologically real, and there is much invested in that belief throughout American culture, now and going back several hundred years. This false belief in the scientific reality of race, and action based on that belief, give race a ***social reality.*** If the social reality of race were not as powerful as it is, the simple realization of its lack of a biological foundation would justify refusing to think or talk about race at all. We might begin putting the general word *race* and its specific types, such as *black, white,* and *Asian,* in quotation marks. However, those gestures would have no impact on the social reality of race unless everyone performed them. In order to think about race, we have to think about the social reality of race. At the same time, we need to keep in mind that there is no scientific basis for racial divisions.

Although Americans believe that biological races exist, many also insist that racial differences are not important. Often, they mean by this that racial difference *ought* not to make a difference in how people are rewarded and punished for what they do or are valued as human beings. Section A offers some clarification of the differences between morally *egalitarian* positions on racial difference. These *normative* positions describe how things should be, rather than how they are. Some *descriptive* positions on the social reality of race are examined in Section B. These positions differ depending on who is doing the describing. Therefore, it might be that the only way to reconcile these positions is to eliminate the idea of race. However, tigers once ridden must be dismounted with care, and Section C addresses the practical problems with an *eliminative* position on race.

A. NORMATIVE POSITIONS ON THE SOCIAL REALITY OF RACE

Anyone who believes in the biological reality of races is a *racialist.* A racialist might think that the differences between races are important or unimportant as human traits. A racialist who thinks that racial differences are unimportant is unlikely to be a *racist. Racism* is the subject of Chapter 5, but we should note here that it involves ill will or harmful action toward people because of their race. A racialist who thinks that human differences due to race are important might or might not be a racist.

Some racialists are *racial determinists.* They believe that as a result of belonging to a biological race, individuals have certain nonracial traits. These traits generally correspond to the aptitudes and skills, virtues and vices, that nineteenth-century hierarchical theories associated with the different races, ranking the white race highest. Historical racial rankings located nonwhites as "inferior" to whites. However, most Americans now accept that human talents and morality are evenly distributed across and within all races. Most racialists now acknowledge that the inheritance of biological race is not accompanied by the inheritance of predetermined sets of aptitudes and skills or virtues and vices. Either racial determinism is false, or it is the normative position that people of different races *ought to have* different nonracial traits—a position that most Americans would now consider racist.

Let's assume that a racialist need not be a racist. Indeed, many nonracist American racialists are *egalitarians.* They believe that racial differences in themselves do not have an effect on fundamental human worth and that therefore racial differences ought not to affect how people are treated by others, how they regard themselves, or how well they do in society. But even a position of racial equality based on universal human equality, or *universalism,* is a description not of how things are but of how they ought to be. This is because it is often very difficult to preserve universal human equality in the face of perceived racial differences. The egalitarian might insist that, despite what happens to people on the basis of racial difference, they are nevertheless equal as people. Such insistence might be based on an abstract, universal idea of a core human being that is present in everyone regardless of race. The idea of this kind of equality would appeal to many, especially those who are religious. But inequalities based on racial difference do not affect core human equality, so it is difficult to see how a belief in core equality could lead to social change. Those who unjustly treat people differently based on race may be prepared to ignore core human equality. The assertion of universal core human equality is somewhat irrelevant to practical inequalities based on race, without the insistence that people of different races be treated equally because of their core humanity. Also, many nonwhites now insist that they be treated equally, not as core humans but as blacks, Asians, Indians, and so forth.

A racialist egalitarian might have a more concrete idea of what a human being is, so that the universal human being is not a core human being without racial traits but a concrete human being who is always a member of some distinct race. In that case, the egalitarian would have to assert that the nonracial differences associated with particular races, such as social or economic status, ought not to exist. The egalitarian would then be committed to changes in the social reality of race that would result in equality. Before we can consider what kind of changes might be necessary to bring about equality in society where there is now inequality based on racial difference, we need to be able to describe the social reality of race.

B. DESCRIPTIVE POSITIONS ON THE SOCIAL REALITY OF RACE

The social reality of race is made up of the ways in which human life differs within the same culture, at the same historical time, according to racial classification. The way that members of racial groups perceive their own and other races is also part of the social reality of race. This reality is more than a matter of difference in the sense of variety, because some racial groups are dominant over others. Dominant groups have more of the goods of society such as money, material possessions, security (including personal safety), health care, education, fulfilling employment, leisure time, and social status. As a result, members of dominant racial groups have more power in society, and the recognition of this power results in their greater *authority.* In the United States the dominant racial group has always been white, and whites generally have more authority than nonwhites.

The ways in which the social reality of race is described depend on the racial perspective of the person doing the describing. General descriptions from the perspectives of whites, blacks, Indians, and Asians seem to unfold along the following lines. Although Hispanics are officially not a race but an ethnic group, many claim that the kinds of discrimination, exclusion, and exploitation they experience is no different from racial oppression.

Most American whites are racialists, but race is not the most important social factor in their daily experience. Race is not a problem for most whites in terms of a history of being dominated or as a present barrier to the development of their aptitudes and the attainment of social goods. From a white perspective, the social reality of race could be described as an element in human interaction that involves the problems faced by nonwhite minorities and the problems faced by whites in dealing with nonwhite minorities. Since whites are still the majority as well as the dominant group, and much of American life is still segregated by race, many whites seem to be unaffected by race. They can grow up, get an education, work, choose companions and spouses, raise families, buy houses, get medical care, go on vacation, retire, and die, without having anything important to contend with on the grounds of race. Among themselves, whites need not be aware of themselves in racial terms at all. So long as all the important people in their lives are white, they have no need to think of themselves in terms of race. In this sense for whites, among whites, race might as well not exist. Nonwhites, by contrast, are often aware of their race on a daily basis, and many would consider it a privilege to be unaware of one's race.

While most American whites acknowledge that nonwhites have been badly treated in the past, they often claim that American society is presently egalitarian and that now justice exists for nonwhites. Past injustices such as black slavery and segregation are assumed to have been corrected by a steady progression of laws, constitutional amendments, and court decisions upholding the civil rights of nonwhites. Some whites now believe that the greatest existing racial injustice in the United States is *affirmative action* policy that appears to favor nonwhites over whites.

In general, American white society in the early twenty-first century honors and idealizes American Indians. Also, in general, Asian Americans are perceived by whites to be a successful racial minority because they have been willing to work hard and they value education. But these are recent historical developments. American colonists viewed Indians as savage heathens, and the nineteenth-century economic and military expansion westward was accompanied by images of Indians as warlike and uncivilized, which accompanied their near-genocide. Asians were shunned by white society in all respects, except as a source of cheap labor, until the second half of the twentieth century.

Present complaints of racism from nonwhites are often considered unjustified by whites. Government assistance to inner-city blacks and court enforcement of Indian sovereignty on reservations may be viewed as undeserved privileges financed by hard-working taxpayers who happen to be mostly white. Indeed, welfare has been replaced by "workfare" in many states. Asian American socioeconomic success may be resented and viewed as the result of unfair cultural advantages or group solidarity in an individualistic society. Native Americans are now often depicted in the media as rich owners of gambling casinos rather than as residents of communities with high unemployment, alcoholism, and despair.

It is odd and surprising for whites to be insulted, hated, obstructed, excluded, or injured because of their race. If it does happen, it may make them aware of being a race for the first time. Many whites are not aware that they belong to the dominant race, and they have no conscious intention of harming anyone based on racial difference. But if they are racialists, they should be aware of what race they are and of the social position of their race, now and in the past.

The description of the social reality of race is very different from a black perspective. Blacks have a tradition of awareness of the ways in which being black influences how they grow up, the education accessible to them, where they work, the stability of their family life, the kind of housing and medical care obtainable, and their social status and authority. They know that as a group they share a history of slavery, segregation, and discrimination implemented by whites on the basis of racial difference.

Black history is embedded in U.S. history, throughout which the federal government upheld local oppression of blacks. In Chapter 1, I mentioned the "three-fifths person" status of black slaves under the U.S. Constitution. In the *Dred Scott* case in 1857, the U.S. Supreme Court ruled that Negroes were not U.S. citizens. It was a crime in slave-owning states to teach slaves how to read or write, and it wasn't until the 1954

Brown v. Board of Education U.S. Supreme Court case that blacks were legally entitled to equal, integrated educational opportunities. Before then, in *Plessy v. Ferguson*
(1896) the Supreme Court had upheld segregation based on community custom. On
the basis of historical examples such as these, as well as ongoing inequities in the
administration of justice, **critical race theorists** who study American culture from a
black racial perspective believe that antiblack racism in the United States has been and
remains an integral part of a false egalitarian political system that favors whites.

At present, blacks value many of the same social goods that come more easily
to whites, and they believe that they do not have the same opportunities as whites to
acquire them. Many blacks believe that one reason for this barrier is that whites
have not implemented all the legal changes that were intended to ensure equal
opportunity after the Civil Rights movements. A second reason is that blacks, in
developing skills for succeeding in society, also have to contend with the results of
centuries of poverty and oppression. From a black perspective, the general effect is
that racial difference is a constant, important aspect of daily life that continues to
work against blacks in every aspect of their lives.

Like the history of African Americans, the history of Native Americans is an
integral part of American history. However, the situation of Native Americans is
complicated by the status of Indian nations as "dependent sovereignties" within the
United States. Since the nineteenth century, these nations have been defined, rede-
fined, legislated out of existence, or encouraged to pursue self-rule. Treaty law was
largely manipulated by Euro-Americans interested in Indian lands and resources.
Efforts at imposed assimilation have not been successful: although over 60 percent
of Native Americans now live off reservations, many in urban areas, rates of unemployment are often over 50 percent.

Contemporary Indian activists affirm traditional values according to their specific
Indian nationalities. They view their people as victims of **genocide,** both physical
and cultural, and express strong repudiation of Euro-American socioeconomic
progress, especially insofar as that progress accelerates the destruction of natural
environments. The cultural differences between traditional Indian societies and
modern American consumer society run deeper than can be described from perspectives based on racial categories.

Although white society has **valorized** Indians, the Indians in question have
not been actual living Indians who struggle in poverty on reservations or in urban
ghettos. Rather, the honor has usually gone to past Indians who fought bravely and
were massacred or driven off their land, or to Indian characters in novels and
movies. Contemporary Indian writers are likely to view such white valorization as
cultural **appropriation.** In substituting Euro-American fantasies of Indians for historical Indians, the reality of Indian life is ignored by whites. For many Indian
thinkers, this denial of Indian life is no different in principle from nineteenth-century
direct genocidal policy against Indians. For nearly a century, in addition to the
massacre of Indian people, Indian culture was directly attacked through laws that
prohibited the practice of indigenous languages, religions, and livelihoods, and
permitted Indian children to be forcibly removed from their families and raised in
schools that would extinguish their language and culture.

Unlike blacks, whose ancestors were brought to the United States in chains, and
American Indians, whose ancestors were here before all other groups, Asian Americans

have ancestors who largely chose to come to the United States, for economic opportunity or to avoid political oppression. During the nineteenth century, Chinese immigrants to the United States were part of a worldwide population referred to as *overseas Chinese,* consisting of poor single men. Extreme legal restrictions were placed on Asian immigration during the late nineteenth and early twentieth centuries, and for decades Chinese women were not admitted. Chinese immigrants were known for hard work, business acumen, and great thrift, but they were denied U.S. citizenship as well as professional employment. This situation began to improve after the 1920s, and Chinese Americans are now considered more successful in the professions than any other ethnic group, given their numerical proportion of the population.

But unlike many European groups that assimilated into the dominant white majority, Asian Americans have generally not completely assimilated. One reason is their desire to perpetuate traditional cultures. Contemporary activists in Asian communities have focused on the ways in which Asians need to organize to achieve political representation commensurate with full civil liberty. Some writers claim that until recently, many Asian American communities have been more attuned to political issues in their countries of origin rather than to American civic and political events that have direct influence on their lives in the United States.

A major external barrier to full Asian assimilation has been racial classification as nonwhite. In addition, many Asians assert that no matter how many generations their families have been Americans, the white majority perceives them as foreigners. The federal government interned Japanese Americans in western states (California, Arizona, Arkansas, Idaho, Montana, Utah, and Colorado) during World War II, ostensibly because the United States was at war with Japan. But many Asian Americans and others still view this as a deeply alienating episode that expressed American xenophobia and anti-Asian racism.

Asian Americans whose families have been in the United States for generations or recent immigrants who arrive with money and education may attain wealth and respected professional and social status. But some claim that this success is limited to rewards for technical expertise and that it lacks social and civic welcome. Asians who arrive without money and education still have to work and study arduously to get out of poverty. Positions against Asian immigration have reemerged in recent years, either because the poor work too hard for other groups to compete against them, or because financially successful Asian Americans have become more visible as owners of property and businesses.

It may seem that the different situations of whites, blacks, Indians, and Asians can be traced to *colorism,* the American belief that white is the most preferred color and black the least, with the skin colors of Indians and Asians falling between. On this view, the basis of the social reality of race is differences in physical appearance that Americans perceive habitually and automatically. It doesn't matter that skin color is a bad predictor of other human traits, of social background, or even of race as it is officially defined, because few people are able to think beyond skin color. Colorism could account for why whites have remained dominant, Indians have been distantly valorized by whites, Asians have been successful in white culture, and blacks have remained at the bottom. The problem with this explanation of the social reality of race is what it ignores: the wide range of skin color within black, Asian, and Native American classifications; the near-genocide of American Indians; the fact that some blacks have lighter skin than some Asians and Indians as well as some whites.

The different racial perspectives on the social reality of race in the United States all have to be considered. But, if belonging to one or another racial group results in a distinctive view of racial difference, then who is to say which group's view is the right one? We could conclude that each group's view is the right view for that group. Such acceptance of difference in social racial perspective can lead to a view of society as a whole as *pluralistic.* On the other hand, a universal egalitarian might insist that since these different perspectives sometimes contradict each other, they cannot all be accurate—at least not at the same time. Therefore, because there are no fair grounds for choosing any one over the others, all the perspectives ought to be discarded in favor of one that could be shared by everyone. One way to do this is to eliminate the false concept of biological race. Without that concept, no one would be able to see the members of groups different from their own as different enough to discriminate against, react to discrimination from, or resent. That is, perhaps we can simply eliminate the false concept of biological race and start from scratch on an unbiased and equal basis.

C. PROBLEMS WITH ELIMINATIVISM

Racial *eliminativism* can be based on principle or on consequences. On principle, the concept of biological race is false and that in itself is reason to eliminate it. Eliminating race would be a simple matter of spreading the truth about the nonexistence of race, beginning with what children are taught in elementary school. The problem with this "argument from truth" is that it's one thing to proclaim that something is true and quite another to insist that people accept that truth. The First Amendment to the U.S. Constitution guarantees freedom of thought, belief, and opinion as part of free speech. Therefore, the truth about race cannot be imposed on Americans against their will. Since belief in races is part of *received opinion,* parents and even teachers would strongly resist an educational program to eliminate ideas of race. Insofar as members of different racial groups believe in the existence of their races, many would strongly resist any forced elimination of racial thinking, especially if they benefit from recognition as being members of the race they are—which almost everyone does, in one way or another. (Indeed, in 2003, voters in California defeated the Racial Privacy Initiative, which would have ended racial identification in public records in that state.) Religious freedom offers an apt comparison here. It is impossible to prove the existence of God based on scientific evidence, but no one therefore proposes that people ought not to be allowed to worship and practice their religions.

Consequentialism is the moral theory that something is good or that an action is right if its results are beneficial. Because human beings are equal in aptitude, it is the perception of racial difference that results in social inequalities based on race. When Americans think of racial difference, they are still influenced by the false nineteenth-century hierarchical theories of race. If Americans were discouraged from thinking in these racial terms or from speaking the language of race, then they would be unable to behave unfairly on the basis of racial difference. Therefore, ideas of race ought to be eliminated because the consequences would be good.

There are several problems with this line of reasoning. First, people may be able to retain false (i.e., scientifically ungrounded) ideas of racial difference without behaving unjustly. Second, if race is unreal—that is, a cultural fiction—then people must be using other things to pick out the different racial groups for unequal treatment, other things such as economic status, culture, country of ancestral origin, and appearance. Without a concept of race, these other things would still be present. This suggests that the problem is not so much with the false folk idea of race as with the uses people make of that idea due to greed and cruelty. But greed and cruelty would not automatically be eliminated if the idea of race were eliminated. For example, even if Native Americans were not racialized at present, Euro-American economic interests in their lands would not change.

Eliminativists might formulate other arguments from principle or consequences. It could be said that Americans have overused their unique cultural structures of racial difference to generate public debates, with the result that more important issues such as poverty, destruction of natural environments, and treatment of drug addiction have been neglected. Giving race a rest might free up energy for dealing with these problems. If the problems masked by race remained when racial categories were no longer in use, then getting rid of these categories would make it possible to confront those problems more directly and openly. Some writers have suggested that the fundamental problem of human relations, generally, is an us-versus-them mentality that has one outlet in false notions of racial difference. So why not get rid of that outlet?

Thus far, we have been discussing proactive eliminative positions. Because the concept of race as we know it did not always exist historically, it could pass out of history on its own without strenuous intellectual effort. People could stop believing in race due to changes in life circumstances. Such changes might include an expansion of the number of racial categories or an increase in the number of individuals unable or unwilling to classify themselves, or to be classified by others, in terms of the three or four currently accepted races. Recent increases in the number of mixed-race people in America, as well as spontaneous grassroots movements in favor of mixed-race classifications, suggest this type of change. Mixed race is the subject of Chapter 3.

D. DISCUSSION QUESTIONS

1. What do you think is the most important aspect of the social reality of race in the United States at this time?

2. Why do people of the same race sit together in college classrooms?

3. Is there any form of racial determinism that can be defended, in your view?

4. How would your life or the lives of people you know change if race were eliminated?

5. What are some general rules that you think everyone ought to follow in relating to people of different races?

E. RECOMMENDED READING

For criticism of racial determinism in the social reality of race, see Ashley Montagu's *Man's Most Dangerous Myth: The Fallacy of Race* and *The Concept of Race.* On the formation of specifically American racial social reality, see Yehudi O. Webster, *The Racialization of America.* For broad and cross-cultural information on the social reality of race, see Oliver C. Cox, *Caste, Class and Race.* On the social reality of race in Latin America, see Richard Graham, ed., *The Idea of Race in Latin America, 1870–1940.* On the formation of racial groups as social entities, see L. Singer, "Ethnogenesis and Negro-Americans Today," in *Social Research.* For philosophical analysis of Western political theory in relation to slavery, see Tommy L. Lott, ed., *Subjugation and Bondage: Critical Essays on Slavery and Social Philosophy.*

Classic sources on the social reality of black race are W. E. B. Du Bois, *The Souls of Black Folk,* and Franz Fanon, *Black Skin, White Masks.* See also Lewis R. Gordon's contemporary interpretation of Fanon in *Fanon and the Crisis of European Man: An Essay on Philosophy and the Human Sciences.* Sources for the legal history of black-white relations in the United States are Derrick Bell's *And We Are Not Saved: The Elusive Quest for Racial Justice* and Joanne Grant's *Black Protest: History, Documents and Analyses 1619–Present.* Useful recent works on legal studies and black critical race theory include Patricia J. Williams, *The Rooster's Egg: On the Persistence of Prejudice;* Richard Delgado, *Critical Race Theory: The Cutting Edge;* Mari Matsuda, Charles R. Lawrence, and Kimberle Williams Crenshaw, *Words That Wound: Critical Race Theory, Assaultive Speech, and the First Amendment.*

Further critical contemporary sources on black social reality include Paul Gilroy, *The Black Atlantic: Modernity and Double Consciousness,* and Patricia J. Williams, *The Alchemy of Race and Rights.* Lewis R. Gordon examines the problematic aspects of existence for black people in white society in *Bad Faith and Antiblack Racism* and *Existence in Black: An Anthology of Existentialist Black Philosophy.*

On Asian Americans, see Robert Olen Butler's *A Good Scent from a Strange Mountain;* Ronald Takaki, *Strangers from a Different Shore;* Maria Hong, *Growing Up Asian American;* Stephen Fugita and Marilyn Fernandez, *Altered Lives, Enduring Community: Asian Americans Remember Their WW II Incarceration.*

Contemporary activist sources on Native American social racial reality are J. Baird Callicott, *In Defense of the Land Ethic;* Ward Churchill, *Struggle for the Land;* Susan Clements, "Five Arrows" in Naomi Zack, ed., *American Mixed Race: The Culture of Microdiversity;* Peter Nabokov, ed., *Native American Testimony: A Chronicle of Indian-White Relations from Prophecy to the Present;* Russell Thornton, *American Indian Holocaust Survival: A Population History Since 1492.* On U.S. government public policy toward Native Americans, see Fremont J. Lyden and Lyman H. Legters, eds., *Native Americans and Public Policy.* On problems of Indian assimilation in urban areas, see Gregory W. Frazier's *Urban Indians: Drums from the Cities.* On indigenous philosophies and worldviews, see Dennis Tedlock and Barbara Tedlock, eds., *Teachings from the American Earth;* D. M. Dooling and Paul Jordan-Smith, eds., *I Become Part of It;* Helmut Wautischer, ed., *Tribal Epistemologies.*

For discussion of what to do given the problems with a scientific basis of race, see K. Anthony Appiah, "Race, Culture, Identity," and Naomi Zack, *Philosophy of Science and Race,* chapter 7.

CHAPTER 3

MIXED RACE

The person sitting next to you on an airplane is reading a novel you just finished. You begin a conversation. This person looks both black and white or maybe something else you can't identify. You are curious about what race your companion is, but you think it might be rude to ask. Why are you curious, and why might the question be rude?

INTRODUCTION

If races were real, most people would be mixed because there have been no lasting situations in history during which entire distinctive groups of people were isolated and bred exclusively within themselves. But races are not real, so racial mixture is not real either. However, most Americans think that races are real. And they do not recognize the existence of mixed-race groups as categories distinct from the four major racial groups—for various reasons.

Traditionally, everyone with mixed black-and-white ancestry has been classified as black, regardless of their amount of white ancestry. From a black perspective, mixed blacks and whites have been routinely accepted as black, especially by black kin. Although American blacks generally acknowledge racial mixture, they take mixed race to be a fact about blackness for some people, rather than an independent racial category. As noted in Chapter 1, the 2000 census allowed for respondents to identify as biracial and multiracial. But, historically, the white majority has been ambivalent about mixed-race classification. In some states during the nineteenth century, mixed black-and-white Americans with one-eighth or less degree of known black ancestry were legally white, and the U.S. census included mixed black-and-white categories such as *mulatto, quadroon,* and *octoroon.* About 1900, the one-drop rule became the law of the land for black classification, and by 1920, mixed black-and-white racial categories were deleted from the U.S. census. At the same time, the term *mulatto,* which originally meant "half black and half white," became a general label for anyone with any degree of black racial mixture. It has been estimated by anthropologists that 70 to 90 percent of American blacks have white ancestry and about 30 percent have Indian ancestry as well. When the census stopped classifying mixed black-and-white Americans as distinct categories within black, ethnic groups previously considered nonwhite, such as Italians, Poles, Spaniards, and Jews, were reclassified as white. Although almost all white Americans now accept these ethnic groups as white, many black Americans restrict the racial classification of white to northern European ethnic whites, such as Scandinavians, Germans, and British.

Mixed race has different structures, depending on racial identities. Mixed Indians-and-whites have been rejected as Indian by the federal government in order to minimize Indian treaty *entitlements.* For example, when Indian tribes have accepted mixed-race Indians as members, the Bureau of Indian Affairs has often not recognized them as Indians if their *blood quantum* has been less than the required 50 percent heritage from one tribe. Moreover, many American Indians themselves place a high value on being "full bloods."

Eurasians have been more easily accepted as white by whites than as Asian by their kin of unmixed Asian ancestry. Indian-and-black and Asian-and-black Americans have been categorized as black by whites and met with varied degrees of acceptance and rejection by blacks, Asians, and Indians. Although American Indians did not have ideas of race before European colonization, and Asian Americans may have different concepts of culture itself as race in their nations of origin, both groups have for the most part accepted the mainstream American system of racial classification.

It should be noted that historically, the state of Hawaii is an exception to the American system of monoracial classification. Hawaiians have a long cultural tradition of public recognition of a multiplicity of mixed-race groups, as well as more social acceptance of mixed-race individuals by all groups on the islands.

Mixed-race Americans are instances of *microdiversity,* because their racial difference exists on the level of an individual person, unlike the *diversity* that is acknowledged to exist between or among the four major racial groups. This microdiversity itself takes different forms. There is a difference between mixed-race people who know they are mixed because their grandparents or great-grandparents were not all members of the same race, and mixed-race people who know they are mixed because their parents are members of different races. First-generation mixed-race individuals are more likely to have intense personal experience of the problems of being mixed in a *monoracial* system and to demand recognition and respect on that basis. In 1967, the U.S. Supreme Court struck down all state laws prohibiting marriage between people of different races. During the 1990s, mixed-race births within marriage were the fastest growing segment of births in any racial group. Present generations of mixed-race Americans, as well as many of their parents, have been visible in grassroots organizations such as Project RACE (Reclassify All Children Equally) that advocate use of a mixed-race classification for schoolchildren on state levels. Since the 2000 census, children who want to be classified as multiracial may check as many races as apply; before, they could identify only as *"other."*

Scholars, psychologists, and other advocates such as members of AMEA (Association of MultiEthnic Americans) have testified before the U.S. Congress in favor of categories for mixed race on the U.S. census. There was a march in favor of federal recognition of mixed race, in Washington, D.C., in July 1995. Although these efforts received broad media attention, and new academic work on mixed race appeared in the 1980s and 1990s, and continues, there is still no comprehensive official recognition of mixed race in the United States. We do not know exactly what the future will hold for mixed-race identity. Mixed-race Americans are an increasingly visible and vocal group. They remain minorities within minorities, but their demands may be more fundamental to human rights and values than is reflected by their numbers alone.

The purpose of this chapter is to consider some of the issues, for both individuals and society, that are involved in microdiversity. Section A presents theoretical arguments in favor of mixed-race identity. Section B outlines different options for mixed-race identity. Section C is a consideration of the problems with mixed-race identity.

A. ARGUMENTS FOR
MIXED-RACE IDENTITY

If people who think they are monoracial have a right to racial identities, then people who are *biracial* or *multiracial* also ought to have that right. To deny mixed-race adults or children identities as mixed is to discriminate against them on racial grounds. Such discrimination is morally wrong and on that basis should be illegal. However, so long as the existence of mixed race is not officially recognized, legally speaking, there is no discrimination.

If mixed race continues to be unrecognized within the United States, arguments for legal change could be based on international human rights. According to the *Universal Declaration of Human Rights* adopted by the General Assembly of the United Nations in 1948, all individuals have a right to choose their religions and beliefs, and no individual can be compelled to belong to an association. When it was assumed that racial identity was a simple matter of a natural category evident at birth, the idea of choice of racial identity would not have made sense. But now that we know race is at best a system of categories created by culture, there is no reason not to revise that system where it is inadequate or repressive for some individuals. Because race is not a natural biological category but something that people affirm or have imposed on them, it resembles a *creed,* a set of beliefs that people live by. Therefore, if people want to identify as racially mixed, they should be allowed to do so, and respected for their choice, as part of their more general human rights to free speech and freedoms of creed and association.

Besides the international human rights arguments, issues of social and psychological *utility,* which includes harm and benefit as well as usefulness, are also relevant. If all mixtures between whites and nonwhites result in offspring being categorized as nonwhite, and if nonwhites have lower status than whites, this reinforces the idea that nonwhite ancestry, especially black ancestry, is a special kind of defect. Black ancestry is the only kind of hereditary categorization that is applied to an entire person solely because it applies to one ancestor. Furthermore, so long as mixed black-and-white racial identification is denied, racial mixtures between nonwhites such as Indian and black, Indian and Asian, or Asian and black will not be taken seriously.

Ignoring the different racial identities of children of nonwhite interracial unions has a depersonalizing and dehumanizing effect on them because it suggests that the unique aspects of their heritage and racial experience are nonexistent or unimportant. Knowing that one is mixed race in a society that doesn't recognize and respect identity can impair self-esteem and social functioning. Children growing up within mixed families may feel ashamed of their "irregular" racial makeup and may experience rejection and alienation in the wider social community.

The idea of monoracial identity has been attached to family inheritance and family descent for cultural reasons, not biological ones. But the result is an assumption that "real" families are monoracial. When children in biracial and multiracial families are not permitted to claim their full family inheritance, the emotionally stabilizing and interpersonally connective aspects of their family life are damaged. Because the culture does not generally recognize mixed race, monoracial family members may emotionally reject mixed-race children and exclude them from broader family life. Thus, as things now stand, racially mixed children are denied a secure social identity and may also be denied those emotionally nourishing benefits of belonging to a family that monoracial children can take for granted.

Adolescents and adults who are racially mixed are put in the position of having to explain basic facts about themselves that are not required from those whose racial identities are recognized. The mixed-race person is often considered a strange and exotic object, not because most Americans are unaware of the existence of mixed race but because they know that there is no official public place for it. Mixed race is presently unacknowledged.

Finally, if mixed-race identities were recognized, the differences between the major racial groups would not be so distancing in human terms, and it would be more difficult for people to think falsely about races as biologically distinct species or subspecies. This might eventually break down essentialist, all-or-none ideas about race. Because what people think of as race is in fact a fluid multiplicity of human traits and types that can change in one generation, a recognition of mixed race would generally result in a more flexible idea of what it is to be a human being. Such a change in how we think about people would make it possible for all individuals to be more expressive about their backgrounds and experience. The present need to fit into rigid, stereotyped categories of appearance, belonging, and what one is expected to say about who one is racially, places an unnecessary stress on all human interactions. Mixed-raced people would be happier if their racial identities were recognized. Monoracial people would also benefit from the removal of some of the burdens that go along with maintaining rigid racial identities, such as obligations to conform to expectations about their own race and hostility toward races different from their own.

B. MIXED-RACE IDENTITY OPTIONS

Let's imagine that mixed race were generally recognized in the United States. It's not clear exactly how mixed-race people would or should identify themselves. Suppose that Jane's mother is white and her father is black and Indian. Jane could identify herself in rough fractional terms as one-third white, one-third black, and one-third Indian. Or she might choose to apply fractions more literally and identify herself as one-half white, one-quarter black, and one-quarter Indian.

On the other hand, Jane may not like presenting herself as "divided" in this way. She could insist that, as a result of a warm and close family life, she has experienced all the racial identities that belong to her parents. She may be unable to determine which "part" of herself is the half, third, or quarter that is white, black, or Indian. As a result, Jane's mixed-race identity could be inclusive, so that she identifies as white *and* black *and* Indian.

By contrast, suppose Jane's friend Dick, who is also black, white, and Indian, grew up on an Indian reservation and learned the oral traditions, ceremonies, and medical practices of his Indian grandparents. Dick wants to identify as a Lakota Sioux, a member of the tribe in which he is enrolled. However, Dick's half-brother Martin was not raised with his Indian relatives, and he now lives in a city with their black father, stepmother, and step-siblings, all of whom identify as African American. Martin has declined tribal enrollment several times and identifies himself as black.

Now, let's return to the complexities of Jane's family life. Jane's parents divorce just after her sister Andrea is born, when Jane is sixteen and secure in her inclusive identity. Andrea grows up in a household headed by her white mother, so she does not have the same experience of black and Indian ancestry from their father that Jane did. When Andrea is eight, her mother remarries, and her second husband is white. Suppose Andrea then wants to identify as white. In a society that overcame its one-drop rule by recognizing mixed race, should she be prohibited from this identification?

Meanwhile, Jane has completed her graduate work in French art history at the Sorbonne, and she marries a fellow student, Johann, who is Dutch. They decide to live in Vermont, where Johann has been hired by a museum that has an excellent collection of eighteenth-century European landscape painters. Jane has been unable to satisfactorily explain the American racial system to her husband and decides to drop her own racial identity completely so they can raise their children as citizens of the world. When Andrea comes to visit them, she tells her sister and brother-in-law about BOMBS, an organization in which she is active in college (Brown's Organization of Multiracial and Biracial Students). Apparently, some members of BOMBS insist that they be identified generically as *mixed* without specifying exactly how they are mixed. Jane and Johann think this is similar to their idea of world citizenship in the human race, but Andrea insists it is distinctly American to be "mixed" in this way.

What these examples, and much of the literary and scholarly work on contemporary mixed race, suggest is that recognized mixed-race identity might take any or all of the following forms: *fractional, inclusive, traditional nonwhite, white, generic,* and *aracial.* Also, mixed-race individuals may want to change their racial identities as their life experience changes, and some scholars of multiracial identity have insisted that they have a right to do that.

C. PROBLEMS WITH MIXED-RACE IDENTITY

The main problem with recognizing mixed-race identity in the United States is that it isn't the way we do things. Although customary and traditional practices are by no means automatically right—slavery was *customary* and *traditional* for hundreds of years—some things in human life seem to be universally decided by custom and tradition (which is custom over time). Globally, racial identity appears to be decided by custom and tradition. Many different racial policies exist from country to country: In South America, racial mixture is an approved and accepted fact of life because it has been for hundreds of years. The Latin American expression *la raza,* "the race," makes of Latinos and Latinas one race despite all their acknowledged mixtures of European, Indian, and African ancestry, that is, la raza is a distinct identity in itself, without reference to its components. In Brazil, although white racial appearance is preferred, racial identity and status can change toward white as mulattoes who do not appear white rise socioeconomically; this has been called the "lightening effect of money." In South Africa, the category *colored* is used to designate mixed race, and it is also a fact of daily life, duly announced in local newspapers, that people can petition the courts to have their races officially changed if their circumstances and the people they associate with change racially. Such flexibility even coexisted with apartheid. In England, East Indians and Pakistanis are known as black; in the United States, they are considered white or Asian. In China, the moral virtues associated with ethnic differences in cultural practices are presumed to be inherited. In India, social status based on membership in a rigid hierarchical caste system is inherited, much as black or white race is in the United States. These differences in what counts as race show that systems of racial classification are culturally relative, the result of long-established practices based on historical circumstances. Therefore, as a tradition that develops over time within a culture, a system of racial classification becomes a fact of history. Although such facts can be criticized, it is extremely difficult for individuals, small groups, or even governments to change them.

American racial identity according to the four major races is a type of identity that is anchored vertically in time. People have "roots" going back for generations in their families that "anchor" their racial identities. Mixed-race identities would be an unsettling disturbance to this kind of human identity structure. If people were allowed to identify as mixed based on just the four categories of black, white, Asian, and Indian, there would be at least fifteen different categories: all four groups combined, each of the four groups taken separately, black-Asian-Indian, black-white-Asian, black-white-Indian, white-Asian-Indian, black-white, Asian-white, Asian-Indian, Indian-white, black-Asian and black-Indian. Indeed, the 2000 census allowed for fifty-seven different racial identities. Also, mixed-race identities would vary, depending on whether it was parents, grandparents, or great-grandparents who were members of the different races in mixed-race ancestry. There are a multiplicity of possibilities for fractional identification and inclusive identification. Those people who want to be known as generically mixed might have to be recategorized according to the ways in which they were mixed, not to mention the task of specifying the racial composition of those who didn't want any racial identification at all. If you add to this the probability of change in individual racial identity over a lifetime, it's clear that wide-scale social recognition of mixed-race identity would make racial identity socially unintelligible. If racial identity were unintelligible, the remaining social barriers against interracial marriage would break down, and the result would be even more racially mixed individuals and more confusion about racial identity and identification. There would be no way to tell the race of a person by looking at him or her. This *rhizomatic,* or multiple-rooted, nature of mixed-race identity, in contrast to the single-rooted nature of monoracial identity, is an unsettling prospect to many Americans. However, that it is unsettling, or upsetting, does not mean that it is morally wrong or that anyone has a right to control or stop it—assuming that it could be controlled or stopped.

A second set of objections to mixed-race identity comes from nonwhite concerns that categories of mixed race would decrease the numbers within minority groups entitled to special treatment on the basis of race. During the *Harlem Renaissance* in black American art and literature in the 1920s and 1930s, the light-skinned segment of the black population, known as the *mulatto elite,* gave up their mixed-race identity for the sake of Negro solidarity. This group had always had more money and education than the darker, less privileged majority of the black population; many were part of what Negro leaders called "the Talented Tenth." Some members of the mulatto elite could trace their ancestry back to white southern aristocrats, and some of their families had been free for generations before the Emancipation Proclamation. (It is often overlooked that not all American blacks were enslaved and that some American blacks are descended from immigrants who arrived after slavery or are themselves naturalized citizens.) Nevertheless, despite the white appearance of some members of the mulatto elite, and no matter their degree of education or cultural refinement, white society had never included them. When the mulatto elite, as a group, came to terms with their exclusion from white society during the Harlem Renaissance, their affirmation of black identity was an important contribution to black solidarity.

To reintroduce mixed-race identity for mixed whites-and-blacks at this time in history could undermine the solidarity based on race that exists in the black population. It would suggest that blacks are no more than a *social group* that is externally constituted and would ignore the ways in which they are a *social entity* that has internal interactions.

As well, solidarity and loyalty based on race are important for American blacks and also for American Indians because whites have traditionally favored the lighter-skinned mixed-race members of both groups and externally appointed them as leaders in order to control their groups from within. That kind of external control can no longer be imposed on either group due to the emphasis placed on positive nonwhite identities since the 1960s. But discussion of mixed-race identity sometimes opens these old wounds of division, corruption, and manipulation.

It should be noted that mixed-race identity is different for American Indians than for African Americans because acceptance as Indian by Indian groups is strongly dependent on cultural practices. Many contemporary American Indians do not appear to be Indian and may in fact have no Indian ancestry in the racial sense. From 1970 to 1995, American Indian identification tripled from 827,000 to 2.2 million. The Cherokee Nation now has no "blood" requirement. What this difference amounts to is that for blacks, mixed-race identity represents leaving the group while for Indians, mixed-race identity represents joining the group.

Finally, some have objected to the recognition of mixed-race identities because they seem to perpetuate scientifically unfounded classifications by race. *If race is unreal, then so is mixed race unreal.* Furthermore, insofar as African

Americans have been a racially mixed group for centuries, a sudden recognition of mixed race would erase this fact because the term "mixed" falsely implies that there are "pure" components.

Traditional arguments against mixed-race identities, for the sake of preserving nonwhite identities (or protecting white identities, for that matter), generally presuppose the value of conformity to custom. They are not arguments based on moral principles or the value of individual rights. I will therefore conclude this chapter by considering ways in which the value of custom in racial issues might be criticized. Custom changes as historical circumstances change. The Civil Rights movement of the 1960s and 1970s was a historical change that was deliberately undertaken because it was morally wrong to practice racial discrimination and segregation in education, employment, housing, and public facilities. The recognition of mixed race for those people who want to be so recognized is simply a further development of the basic civil liberties defended in the Civil Rights movement. Each time a previously unrecognized social group achieves liberation, some people, especially those who benefited from the oppression of that group, are uncomfortable. This discomfort is the price of freedom or of less oppression.

The social confusion that could result from giving free play to all possible racial identities based on mixture might be nothing more than the undoing of the false biological idea of race. Confusion is often a price of social change, but members of the first generation growing up under the new system learn it from scratch in primary school, and by the time they teach it to their children, the confusion is no longer a problem. If we had all grown up without being taught about the three or four main racial groups in America, we would not now be struggling with the problems caused by that false system of racial classification. Mixed-race identity may conflict with ideals based on single roots, but maybe not everyone does or can hold such ideals. Perhaps those with such ideals could continue to practice their traditions and also develop tolerance and respect for those who do not or cannot pursue the same ideals.

The objection that mixed-race identity would perpetuate classification by race fails to fully consider what most people mean by race or racial identity— namely the purity of three or four races. Recognized mixed-race identity would multiply racial categories and undo the assumption that everyone is racially pure. This may, in the process, undo the assumption that race is a meaningful way to categorize people.

D. DISCUSSION QUESTIONS

1. Is there any difference in principle between black-and-white racial mixture and other cases of racial mixture?

2. Do you think that mixed-race individuals have a right to identify as they choose? Support your answer.

3. Why do you think that mixed race has never been officially recognized in the United States?

4. Referring to someone you know, imagine, or have read about, present a case study of being a mixed-race American.

5. If mixed-race people have the right to identify themselves racially, does this mean that anyone should have the right to racially identify in any way at all? Give reasons either way.

E. RECOMMENDED READING

For the concept of universal human rights, see *The United Nations Charter: The Universal Declaration of Human Rights.* Article 2 asserts universal rights of nondiscrimination; Article 20 (2) states, "No one may be compelled to belong to an association."

Historical information on mixed black-and-white race in the United States can be found in John G. Mencke, *Mulattoes and Race Mixture: American Attitudes and Images, 1865–1918;* Paul Spickard, *Mixed Blood: Intermarriage and Ethnic Identity in Twentieth Century America;* Joel Williamson, *New People;* Naomi Zack, *Race and Mixed Race,* Part II. Sources on free blacks during slavery include David W. Cohen and Jack P. Greene, eds., *Neither Slave nor Free: The Freedmen of African Descent in the Slave Societies of the New World;* Ira Berlin, *Slaves Without Masters: The Free Negro in the Antebellum South.* Willard B. Gatewood writes about the "mulatto elite" in *Aristocrats of Color.* See also David A. Hollinger, "Amalgamation and Hypodescent."

On contemporary mixed-race Americans, see L. Funderburg, *Black, White, Other: Biracial Americans Talk About Race and Identity.* See also Karya Gibel Azoulay, *Black, Jewish, and Interracial,* and Jayne O. Ifekwunigwe, ed. *"Mixed-Race" Studies.*

On the possibilities for flexible mixed-race identity, see Maria P. P. Root's "A Bill of Rights for Racially Mixed People," in Root, ed., *The Multiracial Experience: Racial Borders as the New Frontier;* in this volume see also Carlos A. Fernández, "La Raza and the Melting Pot." See Root's affirmation of nonwhite identities for mixed-race people in "The Multiracial Contribution to the Psychological Browning of America," in Naomi Zack, ed., *American Mixed Race: The Culture of Microdiversity.* For aracial mixed-race identity, see Cecile Ann Lawrence, "Racelessness," and Naomi Zack, "Life After Race," in Zack, ed., *American Mixed Race.* Also in *American Mixed Race:* Linda Alcoff, in "Mestizo Identity," explores mixed-race Hispanic identities; Susan R. Graham, in "Grassroots Advocacy," and Carlos A. Fernández, in "Testimony of the Association of MultiEthnic Americans," favor adding a mixed-race category to the U.S. census; F. James Davis discusses mixed-race identity in Hawaii in "The Hawaiian Alternative to the One-Drop Rule." Zack offers philosophical justification for recognizing mixed race in "Mixed Black and White Race and Public Policy," in *Hypatia.* See also Kevin R. Johnson, ed., *Mixed Race America and the Law.*

Sources on mixed-race Native American categories include Jack D. Forbes, *Black Africans and Native Americans: Color, Race and Caste in the Evolution of Red-Black Peoples* and "Blood Quantum: A Relic of Racism and Termination";

David McCord and William Cleveland, *Black and Red: The Historical Meeting of Africans and Native Americans;* William J. Scheik, *The Half-Blood: A Cultural Symbol in 19th-Century American Fiction;* Mariella Squire-Hakey, "Yankee Imperialism and Imperialist Nostalgia," in Zack, ed., *American Mixed Race;* Terry P. Wilson, "Blood Quantum: Native American Mixed Bloods," in Maria P. P. Root, *Racially Mixed People in America.* The data on contemporary tribal membership can be found in *The Statistical Record of Native North Americans.*

David Theo Goldberg, in "Made in the USA," in Naomi Zack, ed., *American Mixed Race,* discusses some problems with mixed-race identity in the context of South Africa. On the 2000 census and mixed race, see Naomi Zack, "American Mixed Race: Theoretical and Legal Issues." For arguments against mixed-race identity, see Rainier Spencer, *Spurious Issues.* On the ethics of interracial marriage, see Anita L. Allen, "Interracial Marriage," in Naomi Zack, ed., *Women of Color and Philosophy.*

CHAPTER 4

ETHNICITY

Your mother's relatives are traditional and they observe the holidays of their forebears. When you are with them at family gatherings, you sometimes feel as though you are in a foreign country in a different historical period. But you still find these family gatherings very satisfying because you think that they are part of *what you are* and *where you come from.* Why is that important? Your father's relatives seem to be typical Americans, with no special family customs. They seem more "normal" and "average." Is that a form of ethnicity, too?

INTRODUCTION

Ethnicity is a characteristic of distinct groups that may or may not be geographically united and that can be identified both across and within nations. For example, Jews as an ethnic group have always been dispersed among different nations throughout their history, constituting a *diaspora;* by contrast, the Lapps in Finland have remained in the same geographical area over many centuries. At this time in human history, there are very few ethnic groups that have no members who have left their ancestral homelands.

Generally speaking, ethnicity concerns all the aspects of daily, family, and cultural life that people with common histories share and find obligatory and fulfilling to teach to their children. In popular thought, ethnicity is a matter of learned behavior with variable connections to biological heredity. Although, as something passed on to people by families and communities, ethnicity is inherited, it differs from race. Few Americans now believe that ethnicity is biologically or genetically inherited in ways that would develop in individuals if they grew up separated from their families or ethnic communities.

In the United States, members of the same ethnic groups tend to be of the same race: Irish, German, Italian, French, English, and Polish Americans are white ethnic groups; Sioux, Mohawk, Pueblo, and Iroquois Indian nations are viewed as different ethnic groups in the same racial category; and Japanese, Chinese, Vietnamese, and Koreans are considered to be ethnic types of Asians. However, the model of ethnicity as a simple subcategory of race has important exceptions: Hispanics are a racially variable ethnic group; most Jews are now considered white but some are black; Native Americans vary racially as well as ethnically; and there are nonwhite members of every European nationality. Many Americans who are *monoracial* are *multiethnic.* Mixed-race individuals are sometimes multiethnic and sometimes monoethnic. Indeed, the fluidity and mixture of ethnicities in the United States is so widespread and commonly accepted that the terms *monoethnic* and *multiethnic* are probably artificial.

Beyond the loose association of ethnicity with culture as opposed to biology, it is difficult to say anything further about ethnicity in general. Some ethnic groups have similar physical appearances among members; others do not. Most ethnic groups share common languages but many do not. Some ethnic groups have strong traditions of solidarity and community, while others are more divided. And so on. Ethnicity, in contrast to race and nationality, is very difficult to account for with generalities. This particularity of ethnicity makes it resistant to any *grand theory.* Instead, the study of ethnicity is a *narrative* discipline, made up of the stories of group relations and histories.

In some parts of the world, ethnic differences are the basis of bloodshed and oppression that have gone on for centuries. In the United States, ethnicity and ethnic difference are less charged than race and racial relations. This seems to allow for tolerance and harmony, if ethnicity is compared to race. For this reason, the word *ethnicity* is often used as a euphemism for *race* when speakers want to refer to race without causing offense to diverse listeners or drawing anger upon themselves. Thus, racial differences, in the sense of false biological differences, may be referred to as "ethnic differences," or reference may be made to an individual's or group's "ethnicity" when what is meant is race in the false biological sense. The reason that *ethnicity* is less charged than *race* is that in the United States, unlike many other parts of the world, ethnic differences have not been as important as racial differences as a continuous ground for prejudice, oppression, or exclusion from the social goods controlled by dominant groups. When ethnicity is a basis for struggle, as it now is for many Hispanics, this is because an ethnic group is viewed as a nonwhite racial group.

In this chapter we will explore the social meaning of ethnicity in comparison to race. Section A is a theoretical discussion of how what people think of as race really is nothing more than ethnicity. Section B presents some of the historical developments of ethnicity as an American form of human categories and *identity.* Section C is an open-ended discussion, through example, of the ethnic complexity in contemporary American life.

A. RACE AS ETHNICITY

Race does not have the biological foundation it is assumed to have, and ethnicity is no longer assumed to have a fixed biological foundation in the social or physical sciences. Thus race is nothing more, and nothing less, than ethnicity. That is, the main nonwhite racial groups that are recognized in American society do not each have biological essences or distinct collections of physical traits that distinguish them from one another. What their members do share are varied degrees of common geographical ancestry, common histories of oppression in the United States, common goals of liberation, and perhaps common stereotypes. It is this kind of common culture that is valued by Indians, Asians, and African Americans. Indeed, it would probably be the main reason that many nonwhites would be reluctant to abandon their racial classification even after a thorough analysis of the false biological foundation of racial classification (see Chapter 1).

An awareness of shared culture and identity among members of a racial group, together with interactions among members of that group that do not take place with members of other groups, makes racial groups *social entities* in the same way that ethnic groups are social entities. The cohesive aspects of racial belonging are the same as aspects of ethnic belonging. Criteria for recognized racial group membership tend to be based on physical appearance and include skin color, hair texture, and bone structure, as well as ways of speaking, dressing, and moving, and styles of behavior. Although black and white Americans associate such criteria for group membership with belonging to a race in the false biological sense, there is little in such criteria that differs from criteria for ethnic group membership. This is especially true when members of the same ethnic group are expected to have a common appearance. That is, because race is biologically unreal, its social reality *reduces* to ethnicity. In popular thought, however, the cultural aspects of ethnicity often are first divided from what are believed to be biological aspects of race. The cultures or ethnicities of different races are then falsely assumed to be biologically inherited. This assumption that ethnicity is inherited *through* race is a remnant of nineteenth-century theories of race that posited racial essences as the vehicle or medium for inherited cultural and behavioral traits, as well as for aptitudes or talents.

Once the idea of race became restricted to biological traits only, the link between racial biological traits and cultural traits, behavior, and aptitude was broken. Without the link to biological heredity, the American notion of ethnicity as cultural inheritance seems to permit support of, and respect for, difference, without the kinds of human distancing that accompany the old false biological essentialist ideas of race. Although members of the same ethnic group may share some traits of physical appearance due to real biological family inheritance, as things now stand, few people believe that they are making racial statements when they say that an individual looks Irish, doesn't look Italian, could be German, or would not be taken for Jewish. People who make such statements probably base them on past experience of the appearance of people whose ethnicities are known to them. Because the projection of racial differences, in the false sense of biological essences, onto differences in human appearance has no foundation in science and causes many social and individual problems, the question is: Why not deliberately *reconfigure* race as ethnicity?

The reconfiguration of race as ethnicity is at this point a theoretical possibility. It would be difficult to accomplish in social reality, mainly due to historical ways in which the success of diverse European ethnic groups in America has been tied to their gradual identification as racially white. Because the white racial group has always been the most successful group socially, economically, and politically, many whites might see the reconfiguration of blacks, Asians, and Indians into ethnic groups, rather than racial groups, as an assault on their own privileged identity as white. By the same token, blacks, Asians, and Indians who still feel aggrieved at past oppression and believe they are still victimized by racism would be wary of such a reconfiguration. From a nonwhite perspective, the danger of changing race to ethnicity in popular consciousness is that whites would still make judgments based on the false ideas of race, which would systematically favor those who used to be called white over those who used to be called black, Asian, Indian, mixed, and so forth. If the same judgments and discriminations were still made in the absence of explicit categories of race, the nonwhite racial groups, after they were considered ethnic groups, would have no recognized grounds on which to seek social justice. The reconfiguration of race into ethnicity would thus be an *eliminative* development of ideas of race that would entail the general problems with eliminativism discussed in Chapter 2.

B. HISTORICAL DEVELOPMENTS OF AMERICAN ETHNICITY

Before culture or ethnicity was conceptually separated from biological race, early-twentieth-century sociologists posited as many different races as would be considered ethnic groups today. Until about 1920, Irish, Germans, Poles, Italians, and other non-northern and non-English European groups were studied as distinct races by social scientists. Jews were also considered to be a distinct race through World War II, especially by the Nazis, who used racist anti-Semitic propaganda to motivate and justify the persecution and genocide of European Jews. This racialization of Jews came to be viewed as anti-Semitic, and today few Americans consider Irish, Germans, Poles, or other non-northern Europeans to be distinct races. Yet racial categories based on non-European ancestry such as Africa, Asia, and even the Americas still stand.

In the United States, from colonial days onward, the dominant economic and social class has been English, Scandinavian, and German in national origin. And in this predominantly Christian country, Protestantism has been the dominant religion (though there are many different branches or sects of Protestantism). Late-nineteenth-century and early-twentieth-century European immigrants who were Catholic faced the task of assimilating to the cultural behavior of the dominant Protestant, northern European ruling class as part of the process of becoming American; the same held true for Jews, especially those from eastern Europe, who did not belong to preferred immigrant nationalities. During the same time, two main models of American national cohesion were in contention. There was the *melting pot* model whereby different ethnic groups would intermarry and share their cultural traditions, resulting in a new American blend. The second model was *pluralism.* According to the early version of pluralism, all citizens would maintain private personal and family ethnic traditions while participating as ethnically neutral Americans in public and civic life. A later version of pluralism, which is more prevalent today, entails that different ethnic groups bring their distinct cultural identities into their roles in public and civic life.

During the second half of the twentieth century, the culture presented as American through the mass media, and the cultural styles that dominated in the upper echelons of business, politics, and higher education, were often presented as

ethnically neutral. Foods, music, and personal styles from distinct ethnicities have been incorporated into images and products for mass popular consumption. However, these nationally consumed items of ethnic diversity are usually more bland than their "prototypes" in ethnicities of origin. Still, it is important to note that the mass-market appropriation and distribution of such material and cultural products display little discrimination on the grounds of ethnicity or, for that matter, race or social class. Any distinct cultural product or practice can be associated with consumer items through advertising. The slang, music, artwork, fashion, and hairstyles of the most disadvantaged and otherwise despised subgroups, such as prisoners, drug dealers, gangsters, lesbians, and gay men, are publicly displayed and personally imitated by members of dominant groups, especially teenagers and young adults—all without apparent prejudice. Although some view this democracy of the marketplace as exploitative, it does diffuse group differences in popular imagination.

But despite ethnic neutrality in the mainstream and egalitarianism in lifestyle accessories, it is not clear to what extent the United States is ethnically democratic at the beginning of the twenty-first century. Ethnically diverse European groups have been able to assimilate as they have risen socioeconomically and sent their children to college. Does this mean that the successful mainstream of American culture is ethnically neutral or that its new members continually acquire the dominant **WASP** (white Anglo-Saxon Protestant) culture? Some critics insist that what appears to be ethnic neutrality is in fact a blend of northern European cultures. On this view, the successful assimilation of American European ethnic groups requires exchanging their distinct ethnicities for the ethnicity of the dominant ethnic groups. In other words, Italian, Irish, Jewish, and even some Asian and black Americans who have joined the mainstream have done so by becoming a different ethnicity, at least in their work or student identities. But the success and assimilation of Jews and Asians often results in new expressions of anti-Semitism and racism against them, precisely on account of their assimilation and success in comparison with other minorities. This suggests that the American elite is still expected to be WASP, an expectation that could be a reflex of tradition, a facet of ongoing anti-Semitism and racism, or both.

We should consider that although the dominant ethnicity of American elites may be northern European, it is hardly a replica of ethnicities in northern Europe but rather is something new. In fact, the desirability of American consumer products is viewed as a threat to tradition in northern Europe, as much as in the Third World. English is the official language in the United States, but it is spoken in a version that has become distinctly American. American high culture—art, music, literature, architecture—is different from that of every other country in the world; American popular culture—music, movies, television, fast food—is even more distinctive (and more in demand internationally).

Finally, one might take the view that the United States, in comparison with most other countries, is still a young nation. American ethnicity, as a distinct way of living that Americans feel obligated and find fulfilling to teach their children, is still being formed. The continual change in this work-in-progress obscures the ways in which American ethnicity is distinctive.

When people from non-northern European ethnic groups, Asians, and African Americans become part of the mainstream, they not only change their own ethnicities but also change the ethnic qualities of the mainstream. This raises the question,

Why should the values and styles of the social, economic, political, and educational elites be definitive of ethnicity in America? Perhaps the ethnicity of those on the bottom and margins of society—those who are poor and undereducated; those whose lives take alternative forms due to disabilities, special talents, nontraditional family structures; those who are not heterosexual, who are in prison, are illiterate, are here illegally, have AIDS, or are homeless—perhaps they and their ethnic groups deserve to be as definitive of a distinct American ethnicity as members of the privileged elite. That is, perhaps an ideal American ethnicity would resemble neither a puree of a melting pot nor a stew of pluralism with identifiable ingredients but a buffet of changing side dishes in unpredictable combinations. Like ethnicity more generally, American ethnicity can be studied only through direct experience or in works of history, literature, and film that record specific events in the lives of particular individuals and groups.

C. CONTEMPORARY ETHNIC DIVERSITY

Americans have always been self-consciously diverse ethnically, even though English and northern European ancestries have predominated among elites. Ethnicity does not exist on its own but in reality *intersects* with both race and religion in varied ways: blacks and whites are ethnically different due to different cultural experience associated with racial difference; Jews, Catholics, and Protestants have different traditions of social and family life; all religious affiliations occur among blacks, whites, Asians, and American Indians. Furthermore, the history of U.S. immigration favored white northern and western Europeans until restrictions on the rest of the world were suspended in 1965. And to this day, white, non-Hispanic immigrants find it easier to thrive than their cohorts from Asian countries and South and Central America. Most illegal immigrants are Hispanic or Asian, and immigrants from the Middle East since September 11, 2001, have faced intense scrutiny. U.S. immigrants have never been immune to the American social reality of race. Throughout American history, especially in wartime, it has been convenient to construct menacing or devalued racial descriptions of "national enemies." Anti-Semitism fueled anticommunism during the 1950s, and since September 11, many Arab Americans have found themselves viewed as nonwhites, when before their whiteness could be taken for granted. As well, many immigrants quickly learn long-standing American practices of white racial aversions.

Dominant ethnic groups are also dominant socioeconomic groups, and people often change or revise their ethnicities as they rise socioeconomically. This suggests that ethnic life in the United States is dependent on nonethnic factors such as money and political power. The technological, capitalistic, consumer-based society in which we function does not have a primary goal of preserving lifestyles that derive from foreign countries of ancestral origin. The economically driven aspects of American cultural life are not so much neutral in ethnic preference as they are *nonethnic.* Ethnically distinctive lifestyles have been further undermined by extensive intermarriage among white European ethnic groups, by the breakdown of extended families, and by high rates of divorce in nuclear families. As a result, many white Americans do not feel "ethnic" at all, although nonwhite Americans may not enjoy this privilege.

Socioeconomic factors may reinforce the ethnic identities of those who are not successful, especially when ethnicity is connected to race. The ways in which race intersects with social class will be discussed in Chapters 7 and 11. As a general rule, we can note here that degrees of non-WASP ethnicity vary inversely with socioeconomic status and political power. Among nonwhites, eastern and southern European, and Middle Eastern ethnic groups, as poverty and disenfranchisement increase, so do ethnic visibility and internal senses of ethnic identity. This is especially true for recent immigrants who remain in their own ethnic communities.

Nevertheless, on all socioeconomic levels, many Americans still identify in terms of their ethnic ancestry. Ethnic differences can spark intense conflicts between groups when combined with perceived racial differences. Consider, for example, debates about whether English is to be the only language taught or used to teach primary school students from Hispanic immigrant families. Or try to construct a reasonable position on the question of whether *Ebonics,* the language composed of current slang and traditional black speech, ought to be used to teach black schoolchildren who can easily express themselves in Ebonics but do not have well-developed skills in standard English. If urban neighborhoods with dominant populations of Asian immigrants have shop signs in Korean and Chinese, should public service information such as traffic signs be provided in these languages as well as in English? Are the benefits from multilingual public speech worth the sacrifice of unity through the imposition of one language? Or is the real issue one of dominance rather than unity? If standard American English is continually enforced as the national language, is this unjustly destructive of immigrant and racial ethnicities?

Suppose that English is the standard American language solely because English speakers have always been the most politically powerful group in the United States. If a wide range of linguistic diversity were publicly represented, many Americans who speak only English might need to become multilingual. However, Americans have a tradition of not wanting to learn "foreign languages." Is that tradition a right?

Language aside, the nondominant ethnicities in the United States lack histories of harmonious intergroup relationships. Rivalries between Italian and Irish Catholics, Cubans and Puerto Ricans, Japanese and Chinese, black Africans and American blacks, and Orthodox and Reform Jews are well-known examples. In recent decades, bitter, racially motivated disputes between American Jews and African Americans have occurred in public forums.

From the turn of the century until the 1970s, American Jews were major supporters of black attempts to secure civil rights and economic and social advancement. American anti-Semites had traditionally excluded Jews from high public office, university and professional employment, and "polite" society. American Jews were also aware of their history of persecution and brutal oppression in almost every European country. Knowledge of this past suffering was reason for Jews to empathize with the struggles of American blacks who had been victims of slavery, segregation, lynching, and other forms of violence, and were denied public social amenities and excluded from higher education and professional employment. More than this, many American Jews were intellectually and morally aware that racial injustice violated democratic principles. Many of the activists who led integration and voter registration efforts in the South during the Civil Rights movement were Jewish. During the 1950s and 1960s, Jewish philanthropists helped fund social justice projects supporting blacks, and Jewish liberals voted for politicians who were committed to programs supporting black advancement from what was called "second-class citizenship."

But by the late 1960s, part of the American black leadership was advocating *separatism* and retaliatory violence against whites as strategies of *Black Power.* This leadership also urged American black solidarity with other groups in the African diaspora throughout the world and with foreign nonwhites generally. For example, support was expressed for Palestinians who viewed Israeli military action against them as racist.

Although few American Jews have been *Zionists,* many have considered support of Israel to be an important part of their Jewish identity. By the early 1970s, insofar as Jews identified both with white Americans and with Israel, there was a broad withdrawal of Jewish interest from black social problems, especially when Black Muslims used anti-Semitic rhetoric. Although many Jews remained Democrats and liberals, some became *neoconservatives* during the 1970s and 1980s. Due to new economic and political concerns, they no longer voted for the government-funded social welfare programs that assisted blacks. Black extremist ideologues countered by resurrecting old European and Nazi myths of Jewish financial conspiracies and exploitation of oppressed groups. Such black-Jewish conflict was driven by economic and political interests that were symbolized by ethnic difference. However, American antiblack racism is more extensive than Jewish antiblack politics, and American anti-Semitism is more extensive than black anti-Semitism. The futility of such disputes is thereby evident.

D. DISCUSSION QUESTIONS

1. Which of these questions do you think most Americans would be more comfortable in answering, and why: What is your race? What is your ethnicity?

2. Why do you think that ethnic difference is less of a problem in the United States than racial difference?

3. Is there a favored American ethnicity? Describe it or explain why it does not exist.

4. What problems, if any, are faced by Americans whose parents are from different ethnic groups? Provide an example from your own experience.

5. Would a raceless society have to be a society without ethnic diversity?

E. RECOMMENDED READING

Source material on specific ethnic groups in American history includes James Paul Allen and Eugene James Turner, *We the People: An Atlas of America's Ethnic Diversity;* Leonard Dinnerstein, Roger L. Nichols, and David M. Reimers, eds., *Natives and Strangers: A Multicultural History of Americans;* Maldwyn Allen Jones, *American*

Immigration; Stephen Thernstrom, ed., *Harvard Encyclopedia of American Ethnic Groups;* Werner Sollors, ed., *Theories of Ethnicity;* and Paul R. Spicard and W. Jeffrey Burroughs, eds., *We Are a People.* See also Gerold D. Jaynes, *Immigration and Race.*

For a history of American social science and ethnicity, see R. Fred Wacker, *Ethnicity, Pluralism and Race.* For political science and literary perspectives on American ethnic difference, see Michael Walzer, "Pluralism: A Political Perspective," in Will Kymlicka, ed., *The Rights of Minority Cultures;* Walter Benn Michaels, *Our America: Nativism, Modernism and Pluralism;* and Milton M. Gordon's *Assimilation in American Life.* On immigration, ethnicity, and legal issues, see Ian F. Haney Lopez; *White by Law;* and Nigel Harris, *The New Untouchables.* See also the PBS documentary series *The New Americans.* On new immigrants segregationist housing preferences, see Camille Zubrinsky Charles, "Neighborhood Racial-Composition Preferences."

Contemporary critical work on ethnicity includes Homi Bhabha, *The Location of Culture;* Claudia Card, "Race, Racism, and Ethnicity," in Linda Bell and David Blumenfeld, eds., *Overcoming Sexism and Racism;* Linda Chavez, *Out of the Barrio: Toward a New Politics of Hispanic Assimilation;* J. Angelo Corlett, "Parallels of Ethnicity and Gender," in Naomi Zack, ed., *RACE/SEX;* Steven Steinberg, *The Ethnic Myth.* On how race does not determine ethnicity, see Franz Boas, *Race, Language and Culture.* On literary multicultural identity, see John C. Hawley, ed., *Cross-Addressing: Resistance Literature and Cultural Borders.*

For accounts of American ethnic identities, see Julia Alvarez, *How the Garcia Girls Lost Their Accents;* Harold Augenbraum and Ilan Stavans, eds., *Growing up Latino;* Raymond A. Beliotti, *Seeking Identity;* Marilyn P. Davis, *Mexican Voices/ American Dreams;* Nazli Kibria, "Migration and Vietnamese American Women: Remaking Ethnicity," in Maxine Baca Zinn and Bonnie Thornton Dill, eds., *Women of Color in U.S. Society.* A primary source on militant black ethnicity and its problems is Louis Farrakhan, "Interview in *National Alliance* Newspaper," in William Pleasant, ed., *Independent Black Leadership in America.* Descriptive and historical works on ethnicity include Mary C. Waters, *Black Identities;* Daniel Boyarin and Jonathan Boyarin, "Diaspora"; Akeel Bilgrami, "What Is a Muslim?"; Kevin R. Johnson, *How Did You Get to Be Mexican?*; Sheng-Mei Ma, *The Deathly Embrace;* and Nazli Kibria, *Becoming Asian American.*

On American Jewish ethnicity and identity, see David Theo Goldberg and Michael Krausz, eds., *Jewish Identity.* A classic literary source is Henry Roth's novel, *Call It Sleep.* Analyses of black-Jewish conflict are presented in Cornel West, *Race Matters,* chapter 6, and Naomi Zack, "On Being and Not-Being Black and Jewish," in Maria P. P. Root, ed., *The Multiracial Experience: Racial Borders as the New Frontier.* See also Lisa Tessman and Bat-Ami Bar On, eds., *Jewish Locations.*

CHAPTER 5

RACISM

Y ou are not a racist. A close friend of yours who
belongs to the same race as you often makes hateful
and hurtful remarks about members of a different racial
group. You have tried to reason with your friend and have
made it clear that you do not share her opinions, but her
behavior hasn't changed. You have known her since junior
high school and have shared many important events of
your life with her, so it wouldn't occur to you to end the
friendship. Is there anything that you are morally *obligated*
to do concerning her racism?

INTRODUCTION

The word **racism** was not widely used before the 1960s. When the hierarchical paradigm
of race was accepted in popular culture, *"n"egroes*—the word was spelled with a small
n until the 1930s—were believed to be genetically inferior to whites culturally, aesthetically, intellectually, and morally. During that time, **discrimination** against Negroes for
jobs, education, housing, and basic civil rights was not illegal or considered morally
wrong by most whites. The same held true for racial discrimination against Native
Americans and Asians. It's easy to forget that the word *discrimination* is an understate-
ment of conditions that included the enslavement, rape, lynching, beating, murder,
unjust imprisonment, and humiliation of American blacks by whites that went on for
hundreds of years. Neither does the word *discrimination* connote the full reality of the
massacre of Indians and their expulsion from ancestral lands, or the exploitation of Asian
laborers in railroad construction and agriculture in western states during the late nineteenth century. Physical **segregation** by race in housing, employment, and public facilities after the Civil War reflected that oppression. That is, those who were mistreated
were also separated and excluded. The situation began to change in the 1960s, but most
nonwhites are probably still aware of deep social differences based on race.

In the 1950s, the possibility of *integration* between blacks and whites became a topic of national controversy. Integrationists thought racial differences were a result of the disadvantages of nonwhites, especially in education, which were kept in place by white *bigotry*. Segregation in schools, workplaces, and public facilities was defended by white southerners on the grounds that integration would result in *miscegenation,* mixed-race offspring from interracial marriage and sex. Popular fears about this threat to *white purity* were based on what would today be called the old racist theory of the hierarchy of the races.

During the 1950s, a distinction was made between *de facto* segregation, which existed unintended, and *de jure* segregation, which was legislated. When the Supreme Court ruled in *Brown v. Board of Education* that public schools had to be integrated, both forms of segregation were struck down in principle. However, it took decades to counteract the will of many white communities to segregate, and de facto segregation still exists throughout American primary education and in housing, because integration never occured or it was met with *white flight* when it did.

After civil rights were legally secured for blacks in the mid-1960s, American blacks began calling themselves "blacks" and "Afro-Americans" instead of "Negroes." The change reflected a resurgence of pride in being black, based on African origins. It was accompanied by renewed commitment to social self-sufficiency within the black community, and new goals for economic and educational advancement. During this period, the concept of racism developed as a way of describing race-based injustice. Racism came to be considered a moral and social evil because people of different races are equal in human worth and potential. Human beings are not responsible for their racial traits, and people ought not to be harmed (or blamed or insulted) for things for which they are not responsible. Racism is a form of injustice in societies and a moral vice in individuals.

Both a denial of the premise of equal human worth and potential across race and advocacy of harm based on racial difference have come to be considered racist views. Direct harm is easy to identify because it consists of insult, assault, and murder by private citizens, and unjust treatment by police, juries, judges, and lawmakers. Indirect harm through lack of opportunity to better life circumstances and denial of earned rewards is more difficult to recognize by those who are not victims of it. The question of where to draw the line between harm that ought to be a matter of private and public morality and harm that ought to be legislated against is a subject of continued disagreement. For example, Americans agree that there ought to be equal educational opportunity for children of all races, but they disagree on what measures government ought to take to implement this. When school integration requires busing or administrative authority over parental choice, many who otherwise endorse equality claim that its implementation violates their liberty. Segregated schools result from the economics of segregated housing. High property taxes in expensive neighborhoods fund better schools for white children, and the lack of comparable education opportunities for black and Hispanic children may restrict their liberty. Good primary and secondary education is good preparation for college, which is now close to a requirement for the benefits of a middle-class life.

Whether *hate speech* ought to be punished because of the *offense* it causes also turns on disagreement about the comparative values of equality and liberty.

Some have argued that censorship of hate speech curtails the right to free speech, which is a greater harm than the hate speech. Those who defend laws and penalties against hate speech have argued that its potential to offend and even cause trauma when it is intended to do those very things entails that it is not speech but action. On this view, hate speech is similar to *fighting words,* language that immediately and directly provokes or incites violence. Censorship of hate speech as a form of action is justified because actions that harm others are not protected by law. Rather, the rights to life and liberty of the victims of such actions are protected by law.

Suppose that hate speech is considered a form of action. Because any speech can be hateful under the right circumstances, all speech, in principle, then qualifies as a form of action. The right to free speech was originally secured to create an area of freedom for individual expression when such expression did not in itself directly harm others. In the liberal democratic tradition, the range of freedom in speech has always been more broad than the range of freedom in action. Some defenders of First Amendment rights have argued that the designation of hate speech as action would blur the important distinction between speech and action. Without that distinction, all forms of protected individual expression would be jeopardized.

If hate speech were a form of action, what distinguishes it from other forms of action is its offensive nature. However, it is not obvious that people have a *positive right* to be legally protected from being offended by others, or even a *negative right* that others not offend them. Conservatives as well as liberals, whites as well as blacks, and heterosexuals as well as homosexuals find many things offensive that others consider it part of their liberty to express or do. It could therefore be a dangerous restriction of everyone's liberty to outlaw hate speech because it is offensive. Of course, this would not mean that hate speech ought not to be condemned according to social rules and moral judgment.

Regardless of where they stand on free speech issues, most Americans today believe that racism is morally wrong. However, whites and nonwhites differ on the amount and extent of racism that they believe exists in American society at this time. Few whites who are not *white supremacists* would identify themselves as racists, and most whites are very indignant at the accusation or implication that their beliefs or actions are racist. Many nonwhites believe that racism against nonwhites, especially blacks, is still widespread and powerful in American life. For that reason, they often do not understand why whites are troubled and distressed when they are called racists, or why whites think that if their beliefs or actions are called racist they are being accused of an unusual moral crime. The purpose of this chapter is to clarify the contemporary concept of racism. Section A is a discussion of *classic racism.* Section B is a discussion of *unintentional* and *institutional racism.* Section C considers the question of whether nonwhites can be racist.

A. Classic Racism

The meaning or concept of racism for the majority of white Americans refers to hatred, hostility, contempt, and harmful intentions in individuals' hearts and minds. According to this definition, a racist is someone who has ill will toward other races and expresses that ill will in speech and action, through racial slurs, insults, unfair behavior, and unprovoked violence. Classic racists in this sense include Ku Klux Klan members, Nazis and neo-Nazis, and anyone else who advocates harming people because of their race. Classic racism is thus conscious and deliberate.

However, classic racism occurs on a continuum. Some racists may never speak their true thoughts and feelings, others may express themselves only to close friends and relatives, and still others may act on their racism whenever they can. Classic racism is not at present acceptable in American white middle-class society, either privately or publicly. Therefore, many contemporary classic racists are *covert*. They either deceive themselves or are discreet, secretive, and subtle about how they harm people of other races. There are two ways to look at this covert strain of classic racism: it's worse than *overt* classic racism because it is hidden and therefore difficult to confront directly with complete and accurate descriptions of what the classic racist thinks, feels, and does; it's not as harmful as overt classic racism because the need for concealment reinforces the public moral position that racism is wrong.

The number or percentage of white Americans who are classic racists is an empirical matter, difficult to measure. However, the charge or accusation of being a racist usually has the connotation of being a classic racist. That is the sense in which most white Americans now consider it a serious insult, bordering on slander, to be called racists.

Strong attempts have been made to understand the causes of classic racism and design remedies for it. Emotional and intellectual causes of noncriminal instances of classic racism have been sought, and criminal instances of it are legally punishable, based on harm done and intent to harm that can be proved.

The probable emotional causes of classic racism vary: compensation for feelings of inadequacy; displacement of anger at persons who are feared onto those who are believed to be vulnerable; projection of one's own shortcomings onto others; cruelty or sadism. Understanding racism as a form of compensation, displacement, or projection requires investigating prior harm experienced by the racist. However, cruelty or sadism are moral and psychological distortions that may not always be understandable as reactions to harm experienced by racists.

The main problem with explanations of racism in emotional terms is that they lack a moral dimension. Victims of racism might be understood to have matching emotional distortions, such as low self-esteem, guilt, or a (possibly unconscious) desire to experience shame, pain, and abuse. Such psychological interpretation is problematic because it imputes pathology to victims in ways that mitigate the injustice of classical racism, especially when its expressions are unexpected or when the victims are children. If racists are judged to be emotionally disturbed simply because they are racists, this lifts their moral responsibility for harm done. People who are not racists tend to hold racists responsible for the harm they do, whereas psychologically disturbed people may not be fully responsible for their mental states and resulting actions. If racists are not responsible for being racists, due to emotional disturbance, then they ought not to be blamed and punished for their racism and its effects.

The appropriate remedies for racism that is judged to be a form of emotional disturbance based on previous suffering or abuse would be to heal the racist and restore his or her self-love and self-esteem so that racism would not be necessary as a form of compensation or reaction. Such remedies would have to be applied in ways similar to other forms of psychotherapy. At this time, there are few, if any, systematic programs of psychological therapy for classic racists. Most nonracists consider racism a moral defect, both blameworthy and punishable. People are responsible for their moral defects because it is presumed to have been within their power not to develop them, or to correct them. Therefore, most nonracists do not advocate therapeutic approaches to racism. And most racists do not consider their racism to be an emotional illness, so they are unlikely to seek such help.

Cognitive psychological explanations of classic racism base it on ignorance. Perhaps classic racists don't know that the objects of their ill will are undeserving of such judgments and actions; perhaps classic racists are unaware of the harm they cause. The ignorance-based explanation of classic racism has structured the traditional educational model for remedying it. On this model, adult classic racists have been poorly taught about human difference and have failed to learn that skin color and other characteristics they associate with racial difference do not have the importance necessary to motivate and justify racist feelings and behavior. Classic racists may be intellectually trapped in a nineteenth-century view of the world that falsely divides human beings into distinct racial hierarchies. They may have a problem with standards for evidence in that they *overgeneralize* from encounters with a few members of a racial group. Such *intellectual errors* of *anachronism* or overgeneralization could result from an unreflective acceptance of views held by parents, neighbors, or peers. Both types of error would be reinforced by limited experience in interacting with people of different races.

On this cognitive model, the remedies for racism are information and education. Classic racists first need to be made aware of facts about people of different races. If this doesn't change their mistaken views, bad habits in reasoning have to be corrected. There has been considerable effort expended throughout the American educational system on such intellectual remedies. Observers differ on the success of teaching primary school, secondary school, and college students ideals and rules of nondiscrimination and racial egalitarianism, as a strategy for eliminating classic racism.

The endurance of classic racism in the United States has led some critics to speculate that racism may be a specific instance of a general human characteristic to respond to difference with hostility. It may be that a certain proportion of the population will always hate and try to harm members of groups different from the groups on which they base their own identity, whether the difference is in ethnicity, race, religion, sexual preference, geographical location, whatever. Short of outright hate, some people may always feel they have to compete with others on the basis of their group identity. If those are constant facts about human nature, then so long as racial difference is generally recognized, there will be classic racists.

Nonetheless, most nonracists view racism as a moral defect. The racist is someone who lacks basic *moral* or *ethical* impulses to *identify* with other living beings. Such identification in the form of empathy or compassion rests on the ability to seriously imagine oneself in the place of another. Those who can identify with others realize that being the object of racism is a painful experience. Because pain is intrinsically bad, it is wrong to cause others pain without justification. Racial difference is not a justification for inflicting pain because people cannot help what race they are. We should blame and punish others only for things that they have done when they could have done otherwise. To hate or harm others on the grounds of race is unfair. This lack of fairness is a moral defect. Those who are fair and who are committed to behaving morally therefore have an obligation not only to continue to behave fairly themselves, but to react negatively to the unfairness of others. It is interesting to note that of all the perspectives on classic racism, only the moral view places a clear obligation on nonracists, as well as racists, to curtail racist speech and behavior. Education and self-improvement may be optional, but sins and vices must be corrected.

B. Unintentional and Institutional Racism

Pernicious and morally repugnant though classic racism is, it is only a small part— and perhaps not the most important part—of what scholars and social critics now mean by the word *racism*. The concept of **unintentional racism** differs from classic racism in that it is defined by the harmful-consequence side of speech and action, rather than by the kinds of motives and intentions that classic racists know they have. Nonwhites may be harmed without those who harm them intending to harm them on racial grounds, or sometimes without intent to harm them in any way. For example, a law-abiding pair of black teenagers may be psychologically harmed when elderly white adults cross the street to avoid them. The same pair may be further injured, this time concretely, when they are arrested for a crime they did not commit because police officers think that the crime was committed by black teenagers and those two happened to be in the area. Or, in another example, Mexican workers may be continually passed over for promotion in a company that has always filled its managerial jobs with whites.

The intention of elderly strollers might be physical safety, that of police officers might be public safety, and that of upper management might be making sure they have competent middle management. Nonetheless, the common effect of these actions is a type of harm to nonwhites that many contemporary Americans, especially nonwhites, would call racist. This type of harm is called racist because it is suffered by nonwhites and not by whites, even though whites who commit it are not classic racists. Also, since racism is wrong, to call the harm racist is at the same time to call for it to stop. The remedy is to educate unintentional racists about how their actions harm nonwhites. This remedy is based on the assumption that unintentional racists would not want to harm nonwhites unfairly.

Institutional racism is a characteristic of public, social, political, and economic organizations and traditions that are harmful to nonwhites. Those who carry out the practices of institutional racism may or may not be classic racists. Some institutional racism is overt, explicitly directed against targeted groups; other forms of it are covert so that the harm does not appear racist. Examples of overt institutional racism are segregated public facilities before the Civil Rights Act of 1964 and the state laws prohibiting interracial marriage that existed before the U.S. Supreme Court struck them all down in 1967. Examples of covert institutional racism are requirements for participation that nonwhites cannot meet as easily as whites and attitudes held or actions taken on the basis of socially undesirable characteristics that occur more frequently among nonwhites than whites. Also, whites may be privileged due to having more social assets than nonwhites (such as college-educated relatives).

Overt, explicit institutional racism is, obviously, intentional racism. But much institutional racism in the United States at this time is not intentional. If blacks and Hispanics live in inner-city impoverished neighborhoods and their children thereby receive inferior social services compared to white children who live in the suburbs, the resulting institutional racism against nonwhite children is not necessarily intended. In a field where job promotion depends on social contact outside the workplace, if a community is socially segregated by race, nonwhites may fail to be promoted even though their supervisors have no racist policies or intentions. In a job situation where whites have always occupied upper-level positions and non-whites, lower ones, tradition alone works against nonwhites in ways that whites may not intend.

A status quo of nonwhite exclusion or underrepresentation tends to be accepted as "normal" in such situations, and most people have to make a special effort in order to change what is normal. Although it could be argued that most of the examples of institutional racism cited thus far do not directly harm nonwhites, they do harm them indirectly by restricting their opportunities for employment and economic advancement. The restriction of those opportunities leads to higher crime rates, higher drug use, and higher dysfunction in family life among nonwhites. American slaves were without education and property after emancipation, and it is not accidental—although it may not all be the result of specific individual intentions—that a large proportion (close to one-third) of African Americans are still poor, undereducated, and without well-founded hope for socioeconomic advancement. Institutional racism continues through a kind of social inertia unless specific measures are taken to change it. When institutional racism is publicly recognized and whites do not want to change it, nonwhites may conclude that those whites who have advantageous positions in institutions within which nonwhites are less successful are classic racists.

Conditions of poverty create further aspects of institutional racism for non-whites insofar as the poor, due to their lack of power and influence, may be victimized by the actions of more powerful groups. For example, places in poor urban and rural neighborhoods inhabited by nonwhites have in recent years been sites for toxic dumps and improperly processed garbage. Inadequate sewage removal, drinking water with high lead and bacteria counts, and vermin infestations are further examples of what has been called *environmental racism* in ghettos and barrios. Businesses that profit from the locations of such pollution defend their actions by claiming that they are acting not on the basis of race but in response to low property values. But whether some of the poor are more vulnerable to environmental depredation because they are poor, or because they are nonwhite, does not really matter in terms of the results. In addition to environmental and health damage, poor nonwhites become further *stigmatized* as people who live in filthy, unhealthful slums. Thus, vulnerabilities due to poverty that may itself be the historical effect of classic and institutional racism lead to further racism of both kinds. Recent scholars have used the concept of *intersectionality* to analyze combinations of disadvantage due to race, class, gender, age, and so forth. Disadvantages combined may make the whole worse than the sum of its parts. For instance, a poor black person suffers greater racism than an affluent black person, and her race may make it more difficult to overcome poverty.

The United States is a culture in which people gain social status and comfort in life by making money. The average middle-class American is impatient with and disapproving of those who fail economically over long periods of time. Because the belief in equal opportunity is strong, the poor tend to be blamed for their own plight. Those, especially nonwhites, who are clients of human service and social welfare bureaucracies, all of which have had funding cuts in recent years, are begrudged this assistance by those who do not need it, although the higher proportion of nonwhites in prison may be more easily accepted. At this point classic racism intersects with another kind of "institutional" racism, this time the ***institutionalization*** of nonwhites.

C. NONWHITE RACISM

The educated liberal ***consensus*** seems to be that racism is something practiced only by whites against nonwhites. But there are objections to this. Black separatist rhetoric in the 1960s and affirmative action programs for nonwhites have led some people to insist that racism has no race. If some blacks, Indians, and Asians vilify whites, or say that all whites are cruel, not to be trusted, and generally evil, why isn't that racism? If black-owned businesses won't hire whites, isn't that a form of discrimination? Suppose a white person gets lost in a black neighborhood and is terrorized and beaten by blacks simply because he or she is white. Is that harm lessened by the fact that the victim's ancestors may have been oppressors? If nonwhites can be racists as well as whites, then why should white people bear all the moral and legal responsibility for being racists? Slavery and legal discrimination no longer exist, and even if blacks and other nonwhites are disproportionately poor, equal opportunity does exist for those who are exceptionally motivated. Therefore, why shouldn't nonwhites take the same responsibility for remedying their own racism that whites have been assigned for remedying theirs?

Answers to these questions depend on what is meant by racism. In the sense of classic racism, which entails individual motive and intent to harm those of a different race, nonwhites can be racists against whites. One objection to this claim has been that whites were the ones who invented the false concepts of race, especially the hierarchical concepts, and that whites are therefore the historically first and primary racists. This objection may be persuasive as a historical or general cultural description, but it does not lessen the possibility that a nonwhite person may be racist against whites in the sense of intending to harm them, either overtly or covertly, simply because they are white. That nonwhites have reasons justifying such harm makes no difference at all in their capacity to be classic (antiwhite) racists, because classic white racists also think they have reasons. Perhaps nonwhites, in having suffered more harm from whites than whites have suffered from them, have moral justification for their racism as a form of revenge. But conscious malice and hatred in the form of revenge are no less malice and hatred. Thus, classic racism would seem to be ***"color-blind,"*** in principle.

However, institutional racism by nonwhites against whites is another matter. Because whites control most institutions and formal structures of power in the

United States, nonwhites are not in a position to instigate, administer, and carry out institutional racism against whites. Apparent exceptions to institutional racism that privileges whites have been affirmative action policies for nonwhites, which will be discussed in Chapter 6. Insofar as most nonwhites who are presently concerned about racism are concerned about white institutional racism, they tend not to have a strong interest in seeking remedies for classic racism by nonwhites against whites. Morally wrong and personally disturbing though such racism is on an individual basis, it does not seem as important a social problem as white racism, either classic or institutional. Still, some critics have insisted that nonwhites behave unethically when they do not apply to their own behavior the same moral standards that they apply to the behavior of whites.

There is another form of nonwhite racism that deserves consideration here, namely nonwhite racism against other nonwhites. Some of it involves racism against members of one's own group, some against members of other nonwhite racial groups. In almost all cases, nonwhite-nonwhite racism involves nonwhites taking up the forms and expressions of white racism and directing them at nonwhites, either by harming them, hating them, or denying them opportunities. Nonwhite groups sometimes develop distinct forms of nonwhite racism based on their own (non-white) perspectives. Nonwhite-nonwhite racism may involve issues of racial authenticity and loyalty that will be discussed under the subject of racial and ethnic identity in Chapter 8. Often, nonwhite-nonwhite racism is based on economic competition—for example, black-Hispanic tensions over jobs, and black condemnation of Asians who operate businesses in black communities.

Nonwhite-nonwhite racism also takes the form of colorism, or preference for light-skinned members within nonwhite racial groups, and self-hatred of one's own nonwhite racial traits or aversion toward them in others. Many writers claim that all forms of nonwhite-nonwhite racism represent acceptance or *internalization* of white-nonwhite racism. That is, victims of racism psychologically become racists as a result of fear of, or identification with, white racists, and denial of their own nonwhite racial identity. However, whatever its causes, nonwhite-nonwhite racism may be more personally damaging than white-nonwhite racism. Most American nonwhites expect whites to be racist some of the time, but they also expect non-whites in other groups to support them, and nonwhites in their own group to accept them, or at least not to display the kind of *aversive* behavior associated with classic white racism. Self-hatred on the grounds of race is an affliction that most people intuitively recognize to be self-defeating.

D. DISCUSSION QUESTIONS

1. In your view, do classic racists suffer from their racism? What do you think is the best remedy for classic racism?

2. Describe an act of covert racism and one of overt racism that you have directly experienced. (*Action* includes speech in this context.) Which do you think is morally worse, and why?

3. If someone accused you of being a racist, how would you try to prove him or her wrong?

4. Describe a contemporary institution or institutional practice that you believe is racist, or explain what is wrong with the concept of institutional racism.

5. Can nonwhites be racist against whites? Explain what you mean by *racist*.

E. RECOMMENDED READING

For a more detailed analysis of the different kinds of racism, see Naomi Zack, "Race and Racial Discrimination," in Hugh Lafollette, ed., *Oxford Handbook of Practical Ethics.*

Opposing sides on punishing hate speech are Stanley Fish, "There's No Such Thing as Free Speech and It's a Good Thing," and Jonathan Rauch, "The Humanitarian Threat," both in Daniel Bonevac, ed., *Today's Moral Issues.* On psychological and social causes of racism, see Michael P. Levine and Tamas Pataki, eds., *Racism in Mind.* See also Philip H. Herbst, *The Color of Words.*

For a primary source on white racism against blacks, see Andrew Macdonald, *The Turner Diaries.* A classic source on racism generally is Jean-Paul Sartre, *Anti-Semite and Jew.* See also: Joel Kovel, *White Racism: A Psychohistory;* Stefan Kuhl, *The Nazi Connection: Eugenics, American Racism, and German National Socialism;* Michael Novick, *White Lies, White Power: The Fight Against White Supremacy and Reactionary Violence;* Patricia J. Williams, *The Rooster's Egg: On the Persistence of Prejudice;* and Michael P. Levine and Tamas Pataki, *Racism in Mind.*

Contemporary philosophical analyses of racism include K. Anthony Appiah, "Racisms," in David Theo Goldberg, ed., *Anatomy of Racism;* J. L. A. Garcia, "Racism as a Model for Understanding Sexism," in Naomi Zack, ed., *RACE/SEX;* Berel Lang, "Metaphysical Racism," and James P. Sterba, "Racism and Sexism: Their Common Ground," in *RACE/SEX;* Laurence Thomas, "Sexism and Racism: Some Conceptual Differences," in *Ethics;* Bernita C. Berry, "'I Just See People': Exercises in Learning the Effects of Racism and Sexism," and Marilyn Frye, "White Woman Feminist," both in Linda Bell and David Blumenfeld, eds., *Overcoming Sexism and Racism.* For a recent analysis of German anti-Semitism, see Berel Lang, *Act and Idea in the Nazi Genocide* and (ed.) *Race and Racism in Theory and Practice.* On racism and black poverty, see Glenn C. Loury, *The Anatomy of Racial Inequality.* On unequal educational facilities for nonwhite children, see Jonathan Kozol, *Savage Inequalities.*

On environmental racism, see Cynthia Hamilton, "Women, Home and Community: The Struggle in an Urban Environment," in Alison Jagger, ed., *Living With Contradictions: Controversies in Feminist Social Ethics;* Laura Westra and Peter S. Wenz, eds., *Faces of Environmental Racism.*

Nonwhite-nonwhite aversion and racism are analyzed in general terms by Iris Marion Young in *Justice and the Politics of Difference,* chapter 5. In *The Bluest Eye,* Toni Morrison presents fictionalized case studies of black self-hatred and colorism. On this topic, see also Virginia R. Harris, "Prison of Color," in Jeanne Adleman and Gloria Enguídanos, eds., *Racism in the Lives of Women.*

CHAPTER 6

PUBLIC POLICY AND AFFIRMATIVE ACTION

Two of your male friends in high school grew up in single-parent households with incomes below the poverty line. Jeff is black and John is white. Both were B students and scored 1100 on their SATs. They applied to the same private college, intending to complete pre-law programs. Each requested full financial aid. Jeff was hoping for a scholarship based on affirmative action. John was hoping for a scholarship because his father had gone to the same college. Do you think that the three of you could have remained friends if only one of them got what he wanted?

INTRODUCTION

Public policy is the spirit and actions of the government and other public institutions regarding issues that affect citizens in important ways. Its literal foundation is a set of laws that have been crafted and passed by legislators who are presumed to represent the people. Its interpretive foundation is the *intent of the law,* or what the goals of those laws are believed to be by government officials and the public. The reality of public policy in everyday life is determined by how laws are implemented by institutional and governmental administrators and interpreted by judges. When laws are just, public policy is the will of the people at their most informed, constructive, benevolent, and optimistic. When laws are unjust, public policy enforces ignorance, destruction, malevolence, and pessimism. During slavery, American public policy regarding race rendered blacks unequal to whites in civic life insofar as they lacked rights or legal status as citizens. During segregation, public policy regarding race was what today would be called racist. In the landmark 1954 Supreme Court ruling in *Brown v. Board of Education,* the practice of racially segregating schools was judged unconstitutional. The Court decided that separate could not be equal, in part because of the effects of racial exclusion on the self-esteem of black children. Current public policy for racial equality rests on three important pieces of federal legislation from the 1960s: the Civil Rights Act of 1964 prohibits discrimination on the grounds of race in all major American institutions; the Voting Rights Act of 1965 protects the voting rights of all Americans; the 1965 Immigration Act forbids exclusion based on race or national origin. However, despite widespread formal commitment to racial egalitarianism, appropriate implementation of these laws remains a matter of controversy.

Resolution of the controversies about racially egalitarian public policy depends on what is meant by equality, how social inequality associated with racial difference is explained, and what people are willing to give up to achieve full racial equality. Recently, these controversies have centered on *affirmative action* in education and employment. At present, affirmative action remains in place in many American institutions and organizations, and the Supreme Court upheld one version of it and struck down another in two University of Michigan cases in 2003. However, on some local levels, such as the California higher education system, affirmative action based on race has been eliminated by referendum.

This chapter focuses on the conceptual foundations for affirmative action and the assumptions behind criticism against it. Section A describes different types of affirmative action and presents arguments in favor of them. Section B presents arguments against affirmative action and considers several of the problems caused by it. Section C develops further discussion of the issues raised by affirmative action and the Supreme Court's 2003 rulings.

A. AFFIRMATIVE ACTION AND ITS BENEFITS

Affirmative action is a proactive attempt to correct inequalities due to race by *affirming,* or taking positive action for, those who are socially disadvantaged on account of their race. Affirmative action assists the disadvantaged, rather than punishing those who may discriminate racially. Before *Brown v. Board of Education* and the 1960s civil rights legislation, racial difference was a basis for discrimination against nonwhites in both employment and education. The 1964 Civil Rights Act outlawed discrimination in employment. The southern filibuster preceding the passage of the Civil Rights Act of 1964 succeeded in depriving the EEOC (Equal Employment Opportunity Commission) of cease and desist authority and the power to sue. After a period of urban riots in 1964, 1966, and 1968, President Lyndon Johnson issued Executive Order 11246, requiring implementation of the Civil Rights Act, by executive departments and federal government agencies. This legal implementation of the act can be understood as the foundation of affirmative action, and Congress extended implementation to state and local government in 1972. However, implementation was never widespread or efficient and the average time of court cases has been a decade. Up to the early 1970s, affirmative action meant positive action taken against discrimination. In the 1970s, through the use of *quotas,* whereby firms and institutions sometimes set targets for the numbers of minorities they wanted to include, affirmative action took the form of *counter-acting* discrimination, instead of opposing it directly. The use of quotas was sometimes accompanied by lower standards for minorities who were not as qualified as whites. In *Regents of the University of California v. Bakke,* the Supreme Court in 1978 struck down the use of racial quotas as an affirmative action strategy for inclusion. Over the years, polls have shown that the American public supports equal opportunity but rejects racial quotas as a way to achieve it.

Affirmative action was originally designed as a strategic remedy for racial discrimination. For example, nonwhite applicants with equal or higher qualifications for admission or employment compared to white applicants could not gain entry, before the 1960s civil rights legislation. Disproportionately small numbers of nonwhites attended college and even fewer were managers or professionals. But after the 1960s legislation, continuing discrimination on the basis of race often could not be proved when policies of exclusion were covert, either because no records were kept of qualified nonwhite applicants or because admitting and hiring authorities could claim to reject nonwhite applicants for reasons unrelated to race.

The broad assumption behind affirmative action as a strategy against discrimination is that human abilities are equally distributed across races. If there are situations in which members of one racial group seldom or never get chosen when they apply for entry, or if significantly fewer members of that racial group, relative to their proportion of a larger population, get chosen than of another racial group, the unequal *outcome* is considered evidence of racial discrimination. Overt racial discrimination is simple to prove because it proves itself: those who practice it say that is what they are doing. But covert racial discrimination is very difficult to prove in any one particular case because people who discriminate can conceal the real reasons and motives behind whom they choose and whom they reject. Furthermore, institutional traditions that favor whites over nonwhites, or institutional racism, may foreclose opportunities for nonwhites in the absence of any kind of racial discrimination in the hearts, minds, or practices of individuals. Therefore, given evidence of discrimination or exclusion in outcomes, the remedy is to deliberately increase the hire or admission of individuals from the groups that are known to have suffered discrimination in the past and that are "underrepresented" in the present context.

Affirmative action has been implemented in a variety of ways where the groups affirmed have been white women, and black, Hispanic, and Indian men and women. Usually, when women were the affirmed group, white women tended to benefit. If nonwhite races were the affirmed groups, both nonwhite men and nonwhite women benefited. Some writers claim that when institutions are reluctant about affirmative action they prefer to hire nonwhite women over nonwhite men because each hiree can be counted as a member of two underrepresented groups. But if institutions are sensitive to the high unemployment statistics for black men, they may prefer to hire them over black women who are equally qualified. Which group will be affirmed may also depend on the existing racial and gender balance in the particular context. For example, a company with all-male management of all races might focus on promoting women, but one with few people of color might focus on increased racial representation regardless of gender.

Different types of affirmative action have been applied. In some situations, it was decided that a specific number of women or nonwhites needed to be included. This policy of aiming for quotas of women or nonwhites has drawn the heaviest opposition on the grounds that a predetermined quota of women or nonwhites means that a certain number of white men will not be hired or admitted even if they are the most highly qualified applicants. As an alternative to quotas, special job lines or educational programs have been created for nonwhite applicants, in addition to the places that previously existed. The rationale is that the total number of positions is increased rather than redistributed.

Besides quotas and added places for nonwhites, affirmative action strategies have involved a reconsideration of criteria for entry. It has been argued that some of the criteria for entry privilege whites over nonwhites in ways that are not related to job or educational performance. For example, the high cost of private education may be more difficult for families of nonwhite students to afford. Standardized tests may presuppose that applicants have had cultural experiences that whites have had more often than nonwhites. Indeed, recent research on SAT exams suggests that foreign and African American students get higher scores on the more difficult questions on these tests. The explanation is that the material presented in the hard questions is learned in classrooms or from textbooks. The easy questions use words that are part of everyday life in contexts that are shaped by white middle-class experience. (SAT scores are not now weighted in favor of the more difficult questions.) Sometimes there have been deliberate policies of *preferential treatment* so that race is counted as a criterion for entry, with the result that successful nonwhite candidates may, apart from race, be equally or less qualified for the position than some unsuccessful white candidates.

Finally, there are business and institutional practices of recruiting applicant pools that are racially diverse. Such applicant pools may have a higher percentage of nonwhites than usually apply or than are present in the wider population. The most highly qualified applicants are then chosen, regardless of race. The rationale for these practices is that it gives nonwhites greater opportunities to be considered for desirable positions.

We will now consider four main arguments for affirmative action in the context of race. First, in situations where discrimination was practiced, qualified nonwhite candidates were often passed over solely because they were nonwhite. Such practices were unjust, and affirmative action in all of its forms was a remedy for them.

Argument two is the *role-model argument.* Nonwhites in educational and professional positions where they were previously not present function as models for other, especially younger, members of their racial group who can identify with them and form realistic goals to occupy the same roles themselves. Eventually, this role-model emulation process will create social and economic equality across race.

Argument three for affirmative action is based on the concepts of *compensation* and *reparation.* Members of a society who are disadvantaged through no fault of their own, such as earthquake victims and people who have a history of racial discrimination and oppression, ought to be compensated so that they have the same opportunity for success as members of society who are not thus disadvantaged. Quotas based on race, extra places, and preferential treatment provide this kind of compensation to nonwhites. Reparation entails both compensation and the recognition of past injustice, in that benefits given now are intended to acknowledge unjust harms in the past.

The fourth argument for affirmative action is that it gives places and opportunities to particular nonwhite individuals who might not otherwise have them. The benefits to those people are concrete and direct and enhance their chances for security, fulfillment, and happiness in life. If one can't change the whole of society, sometimes the best that can be done is to make life better for particular individuals, one at a time.

Finally, all forms of affirmative action positively affirm individuals and groups who have been otherwise passed over and rejected. Such affirmation satisfies human needs for honor and esteem among those previously deprived of that kind of attention and respect.

B. ARGUMENTS AGAINST AFFIRMATIVE ACTION

There are arguments against affirmative action from those who think it does not go far enough in correcting racial inequality and from those who think it goes too far. We'll start with the first group. It has been claimed that affirmative action does not really address discrimination. Nonwhites who gain entry to employment and educational institutions through affirmative action may still experience racial discrimination after they are included. Also, all who benefit from racial affirmative action have to be identified and selected on the grounds of nonwhite race. Since nonwhite race already bears a social stigma in American society, affirmative action candidates are marked as less desirable than whites from the beginning. Many Americans believe that nonwhites are less competent or less qualified than whites and thus need affirmative action in order to be admitted or hired. Therefore, the presence of nonwhites in contexts where affirmative action is known to be in effect will cloud future perceptions of their performance and create new forms of racial discrimination.

As a form of reparation, affirmative action doesn't begin to make amends. A stigmatized place in an Ivy League college that a black student might otherwise be academically qualified for is not adequate reparation for the rape of a slave great-grandmother or the lifelong labor of other enslaved forebears; neither does it repair the damage suffered during a childhood in a ghetto. A job on a construction site, as part of a quota, does not adequately repay a Native American for the loss of the unspoiled natural environment that his ancestors may have got their living from on that same site.

Finally, affirmative action does not affect the situations of poverty and social dysfunction in American inner cities. Most affirmative action programs benefit mainly nonwhites who are already part of the middle class. Affirmative action does not help the black underclass to gain entry into the middle class or even into the working class. There are no affirmative action policies in businesses that hire unskilled laborers because minority workers are typically already overrepresented on the lowest rungs in such firms; promotion to managerial positions in these firms is often not monitored in terms of race even though such firms may embody the most extreme forms of institutionalized racism. Young people growing up in violent, impoverished, drug-trafficking neighborhoods have little reason to believe that they can ever emulate the few nonwhite role models in prestigious professional positions. The values held by nonwhites in those affirmative action positions do not speak to immediate underclass needs for survival; and the rewards for the hard work and self-discipline necessary to fit into the white mainstream must compete with the immediate gratifications of drugs and violence to which inner-city youth are continually exposed. Affirmative action may be no more than a pressure valve for those nonwhites who might otherwise direct their energies toward helping their entire disadvantaged groups. Indeed, the Kerner Commission's 1968 reports on riots in American inner cities may have provided the motive of social stability to some architects of subsequent affirmative action programs. The most radical view that affirmative action does not go far enough would interpret it as a white conspiracy to entice talented and enterprising nonwhites to "sell out." On this view, the beneficiaries of affirmative action exchange their real positions as members of oppressed and despised groups for the opportunity to reap material rewards as *tokens* of these groups in what remain white racist institutions. The presence of tokens does not help those who remain excluded or change the bias of white majorities.

The arguments against affirmative action on the grounds that it goes too far proceed from American values of fairness and a belief in *meritocracy.* Affirmative action is unfair because it takes race into account where rewards should have nothing to do with race. If it is wrong to discriminate *against* people on the basis of race, then it is also wrong to discriminate *for* people on the basis of race. Because discrimination for nonwhites appears to be discrimination against whites, affirmative action has been called *reverse discrimination.* Quotas and preferential treatment would be examples of such reverse discrimination. Where special places are created for nonwhites, there is no unfair discrimination against whites. However, the special-place form of affirmative action is unfair in rewarding people on the basis of race, and it may "make work" or create a tier of performance in which standards are lower, both of which waste resources.

For thousands of years, philosophers have defined *justice* as equal treatment for equal actions, virtues, vices, talents, and so on. In education and employment, what ought to count for advancement is ability and merit. Race is not a mark of ability or merit. Therefore, race ought not to count. This argument against affirmative action goes further. If ability and achievement are strong positive values, then affirmative action is a social evil because it fails to reward excellence for both whites and nonwhites. Nonwhites do not have to be excellent under affirmative action policies because they can succeed on the basis of race alone. Whites may not be rewarded for the attainment of excellence because less qualified nonwhites may be rewarded instead. If excellence is not rewarded, then individuals have no incentive to cultivate it. Part of the cultivation of excellence requires a willingness to seek out opportunities for advancement based on one's merits. And all forms of affirmative action discourage this kind of enterprise.

The arguments against affirmative action as forms of compensation and reparation rest on the claim that since discrimination and segregation on the grounds of race are now illegal, equal opportunity for nonwhites exists. If nonwhites remain underrepresented in mainstream American institutions and are disproportionately poor, it is their own responsibility and ought not to require sacrifice from members of other racial groups. Therefore, there is no need for compensation on the grounds of race and that justification for affirmative action collapses.

Reparation has been rejected by affirmative action critics because the white individuals alive today are not the individuals who committed the exploitative and oppressive acts against nonwhites in the past. Therefore, it is morally wrong to expect contemporary whites to give up benefits they deserve in order to redress the injustices of some of their ancestors. Human culture develops and progresses by putting the past behind it. If it were the responsibility of every generation to correct the wrongs of every past system of oppression that took place in history, then none of us would be able to make plans and carry on with our own lives in the present. If it is argued that whites alive today still enjoy privileges that they have inherited as members of a group that has historically oppressed nonwhites, the question arises of where reparation is to begin. The crimes and exploitation against blacks took place on land that whites had stolen from Native Americans. Shouldn't we therefore return the land to the Indians as a first act of reparation? But even this would be inadequate because much of the land has been changed, so it would no longer be possible for Indians to live on it as their ancestors did. Because the past cannot be undone, we have to accept things as we've inherited them, behave fairly in the present, and move on in a system where people are rewarded based on their merit alone.

The role-model argument for affirmative action twists the meaning of *role model*. Suppose a nonwhite is hired as a teacher through affirmative action. The role in question is the role of teacher. So why should the race of the teacher make a difference? If the role is the role of a nonwhite, the social value is dubious because it further divides people along the lines of race and distracts from job performance that has nothing to do with race. The proper roles of teachers, other professionals, students, and employees is to do the work their jobs require, not to "model" their jobs for other members of their races.

Concerning the benefits to specific individuals who are successful affirmative action candidates, although good is done in the short term, it is unearned gain. Such benefits from affirmative action are no different from winning a lottery or finding money in the street, and we have a right to expect skill and not luck to decide who will participate in education, the professions, and management.

C. FURTHER DISCUSSION
AND RECENT CASES

A big difference between the arguments for affirmative action and those against it is the time frame assumed. Those in favor of affirmative action consider the history of nonwhites in American society and assume that present public policy ought to take that history into account. Those who are against affirmative action based on its unfairness are focused on the present. The question of the extent to which present generations are responsible for past history turns on the extent to which that history still has an effect. If one believes that the reason African Americans do not do as well as whites in education and employment is that they are still hampered by a history of exploitation and oppression, then that history is by no means behind us. If one believes that there is broad institutional racism in contemporary American society, then the objection to affirmative action that is based on present equal opportunity collapses.

The disagreement about the appropriateness of reparation is another matter. Although those whites who lose out to affirmative action candidates are not directly responsible for past racism, they are members of a group that has generally bene-fited at the expense of victims of past racism. In this sense, it could be argued that whites have a *collective responsibility* for past harms done to blacks, just as con-temporary Germans have accepted a collective responsibility for harm done to Jews by the Nazis during World War II. Also, some defenders of affirmative action insist that reparation needs to be made for *contemporary* institutional racism.

Although the appeals to merit are ethically sound, there is a real question of whether American society does generally dispense rewards on the basis of merit. Those (known as "legacees") who apply to colleges that their parents and grandparents attended are routinely given preferential treatment over other applicants. Besides legacees, many colleges and universities give preferences for athletes, veterans, in-state residents, and candidates with rare talents. Fewer nonwhites than whites have parents and grandparents who went to college, because it is only recently, since the 1960s, that American colleges have not discriminated against nonwhites. Entry into, and subsequent success within, business and professional fields is to a large extent dependent on family and friend networking that traditionally has excluded non-whites. If such examples of preference for whites, which are built into the system, constitute institutional affirmative action for whites, then why shouldn't there be a proactive public policy of affirmative action for nonwhites? To this, it might be countered that two wrongs do not make a right. But in that case, it would seem to be up to the critics of affirmative action to propose an alternative counterbalance to institutionalized white affirmative action.

The criticism of the role-model argument for affirmative action, like the argu-ment from merit, fails to take existing social reality into account. In many fields, whites have dominated historically and there have been very few or no nonwhites. The new presence of nonwhites in such fields is very likely to send a motivational message to other nonwhites that race is not a barrier to entry. Such messages are important because many nonwhites assume that situations in which members of their race are not present are deliberately racist against them. Role models also work as points of identification. Young people, especially, look to older persons with whom they can identify as inspiration for their future goals. Such identification also furthers senses of belonging to successful groups. In a society as divided by race as ours is, many young people can only succeed in identifying with members of their same race. While the role-model argument in favor of affirmative action does depend on shifting the meaning of "role" from job role to racial role, racial role models may be more effective than job role models, given socially real racial divi-sions. That is, the socially real irrationalities of race form *psychologies of race* in individuals. Advocates of social change have to *work with* these psychologies of race, through an understanding of existing human motivation rather than abstract argument.

While scholars and social critics have been debating the merits of affirma-tive action, many American businesses have instituted affirmative action policies on their own, for several reasons. One reason is an obvious desire to avoid the appearance of discrimination and to decrease exposure to lawsuits based on discrimination. But another reason is that the placement of minorities in positions where they were not present before is good for business and for the image of business in the community. Many American consumers are nonwhite, and the American economy is two-thirds driven by consumer purchases. The image of business as socially responsive is not merely a pragmatic asset that enhances profit. Some members of the corporate community believe that due to the major effects of American business and its practices on American life, American corporations have a moral obligation to behave well, as social entities in their own right. In addition, the U.S. military has been racially integrated for decades, partly due to its own affirmative action policies.

It should be noted that in all institutions where there are affirmative action programs, applicants, students, or personnel are automatically categorized by race. Except for nonwhites who *pass* for white, nonwhites who identify racially have no choice about whether or not they will be the beneficiaries of affirmative action in such institutions. It is therefore unreasonable to expect individual nonwhites to develop positions on affirmative action as though they were personally responsible for it.

In conclusion, let's consider how the U.S. Supreme Court argued and decided in 2003. On June 23, 2003, in *Grutter v. Bollinger* the U.S. Supreme Court ruled 5–4 in favor of the admissions policy of the University of Michigan Law School. At the same time, in *Gratz v. Bollinger* the Court ruled 6–3 against the University of Michigan's undergraduate admissions policy. In both *Grutter* and *Gratz,* the Court recognized the value of a racially diverse student body, so it did not so much question the goal of affirmative action admissions policies as it scrutinized their methods. The ruling for the university in *Grutter* was based on a decision that minority racial identity can be a favorable factor for admission, provided that it does not automatically overrule other factors. The ruling against the university in *Gratz* held that race alone cannot be used as a favorable admissions factor, in a mechanical way. The Court upheld as constitutional the University of Michigan Law School's practice of considering race in conjunction with other factors and making a resulting judgment about individuals. The Court rejected as unconstitutional the undergraduate admissions policy of always assigning the same number of points to minority racial identities.

It is interesting that in light of several decades of **critical race theory,** the Court implicitly rejected the central claim of this theory, which is that historically and to the present, nonwhite racial identities have had preemptive influence on the social and civic identities of individuals in the United States. According to critical race theorists and to many others across the scholarly humanities who criticize racism, there are no important political or institutional contexts in which the race of individuals can be discounted or subtracted so that "individuals" can be discussed without their racial identities. Nonwhite racial identity is understood to make it impossible to function neutrally in society in the same way as whites. On this view, it would not make sense to consider a nonwhite college applicant's nonracial attributes independently of her racial identity, because her racial identity will have already conditioned all of her other attributes through racism existing in the culture.

However, it should also be noted that the Supreme Court did not endorse complete race neutrality as an admissions principle, a position that the Bush administration supported in an amicus curiae brief. A position of complete race neutrality would prohibit considering race as even a contextualized factor. Rather, the Court supported consideration of race in flexible, individualized ways, as a necessary means for achieving the kind of racially diverse student body that, in a society without racism, would be expected to exist without affirmative action. In other words, the Supreme Court supported race as a factor in admissions so that in the future there will be a racially diverse student body and no necessity to consider race as a factor in admissions. The Supreme Court implied that use of race to further integrate the student body will lead to the abolition of racism in society outside academia.

Let's turn to the principles behind the Court's decisions. The Supreme Court has repeatedly expressed its fundamental requirement that race-conscious policy is subject to **strict scrutiny.** Strict scrutiny is the highest standard of constitutionality applied under the equal protection clause of the Fourteenth Amendment, and it poses two questions: Does the goal of a race-conscious policy constitute a compelling government interest? Is the policy *narrowly tailored* to advance that interest?

The Court's answer to the first question regarding affirmative action admissions policies was yes. In *Grutter v. Bollinger* the Court relied on Justice Lewis Powell's 1978 *Regents of the University of California v. Bakke* opinion—namely that a university's interest in broad **diversity** in its student body is based partly on principles of academic freedom and also constitutes a compelling government interest. However, the Court had ruled in 1989 that although institutions may promote diversity to correct their own past discrimination, they may not do so to remedy wider social discrimination, and it had also ruled in 1986 that diversity among K–12 faculty may not be promoted for the sake of providing role models for students.

The Supreme Court's *Grutter* opinion is based on the forward or future-looking view that student body diversity has educational benefits for all students, helps break down racial and ethnic stereotypes, and develops a diverse, racially integrated leadership class. One could reinterpret the Supreme Court's position as follows: Insofar as universities create the culture of the future leaders of society, they have the right to ensure that such leaders will have been educated for leadership as a racially diverse group. There is some ambiguity in the Court's language about leadership, which could mean either that the leadership class should be constructed within higher education as a racially diverse class or that the leadership class will remain white but needs to be educated among nonwhites. Still, the Supreme Court did note in *Grutter* that the benefits of diversity cannot be accomplished with "only token numbers of minority students," and it emphasized the importance of diversity in Congress, federal judgeships, business, and the military.

The Supreme Court's answer to the second strict scrutiny question of whether a race-conscious admissions policy is *narrowly tailored* is reflected in the finding against *Grutter* but in favor of *Gratz* in the Michigan cases. According to the Supreme Court, the policy "must be calibrated to fit the distinct issues raised by the use of race to achieve student body diversity in public higher education." Relying again on Justice Powell in *Bakke,* the Supreme Court wrote against the constitutionality of race-based quotas, although institutions may have a range of numerical objectives for minority enrollment beyond a token number. Individual consideration of applicants requires that their race or ethnicity not be viewed as their defining feature; other diversity factors besides race are to be counted. Race-neutral alternatives are to be adopted if they can be more effective in serving diversity goals. If the admissions policy is flexible, then nonminority applicants are competitive with minorities and not unduly burdened.

To sum up, the Supreme Court in the Michigan cases recognized the value of diversity on college campuses, a value that for over a generation has been preserved by administrators in higher education, and implemented through affirmative action admissions policies. The Supreme Court recognized this value in terms of the effect of higher education on the larger society. However, the Supreme Court's recognition of the value of diversity is qualified, and the Court laid down safeguards so that the implementation of diversity will not occur at the expense of implementing other values, such as fairness and academic excellence within the student body.

To an extent, the concept of diversity works to mediate between uniform extra points for race and the kind of race neutrality that the Court believes would be optimal. Students may get extra points for their contribution to diversity, a contribution that white as well as minority applicants may make. However, in the long run, the test of whether diversity is achieved will be whether or not the student body is racially integrated beyond tokenism. Nonetheless, it is important to note that the emphasis placed on diversity by the Court, and its rejection of quotas, reparations, compensation, and role models as unconstitutional, will likely change the framework of debates about affirmative action in the future.

D. DISCUSSION QUESTIONS

1. What in your view are the strongest arguments in favor of affirmative action for nonwhites and against it?

2. Distinguish between compensation and reparation. When is each justified?

3. Does affirmative action address racial discrimination? Why or why not?

4. Can you think of a remedy for racial discrimination other than affirmative action? Explain what its benefits might be.

5. Explain how the U.S. Supreme Court supported affirmative action with the concept of diversity.

E. RECOMMENDED READING

On the notions of affirming and affirmation, see Laurence Thomas, "Moral Flourishing in an Unjust World," in *Journal of Moral Education.* On the social stigma of black race in the United States, see Glenn C. Loury, *The Anatomy of Racial Inequality.*

For discussion of general social and political assumptions that underlie debates about affirmative action, see James P. Sterba, *Contemporary Social and Political Philosophy* and Carl Cohen and James P. Sterba, *Affirmative Action and Racial Preference: A Debate.* Relevant core political issues involving individual and group rights can be found in William Alonso and Paul Starr, eds., *The Politics of Numbers;* Derrick Bell, *And We Are Not Saved: The Elusive Quest for Racial Justice;* Nathan Glazer, "Individual Rights Against Group Rights," in Will Kymlicka, ed., *The Rights of Minority Cultures.* For philosophical and race-based discussions of justice, see Rodney C. Roberts, ed., *Injustice and Rectification.*

Additional sources that directly take up affirmative action include Anita L. Allen, "The Role Model Argument and Faculty Diversity," in John P. Pittman, ed., *African-American Perspectives and Philosophical Traditions;* Bernard Boxill, "The Morality of Reparation," in *Social Theory and Practice;* Gertrude Ezorsky, *Racism and Justice;* Andrew Hacker, "Goodbye to Affirmative Action?" *New York Review of Books;* J. Edward Kellough, "Affirmative Action in Government Employment," *The Annals;* Lisa H. Newton, "Reverse Discrimination as Unjustified," in Allison Jagger, ed., *Living with Contradictions: Controversies in Feminist Social Ethics;* Norma M. Riccucci, "Merit, Equity, and Test Validity," in *Administration and Society.*

On the pressure valve motive for affirmative action policy, see *The Kerner Report on Civil Disorders* and *The Kerner Report Revisited.* For discussion of socioeconomic problems that are untouched by affirmative action, see the following: Thomas Sowell, *Civil Rights: Rhetoric or Reality?;* William Julius Wilson, "Studying Inner-City Dislocations: The Challenge of Public Agenda Research," in *American Sociological Review;* and *The Truly Disadvantaged.*

On data that foreign students and minorities out-perform whites on hard SAT questions, see Roy O. Freedle, "Correcting the SAT's Ethnic and Social Class Bias," and Jay Mathews, "The Bias Question." On reparations, see Angele Corlett, *Race, Racism and Reparations.*

CHAPTER 7

WHITENESS

You are a college senior. A sophomore who has just declared the same major as yours asks you about professors whose courses you've taken. Under what circumstances would you volunteer the race of the professors in your descriptions of them?

INTRODUCTION

According to the *taxonomy* of race, over three-quarters of the world's population is nonwhite: Asian, Indian, black, and mixed. Even if one begins by viewing races as no more than biological types, it immediately becomes clear, on a global socioeconomic basis, that racial difference is not mere biological variety. Racial differences are accompanied by significant differences in wealth, military power, comfort in lifestyle, access to the most up-to-date consumer products, and technological expertise. Even though racial taxonomy is biologically false, it is a remarkably accurate device for picking out the socioeconomic differences. That this should be so is the result of historical events. The descendants of the groups of people whose members invented the racial taxonomy according to which they were white, are now the groups of people who have the most wealth, power, possessions, and technology. If we define the world by its dominant groups, the world is white. If we define a country by its dominant groups, the United States is white. Notice that in the case of the world, white dominance is not a matter of numerical majority. As a result of intermarriage with Hispanics and Asians and increased immigration from Asia and Latin America, American whites, who were 75 percent of the U.S. population in 2000, may not always remain a majority in the United States.

The world was not always white, and the United States did not automatically become white in the sense of dominance. American whiteness was constructed in several ways: through cultural ideals about whiteness, the development and enforcement of ideas of nonwhites as humanly inferior to whites, the exclusion of nonwhites from positions of public authority, and the imposition of the cultural norms of white people on all racial groups.

If one values the achievements of Western culture over the past three hundred years, and one accepts or makes a commitment to a mainstream American identity, the tragedy of whiteness is that blacks, Asians, and Indians have not been able to fully participate in it—that is, the tragedy of whiteness is that not everyone is white. But if one thinks that Western culture, particularly American culture, represent a long wrong path in human history because it has been taken at the expense of non-whites, then the tragedy of whiteness is that anyone is white. Most people take a position somewhere between these extremes, which distort the realities of how non-whites have contributed to the wealth and culture of Western civilization generally and of the United States in particular. The often unrecognized contributions of labor from Asians and Africans, of land and resources from indigenist and colonized people, and of art and other cultural products from all nonwhite groups entail that all so-called racial groups have been part of European and American history.

The purpose of this chapter is to focus on whiteness. Section A presents a brief intellectual history of ideas of racial whiteness. Section B is an analysis of the ways in which whiteness has acquired a moral force in American culture. Section C is a discussion of issues and identities that have arisen in reaction to recent criticism of whiteness.

A. THE HISTORY OF IDEAS OF WHITENESS

Before the 1970s, historians, sociologists, and cultural critics often did not take racial difference and racism into account in studying American society. More recently, scholars in the humanities and social sciences have addressed the cultural formations of white racial identity, as a distinct subject, under the framework of *whiteness studies.* Some of the main themes of that multidisciplinary subject will be explored in this section.

The modern idea of the white race began not as a biological concept but rather as a religious identity for most Europeans and as an intellectual identity for the English. A small European slave trade in Africans filtered through Mediterranean countries from the time of ancient Greece and Rome until the beginnings of the industrial revolution and the modern colonial period. Africans were not the only groups enslaved, and the moral justification for enslavement, when justification went beyond simple rights of conquerors, was that those enslaved were heathens, or non-Christians. This justification was an effect of the importance of Christianity as a basis for identity in the European groups that later became known as white. After the Copernican revolution, during the formation of modern science as a systematic enterprise in the mid-1600s, the founders of The Royal Society of London for the Improvement of Natural Knowledge described the English as a race possessed of a special intellectual genius.

The English led the European slave trade by the end of the seventeenth century, and, at that time, ideas of biological whiteness were not yet developed. At the beginning of the English slave trade, Queen Elizabeth I expressed concern about whether

African slaves had consented to their captivity. Some early English slave-traders had qualms about enslaving those who had the same "form" or human shape that they did. This suggests that whiteness was not at that time a designation referring to skin color, and that skin color did not yet symbolize white racial identity. Neither was whiteness fully based on natal Christianness because slaves and other non-Christians could be converted to Christianity. Although the equation of animality with non-Europeans began early in Western history, claims that Africans, Indians, and Asians lacked souls did not prevail in the Christian tradition.

The modern racial definition of whites as a superior human subspecies had three main sources: development of the science of biology as a system for classifying life forms; new biological and geographical interpretations of the Bible; and colonialist domination of non-Europeans by Europeans. In the heyday of nineteenth-century *biologism,* whiteness was a matter not just of physical traits but of cultural superiority as well. Scholars of the period were steeped in the tradition that held ancient Greece and Rome to be the source of western European achievements in the arts, technology, government, and science. Both the Greeks and the Romans had described themselves as naturally superior to other groups, but the Greeks recognized cultural debts to Hebrews, Phoenicians, and Egyptians, who in modern racial terms were not the same "race" as they. Inspired by the new (false) biological taxonomy, nineteenth-century European classicists redescribed ancient culture as the product of white Greeks only. On this interpretation, Greece and, through Greek influence, Rome became the racially white source of racially white modern European culture.

In the United States, by the mid-1800s, the white race was constructed by scholars in the top colleges and universities as "the Great Race," the only race responsible for all of the magnificent achievements of human history and the only race fit to rule itself and all others. There was some empirical attempt to give these claims a biological basis through measurements of human cranial size, brain size, and limb proportions. However, the data collected on anatomical comparisons among whites, blacks, and Asians is now recognized to have been flawed from the outset: comparisons of brain size did not take body size into account; evidence contradicting the hypothesis that white men had the largest brains was discarded; and there was outright falsification as well as reports of measurements that had never been made.

During the late nineteenth and early twentieth centuries, whiteness, as opposed to blackness, immigrant Europeanness, and American Indianness, became the rallying point and foundation for American patriotism. Twentieth-century southern and eastern European immigrants were not considered fully white until they became fully American. White identity as a political national identity was also used to override U.S. regional differences that might have prevented national unity if people who were not conscious of themselves as white expressed primary loyalties to their immediate communities. At the same time, the one-drop rule became the effective social criterion for blackness, so that whiteness came to mean pure whiteness (see Chapter 1). The result of the combination of nationalism with biologism was that white purity became a moral, social, and civic hereditary virtue.

As the United States expanded west and south and built up the wealth that would make it a world power, the center stage of American public events was occupied by white leaders, white heroes, and white achievers. The history of the United States as taught to schoolchildren was a story of deeds accomplished by heroic white people. The main characters were men because history was public and the proper sphere of women was private. The approved roles for nineteenth-century white middle-class American women were restricted to domestic duties, the enforcement of sexual morality, the spiritual uplift of men, and ruling the world by rocking the cradle. Christianity was the spiritual dimension of whiteness, and God and Jesus were pictorially depicted and popularly imagined as white men.

By the time of World War II, whiteness had become fully attached to the masculine virtues of Americanness, which included enterprise, individualism, self-reliance, courage, and fairness. After the majority of Americans publicly aspired to and gave a semblance of living up to these ideals, the false biological racial aspects of whiteness no longer required as much emphasis as a foundation for white identity. Whiteness had become the American human norm: it seemed to white folk as though they were the only folk, because they were the decent, law-abiding, hardworking, church-going, money-making, family-raising people in the United States—the American people. The connection between whiteness and Americanness has always been most intense during wars. The Germans were depicted in the media as an inferior racial group during World War I. During World War II, the Japanese were stereotyped as a menace. Since September 11 and the "War on Terror," people from the Middle East are imagined as a distinct "menace" in ways that focus on their non-Christian and nonwhite ethnicities and race.

B. White Normativity

The term *normativity* captures an attitude that things ought to be a certain way and that their being that way can be taken for granted. Three aspects of white normativity will concern us here: the normalness of whiteness to American whites; the goodness of whiteness to American whites; and the imposition of this normal and good whiteness on nonwhites and its use as a standard for evaluating them.

The normalness of whiteness results from the simple fact that in a culture that is still largely segregated by race, white people interact with other white people in all of the important private and public aspects of their lives. If your family members are all white, if your friends are white, if most of your classmates are white, if the people you date are white, if the person you will marry is likely to be white, if the leaders of your society are white, if your teachers are white, and if the person hiring you for your first job is white, two things happen simultaneously. First, you are not aware of your whiteness and the whiteness of those around you during most of your daily activities. Second, whiteness is the accepted and expected racial condition for you, and nonwhiteness and nonwhite people seem to be unusual. The result of taking whiteness for granted and reacting to nonwhiteness as an exception is that in the minds of white people, *persons,* those beings who can take effective action and are worthy of respect, are white.

The general, often unspoken sense of the moral goodness of values held by white Americans has complex, changing sources. Whiteness was defined as moral superiority by nineteenth-century race theorists, and it continues to be assumed by many that there is a white monopoly over spirituality, rationality, intelligence, technological inventiveness, enterprise, and general competence. Even environmental preservation has been mainly associated with whites, although environmental pollution has in recent years become an activist issue for people of color who live close to sources of industrial pollution. The color white also symbolizes virtue, as opposed to sin, in Christian theology. In the visual arts, including contemporary film, video, and print media, most of the people who are presented as examples or embodiments of human beauty have been white. But the most important foundation for white goodness in American culture probably concerns money.

Americans have always been materialistic and entrepreneurial. Slavery was above all an agrarian business form, and the frontiers of the West were pushed back due to farming, mining, and other commercial interests. The discrimination against newly arrived immigrants has always coincided with their exploitation as sources of cheap labor. Some scholars believe that the American working class never united in a politically self-conscious way because the low wages of nonblack groups, such as poor whites in the South and immigrants from Ireland in the early 1900s, were supplemented with the label of whiteness. Whiteness in turn allowed them to continue to work hard for further material rewards. Nonwhite groups beginning from poverty worked as hard as poor whites, and often under worse conditions, but without the reward of full entry into the economic system. Full entry into the economic system usually results in managerial and professional employment. Some of this "white collar" occupation would be pursued for its own sake, but the rewards most broadly recognized are things that can be bought: bigger houses, finer cars, up-to-date appliances, electronic gadgets, fashionable clothes, exotic vacations, tuition for children at private schools, and better care of the body through state-of-the-art medical treatment, diet, exercise, and cosmetics.

Even relatively *nonmaterialistic* lifestyles require money: artists, writers, and musicians need jobs or patrons in order to sustain their creative efforts; ministers, social workers, and teachers need institutions to subsidize their callings; intellectuals require livelihoods. Because money is a value, the asset of whiteness for obtaining money further reinforces the goodness of whiteness.

The imposition of white values on nonwhites has two dimensions. First, it expresses an inclusive aspect of Americanness. White Germans offer an interesting contrast. German Jews who spoke German and had been part of German civic life for generations were not considered Germans by the Nazis, and German Turks who have been in Germany for generations are not recognized as Germans by many white Germans today. But the white American ruling classes, in what amounts to a separation of race from ethnicity, expect and demand that everyone living in the United States be an American. (Even members of groups that are considered foreign, such as Asian Americans, are expected to try to be Americans.)

The second dimension of the imposition of white values on nonwhites applies to poverty and a history of oppression, which have led to cultural characteristics that depart from white ethnic norms. The historical causes of the cultural differences are overlooked by white Americans, and the departure itself is seen as morally bad and pathological. The kind of attention paid to black family life in the twentieth century by social scientists and public administrators is a compelling example of this normativity. During slavery, American blacks were not permitted to stay together as nuclear families. After slavery, in a culture where men were expected to financially support their families, black men did not have the same employment opportunities as white men. The result has been a black family structure that is different from the traditional white ideal. Black mothers have always had to work outside the home, black families are often extended in multigenerational and *collateral kinship* directions, and there are proportionally fewer black than white male heads of household. However, these adjustments to historical circumstances have been viewed by white observers as the willfully deviant cause, rather than the adaptive effect, of black people, especially black males, not succeeding in white American society.

C. POST-CRITICAL WHITE IDENTITIES

As nonwhites have affirmed and asserted their cultural differences from whites, many whites have come to believe that their whiteness is under attack. If whiteness is defined as superior group and individual identity, and if the values of white culture are believed to be proper values for all human beings regardless of their culture, then this belief is justified. But in an egalitarian society, there is no reason to regard any group as superior on the basis of false biological ideas of race or the results of unjust dominance. In a democratic pluralistic society, values arising out of distinct historical group circumstances become subject to public examination and debate if they are presented as values that everyone should hold. The values that are to be shared by all, except for foundational values of equal civil liberties and respect for human rights, become subject to negotiation. In these senses, it is unfair white privilege that is under attack and such privilege is difficult to defend.

There are other ways in which whiteness is presently perceived to be under attack. If whites will no longer be a numerical majority due to white-nonwhite intermarriage (which results in more children being classified as nonwhite) and nonwhite immigration, then the result is fewer white people in the population. But it's not clear that this "browning of America" is an attack on whiteness unless it is assumed that the main strength a group has is the size of its membership.

If nonwhites have the same *citizenship rights* as Americans that whites have, then an automatic association of whiteness with Americanness can no longer be justified. The same thing happens if nonwhites have the same *moral status* that whites have—it can no longer be assumed that whites are morally superior to nonwhites. Again, in an egalitarian society, this is not an attack on whiteness. But if the specific cultural practices and styles arising out of the ethnic groups to which whites belong, including WASP ethnicity that appears to be ethnically neutral, become devalued, driven underground, and suppressed, then whiteness is under attack. Such an attack against ways in which people live that do not harm others can be objected to by appeal to the same principles of justice that nonwhite groups use to protect their ethnicities.

Except for the last case, the foregoing perceived attacks on whiteness are not real harms because they do not deprive whites of basic rights or liberties. Rather, these affirmations of nonwhite cultural practices directly relate to improvements in the quality of the lives of American nonwhites. However, many whites have felt under attack as whites because they have been accused of being racist (see Chapter 5) and have been held *collectively responsible* for harms done to nonwhites by their ancestors (see Chapter 6). There have been two lines of defense. The first points out that not all whites, now or in the past, have lived the carefree lives of affluent oppressors or have held the values of the ruling class. Some contemporary whites have ancestors who were peasants in Europe or who suffered religious persecution. The second line of defense concerns the present status of whites. Most whites are not part of the most affluent class, and many are not even middle-class. Numerically, there are more poor whites than poor nonwhites. Some whites who are not middle-class have affirmed themselves as *white trash;* some whites who do not want to be identified as white, insofar as this means being oppressive against nonwhites, have identified themselves as *white-race traitors.*

The label *white trash* used to be a form of abuse for poor whites who failed to conform to the moral standards and tastes of middle- and upper-class whites. Illegitimacy, alcoholism, drug addiction, incest, crime, illiteracy, domestic violence, irrationality, cheap personal possessions, substandard dwellings, sloppy housekeeping, dirty habits, undisciplined sexuality, and low IQ: these were the components of traditional stereotypes of white trash. The label and its stereotypes were ways of dismissing whites who failed to come up to middle-class white values and norms. Because they did not have the traits that were assumed by middle- and upper-class whites to distinguish whites from nonwhites, they were considered trash, beings of low value to be cast aside, discarded, not taken seriously.

Contemporary white-trash affirmation is a sophisticated conceptual move against both affluent white discrimination against poor whites and nonwhite attacks on white identity. By affirming the tastes and lifestyles of poor whites, which are often determined by external economic conditions over which individuals have no direct control, a self-righteous aspect of white middle-class cultural mores is mocked. By affirming the whiteness of poor whites, white-trash advocates ask nonwhites to consider the fact that not all American whites belong to the social classes that are in positions of privilege and dominance over nonwhites. That is, some white people live in slums (both rural and urban), cannot afford adequate nutrition or health care, do not have home environments that can support their children's success in school, have friends and relatives in prison, and so on. White-trash affirmation also constructs positive points of identity for some poor whites, as well as for some well-off whites who have "lowbrow" cultural tastes. However, white-trash affirmation retains an edge of racialist, if not racist, advantage. To be proud of being white trash is, at least in part, to be proud of being white.

White-race traitors are contemporary writers and social critics who publicly accept responsibility for belonging to a group with a history of racism in both the classic and the institutional senses (see Chapter 5). The acceptance of this responsibility is intended to relieve nonwhites of the burden of instructing whites on how not to be racist. The element of treason rests on a deliberate refusal to benefit from belonging to a group that sets the norms for all other groups. This is presented as a position of disloyalty toward other whites who accept the benefits. The term *traitor* also evokes the political nature of white racial identity insofar as the American ruling classes are white. (White supremacists call whites who support nonwhites "traitors.") Nonetheless, the polemical effectiveness of white-race traitors depends on their retention of white racial identity at the same time that they disparage that identity and point out its injustices. If white-race traitors renounced their whiteness in action, by passing as nonwhites, they could not attack whiteness from within.

There are touches of playfulness in both white-trash affirmation and white-race treason. A more serious note is struck by contemporary white supremacists because they believe that racism against nonwhites has factual, aesthetic, and moral justification. Militant white supremacists advocate violent reaction against individuals who attack whiteness, as well as armed resistance, terrorism, and rebellion against federal and state government and other mainstream institutions that they think support nonwhites against whites. Many white supremacists value what they believe is biological white racial purity. Some are *fundamentalists* concerning individual rights in their interpretations of the U.S. Constitution and are committed to lifestyles that are independent of the contemporary American "system." A significant part of their ideology consists of the vilification of American blacks and Asians, and many believe in the existence of antiwhite and anti-Christian international Jewish conspiracies.

White supremacist groups partly overlap with libertarians, anarchists, Christian fundamentalists, and state and local constituted militia. Nonwhites, Jews, and mainstream political liberals and conservatives react to these types with varying degrees of fear, anger, and admiration. Contemporary ideologies of white supremacy are a nineteenth-century anachronism and, as such, are *radical* (in the sense of returning to roots) reconstructions of whiteness under the stress of egalitarian gains made by nonwhites. The practical outcome of this extreme "neo-whitest" contribution to American history is presently undetermined, although white supremacists do not seem to count as a major threat in the "war on terror" since September 11, 2001.

D. DISCUSSION QUESTIONS

1. How do you think whiteness should be defined?

2. In your view, what moral justifications are there for the historical benefits that have accrued to white groups?

3. Describe some ways in which white culture has put itself on center stage.

4. Describe one or more white norms that you think ought not to be imposed on people with nonwhite cultural backgrounds or on poor whites.

5. Do you think whites ought to "betray" their whiteness in the interests of social justice? What do you think would count as betrayal?

E. RECOMMENDED READING

On historical and global relationships between racial difference and money and power, see Thomas Sowell, *The Economics and Politics of Race: An International Perspective.*

David Stowe provides a useful survey of the relatively new field of whiteness studies in "*Un*Colored People: The Rise of Whiteness Studies," in *Lingua Franca.*

Scholarly analyses of the formation of the white racial category over modern history include Virginia Domíguez, *White by Definition: Social Classification in Creole Louisiana;* Martin Bernal, *Black Athena: Vol I, The Fabrication of Ancient*

Greece, 1785–1985; Reginald Horsman, *Race and Manifest Destiny;* Noel Ignatiev, *How the Irish Became White: Irish-Americans and African-Americans in 19th Century Philadelphia;* Michael Omi and Howard Winant, *Racial Formation in the United States: From the 1960s to the 1980s;* David R. Roediger, *The Wages of Whiteness: Race and the Making of the American Working Class;* Naomi Zack, *Bachelors of Science: Seventeenth Century Identity, Then and Now,* chapter 12. On culture and class within white America, see Lawrence W. Levine, *Highbrow/Lowbrow: The Emergence of Cultural Hierarchy in America.*

Recent works on contemporary whiteness include Crispin Sartwell, *Act Like You Know: African-American Autobiography and White Identity;* Kate Davy, "Outing Whiteness: A Feminist/Lesbian Project," in *Theatre Journal;* Noel Ignatiev and John Garvey, eds., *Race Traitor;* Matt Wray and Annalee Newitz, eds., *White Trash: Race and Class;* Ruth Frankenberg, ed., *Displacing Whiteness: Essays in Social and Cultural Criticism*; Paula S. Rothenberg, ed., *White Priviledge.*

Popular works on white-trash affirmation include comedian Jeff Foxworthy's *Red Ain't Dead* and Dorothy Allison's novel, *Bastard out of Carolina.*

James Ridgeway, in *Blood in the Face,* chronicles recent grassroots ideas of whiteness that many critics would consider racist.

CHAPTER 8

RACIAL AND ETHNIC IDENTITY

In the place where you work or go to school, a group of your own race or ethnicity bands together. You are accepted by them but you also associate with people who do not band together on the basis of race or ethnicity. A member of your group becomes the subject of a disciplinary investigation. You do not know if this person is innocent or guilty and decide to keep an open mind. But other members of your group are expressing support "no matter what." You explain your position and are told in return that some members of your group have always wondered whether you really were one of them. What does this attack on your racial or ethnic identity mean? How does it make you feel?

INTRODUCTION

Racial and ethnic identity is perhaps the leading scholarly topic in current *emancipatory* studies. The term *identity* is ambiguous, however, because it is used to mean both subjective experience and shared group membership that includes history and group self-image. For our purposes, a distinction between identity and *identification* will be useful. Identity is that about an individual that he or she reflects on, accepts, and develops, in the self. A person's identity is his or her private ideas about who or what he or she is. An individual has a range of choice about how to accept and develop his or her identity and it is unlikely to be based on any one thing. Profession, gender, family roles, race, ethnicity, and even sports, hobbies, and possessions might be part of identity. Identification is what others, typically those who do not know an individual well, use to distinguish that individual from others. Thus, *black, white, Hispanic, Asian, woman, man, mother, teacher, lawyer,* and *cop* are all terms of identification.

Despite this distinction between identity and identification, the sense of identity that is relevant to race and ethnicity is not entirely free of identification. To further specify how race and ethnicity relate to identity, racially and ethnically neutral meanings of *identity* are relevant. Psychologists and psychiatrists work with therapeutic notions of identity that refer to the feelings a person has about his or her self. For instance, someone confident and optimistic, who sets attainable goals, achieves them, and is capable of self-assertion, has a strong identity. A strong identity is connected with self-esteem and self-love, which are based on trusting, nurturing interactions with caregivers early in life. Sociologists would be more likely to consider the identity of persons in terms of the roles they play in interacting with others in both personal and impersonal contexts. Theologians, by contrast, might locate personal identity in the soul or in the soul's relation to God.

Philosophers have approached identity by looking for something in persons that would persist when everything else is changed. Sometimes it seems as though having the same memories is the criterion for someone being the same person. But lapses of memory or even amnesia do not change personal identity, from the perspective of others. Another philosophical position is that the sameness of a person is determined by a continuous path, through physical space, of the same human body, beginning at birth. Observers could, in principle, track that path of a person as a physical object, and the continuity of the path would guarantee the sameness (identity) of the person. In addition to criteria for the sameness of persons, philosophers have addressed questions of what it is about persons that best characterizes them to themselves in an enduring way over time. Is it a mind, a body, a mind and a body, the ability to think, the ability to choose, memories? This philosophical concept of what one is to oneself, over time, is helpful to keep in mind when thinking about racial and ethnic identity. For example, if one could be the same person even though one's race changed, then racial identification would not be part of personal identity.

In Section A, the construction of nonwhite identities in *emancipatory traditions* is considered. The topic of identity is further explored through the idea of *authenticity* in Section B. The complexities of *American Jewish identity* in contemporary life are taken up in Section C as an example of ethnic identity.

A. NONWHITE EMANCIPATORY IDENTITIES

Throughout American history, nonwhite emancipatory identities have been deliberately forged as resistance to and liberation from oppression. These emancipatory identities have included the moral virtues of courage against oppression, altruism toward other members of the group to be emancipated, and dedication to greater social justice in the future. Emancipatory identities cover the spectrum from fighting in political revolutions to religious uplift. Such identities are often based on a rewriting or retelling of historical events from the perspective of the oppressed group. We will consider such *socially constructed* aspects of emancipatory identities in this section.

When groups of people are oppressed—for instance, as slaves, low-paid laborers, or victims of racism—they are not automatically aware of their oppression as such. Those who are oppressed materially are often required to expend all their energy on the tasks of physical survival, getting the basics of food, clothing, housing, and safety in order to be able to carry on for another day or another week. Those who are psychologically degraded by racism may believe that they have the traits ascribed to them by dominant groups. At first, only a small number of the oppressed group, or members of another group who sympathize with their situation, find the words and do the deeds to create self-awareness of the conditions of oppression. Some form of group identity is necessary before an awareness of group oppression is possible. The most convenient and socially intelligible identity is often the identification made by oppressors: "n"egro, Negro, black, Jewish, Indian, "Oriental," Mexican, Hispanic, Asian, and so on.

The externally imposed group labels may be changed as the stereotypes associated with them by oppressors are repudiated by group members. For example, early-twentieth-century African American leaders believed they had a mission to instruct their people, as well as whites, that they were entitled to education and the right to vote because they were not inferior to whites in the ways white society had constructed them to be. At that time they insisted that the word *Negro* be capitalized as the names of other American ethnic groups were. Similarly, Chinese Americans and Japanese Americans now want to be known as *Asians* because the earlier designation *Oriental* was used to refer to imported objects as well as people and its literal meaning, "east of Europe," suggested that Europe was the center of the world. Indians have at different times preferred being called *Native Americans* in reference to their own origins, rather than to the place (India) after which Europeans named them by mistake. Sometimes a new emancipatory group name is chosen in order to accept with pride what was intended to be a derogatory label, for example *black* or *queer*.

When labels are changed as parts of stereotypes are discarded, emancipatory identities are used to encourage and motivate actions that it is believed will result in social change. In a ***pluralistic society,*** they become the basis for what is known as ***identity politics.*** A general public policy commitment to pluralism presupposes that full social justice can best be obtained not if human rights are enforced on an individual basis, but if individuals receive protection and benefits as members of groups. This means that even though it is individuals who vote, the practical political unit is a group whose members share a common identity. Politicians running for office thus become concerned about securing the black vote, the Hispanic vote, the white working-class vote, the women's vote, and so on. Once elected, they are expected to support policies and legislation that will benefit the groups that helped put them in office. (Although their constituencies after election include those who voted against them as well—the president of the United States is president of all the people.)

Identity politics extends beyond the politics of public office. People within institutions or communities form groups that are based on racial or ethnic identities. Group leaders and members then advocate for specific interests. Contemporary debates over ***multiculturalism*** in education, the arts, and cultural life generally are a form of identity politics. The rationale behind multiculturalism is that members of a pluralistic society who identify as members of minority groups ought to have an opportunity to see people like themselves in educational curricula and on the stage of public events. This speaks to a psychological need to be able to ***identify,*** that is, see oneself in the place of another. Multiculturalism also has a goal of universal intellectual and aesthetic enrichment through exposure to works and traditions from racial and ethnic groups other than one's own. The centrality of white European cultural products and people, in a society where white Europeans are the dominant group, can make it seem as though only these people and their products are of value and interest.

Even though emancipatory identities are deliberately constructed, this does not mean that they are experienced as superficial or artificial. Emancipatory identities are woven into racial or ethnic experience, such as traditions, shared circumstances of poverty over which members do not have the same control as more privileged groups, and most important, they may be part of family life. It seems to be a universal fact for all societies in recorded history that human beings come into life in families, are raised in families, and look to family members for some of their deepest personal satisfactions as adults. In the minds of individuals, the racial aspects of their identity become welded to the nurturing qualities of family life. Racially nonwhite and non-WASP Americans think of their families as black, Chinese, Mexican, Jewish, Irish, Italian, or multiracial or multiethnic, in ways that humanly redeem the malign origins of such categories as labels connoting inferior difference. Thus family life as well as public life can add a further dimension to the ways in which emancipatory identities counteract the alienation that accompanies membership in nondominant groups.

It should be recognized that not all aspects of racial and ethnic identity arise from situations of oppression or are deliberate reactions to oppression. Many people live in racially or ethnically *homogeneous* communities that have distinct practices passed on from generation to generation. These traditions, and the feelings of belonging and claiming that accompany them, are found rather than made or deliberately chosen by the individuals who grow up within them. And these individuals in turn pass them on to subsequent generations simply because it is the way they have been taught to conduct and celebrate their lives.

Reactive liberatory identities, family-based racial and ethnic identities, and positive identities based on community homogeneity all work together in dynamic processes that change as historical circumstances change. Each generation in a racial or ethnic tradition inherits the project of reinventing and discovering a shared group identity. A generation may break with its parents and relatives at the same time that it changes what it accepts from them in order to deal with changes in the wider society.

B. AUTHENTICITY

Indians, blacks, Asians, Jews, Chicano[/as], Latino[/as], and members of other groups that have experienced oppression in Western history have been expected to be *authentic.* Racial and ethnic authenticity is usually presented as an obligation by those who are in a position to attach moral values to the racial and ethnic identity of the group in question. As a result, authenticity tends to be accepted as a duty by group members, especially younger people. The "authorities of authenticity" for any particular group vary from the immediate peers of teenagers, to family elders, community leaders, and intellectuals. If the community is geographically scattered, its members are nonetheless expected to behave like group members through religious practice, marriage within the group, holiday celebration, dietary habits, and so forth. But perhaps more important than conformity to custom, an authentic group member is expected to help and support other members of the group simply because they are members of the group. An authentic group member is expected to feel fulfilled and gratified by his or her own authenticity; someone who is inauthentic is expected to feel ashamed, inadequate, and morally weak.

However, the term *authenticity,* with its moral connotations, is ambiguous. People can be racially or ethnically authentic in one or more of at least five different ways. Let's suppose for the sake of this discussion that there is a racial or ethnic group—call it the Quicks—whose members have been stereotyped as follows: they are bald; they love to eat radishes; they traditionally collect insects; they listen to classical music at all major holidays and family gatherings; they are very generous; they are skillful liars.

One way of defining authenticity is as ***provenance.*** An authentic painting by Picasso has to be traced to the artist's studio through its successive owners, as well as certified to be a Picasso by examination of its brushstrokes and its recognition as a Picasso by knowledgeable art dealers. A Quick with authentic provenance would be someone who had Quick ancestry and was known by members of his or her community to be a Quick. But suppose that this person—call her Winifred—did not like to be with other Quicks or to help them, claimed to hate radishes, preferred jazz to Bach, was seen wearing wigs, and was known to be stingy. Peers and elders might then pronounce her inauthentic, despite her provenance, because she would not have an ***authentic appearance*** as a Quick.

Suppose that Winifred changed so that, in addition to her authentic provenance, she displayed the right kind of behavior—that is, she threw out the wigs, collected the insects, ate the radishes, rhapsodized over Bach, and lied elaborately—with the result that non-Quicks immediately recognized her as a Quick. If, in addition to this authentic Quick appearance, other Quicks knew they could count on Winifred's support and loyalty as a Quick, then Winifred would have ***authentic solidarity.***

Now let's imagine that economic conditions in the culture change and Quicks, who previously lived in peace with other racial and ethnic groups, become a hated minority because they own (in perpetuity) exclusive patents to newly engineered genes for radishes that reverse aging and make people smarter. The majority group in society, the Dead, controls the mass media and thereby makes it common knowledge that the distinctive traits of Quicks are pathological signs of social dysfunction and moral degeneration. Over the next generation, during which Winifred's son Fred grows up, strong social pressures develop for Quicks to assimilate to mainstream Dead society, even though their civil liberties are legally protected and no one stops them from continuing in their traditional ways. Fred receives an elaborate glass ant farm on his sixteenth birthday and has a collection of 112 live crickets in gold filigree cages in his room. However, when his Dead friends come to hang out, he hides the insects in the garage. Fred loves radishes, but when he is offered radish dishes at other people's houses, he pretends to be allergic to them. And, working against the stereotype of lying, Fred becomes known as a compulsive truth teller.

Winifred arrives at the painful realization that her son is inauthentic because he lacks the courage to express his real identity. She sadly reflects that even if truth telling were a virtue, Fred could not be considered virtuous because he tells the truth not because he thinks it's right, but because he doesn't want Dead people to dismiss him as a stereotypical Quick. If he just went ahead and allowed himself to *be* what he really was, he would have ***personal authenticity.*** But when Winifred tries to talk about this with Fred, his response is that it's very important to him to feel accepted by friends and to "blend in." He points out that many Quicks do the exact same things he does in order to "get along."

By contrast, Fred's sister Winnie hates radishes, is frightened of insects, likes rock n' roll, and refuses to lie because she believes that lying is wrong. Furthermore, Winnie insists that she has a right to be herself and that she will even marry a Dead man someday if she should happen to fall in love with one and he asks her to marry him. Although Winifred disapproves of Winnie and recognizes that she lacks authentic solidarity as a Quick, she nonetheless concedes that Winnie, unlike Fred, is personally authentic.

Referring back to the chapter introduction and Section A, we can draw the following conclusions about authenticity: authentic provenance is racial; authentic appearance is both racial and ethnic; authentic solidarity is political, in a broad sense; personal authenticity is a matter of strong psychological identity. Ideally, personal authenticity need not conflict with racial or ethnic authenticity. However, complexities of circumstance and individual personality make it difficult to generalize about the desirability of racial and ethnic authenticity. In fact, authenticity as it relates to membership in racial and ethnic groups varies as personal ***narratives*** or life stories vary. Because individuals are unique, they may be the best judges of what it means for them to be authentic members of their racial or ethnic groups. Thus, perhaps the forms of authenticity other than provenance ought to be subject to individual ***autonomy.*** In that case, the concept of authenticity, insofar as it means "genuineness" that is evident to others, loses much of its moral force.

From social perspectives, however, there is a stable meaning of authenticity that requires having knowledge of the history and values of one's group and displaying the knowledge and affirming the values. Such ***cultural authenticity*** may impose limits on individual autonomy, especially when individuals can benefit by downplaying the history of their racial or ethnic groups and affirming the values of the dominant group. Thus, cultural authenticity may be opposed to ***assimilation.*** If individuals have a moral right to choose between cultural authenticity and assimilation, then the value of individual autonomy overrides the values of both cultural authenticity and assimilation.

C. Contemporary American Jewish Identity

Contemporary American Jewish identity is a complex result of identity choices based on identity politics and all the different kinds of authenticity. Most other ethnic groups tend to place their religious, racial, or national origin labels before the word *American*. However, it seems to be customary to speak of American Jews, rather than Jewish Americans. American Indians are another exception to the general usage (although when the label *Native Americans* is used, the second word does not mean the same thing as it does for non-Indian, U.S.-born Americans). The exceptions might be accidental, or they might indicate that both Jewish and Indian identities are considered primary or prior to American nationality.

Since World War II, American Jews have largely been successful in projects requiring assimilation to mainstream American life. At the same time, many American Jews still value their identities as Jews and struggle with questions about what it means, exactly, to *be* a Jew in the United States. Although Jews today generally define themselves as a religious group, there is religious difference among Orthodox, Reform, and Conservative Jews. Criteria for who is a Jew extend beyond religion to ancestry. According to Talmudic law and Israel's immigration policy, which in principle keeps an open door to all Jews, a Jew is someone whose mother is or was a Jew or someone who has converted to Judaism according to Orthodox criteria. However, Reform Jews hold that anyone whose father is a Jew is also a Jew. The religious aspect of Jewish identification entails that people whose mothers were not Jewish can convert to Judaism and thereby become Jews. The maternal heredity aspect of Judaism entails that people whose mothers are Jewish are Jews even if they are **nonobservant,** that is, do not practice the Jewish religion. Furthermore, some American Jews see no contradiction in claiming both an **atheistic** belief structure and a Jewish identity.

The formation of the state of Israel in 1948 allowed Jews worldwide to claim a homeland. Israel has been accepted as the original homeland of Jews since biblical times. But throughout Western history, Jews dispersed to almost every country on earth, mainly as a result of their periodic persecution and expulsion from Christian countries, as well as Palestine, during crises of anti-Semitism. **Zionism,** as opposed to the different forms of Jewish religion, is partly a political ideology that privileges Israel as the center of Jewish life for all Jews. Since Israel is a small country whose neighbors resist its existence as a state, Israel has been involved in political and military actions that many Jews do not support on other political grounds. Some Jews insist that political support of Israel is now necessary for Jewish authenticity. Other Jews believe that their Jewish identity is independent of politics.

The success of Jews in mainstream American life has been accompanied by the abandonment of traditional cultural practices that derived from the lives of Jews in the specific European countries from which many emigrated in the late nineteenth and early twentieth centuries. Early-twentieth-century Jewish immigrants in New York City had their own press and theater in **Yiddish,** a dialect of High German that is written in Hebrew letters. Today, few American Jews speak, much less read Yiddish, although some adults can remember their grandparents' use of it. The official language of Israel is modern Hebrew, and only a minority of American Jews are fluent in that.

Given that religion, ancestry, homeland, customs, and language are such variable components of Jewish identity, the question of Jewish identity is extremely problematic. Almost 50 percent of all Jews who marry, marry non-Jews. Jewish identity is not imposed on American Jews in the same way that black identity is imposed on any American with black ancestry, so this rate of intermarriage may represent further loss of Jewish identity in family life.

For many Jews, thinking about the Nazi attempt at genocide intensifies Jewish identity; even casual, "polite" American anti-Semitism that imputes stereotypes of appearance and behavior to Jews can become a personal reason to retain Jewish identity. The psychological dynamic of Jewish identity is often reported as a process of discovery based on strong emotional reactions of horror, shock, fear, and grief in response to finding out about Jewish suffering. However, some Jews question the validity of an identity based on suffering. Others insist that the persistence of Jews, as Jews, in the face of such suffering is inspiring in universal human terms, so that remembering that they are Jews makes them better people.

Finally, race intersects with Jewishness in complicated ways. Although most Jews and non-Jewish white Americans consider Jews to be white, some black Americans and some Jews believe that Jews are nonwhite because they are traditionally *Semites,* who were considered nonwhite throughout the nineteenth and part of the twentieth centuries. Most American Jews are of European origin but a small number have black ancestry. Jews with black ancestry who live in Jewish communities tend to identify as Jews first and African Americans second. Jews with black ancestry who have been raised in or as adults live in African American communities tend to identify primarily as black. But blacks who have become Jewish through conversion tend to proclaim encompassing identities, that is, black and Jewish. The operative word in all this is *tend,* because there are many exceptions to such generalizations.

D. Discussion Questions

1. Name at least one leader of an emancipatory tradition, and show how that person exemplifies the description of emancipatory identity in Section A or fails to do so.

2. How would you defend multicultural innovation in an educational curriculum for high school students to someone who opposed it on the grounds that it would detract from teaching the classics of Western civilization? Or, if you wouldn't defend such innovation, why not?

3. What could be lost in a fulfilling life if one constructed an identity for oneself mainly based on authentic membership in a racial or ethnic minority group? What would be gained?

4. How would you explain Jewish identity to an intelligent seven-year-old?

5. What are the components of your own identity?

E. Recommended Reading

For philosophical analyses of personal identity, see Harold W. Noonan, *Personal Identity,* and Naomi Zack, *Bachelors of Science: Seventeenth Century Identity, Then and Now,* introduction, chapters 4, 5, 6. For psychological discussion of identity, see Erik Erikson, *Identity and the Life Cycle;* P. Hines and L. Berg-Cross, "Racial Differences in Global Self-Esteem," in *Journal of Social Psychology.* For philosophical and psychological issues relating to racial identity, see K. Anthony Appiah's *In My Father's House* and "'But Would That Still Be Me?'" in Naomi Zack, ed., *RACE/SEX;* Helena Jia Hershel, "Therapeutic Perspectives on Biracial Formation and Internalized Oppression," in Zack, ed., *American Mixed Race;* Howard McGary, "Alienation and the African-American Experience," in John P. Pittman, ed., *African-American Perspectives and Philosophical Traditions.*

For an overview of the issues involved in identity politics, see Iris Marion Young, *Justice and the Politics of Difference,* chapter 6. For a theoretical discussion of multiculturalism, see David Theo Goldberg, ed., *Multiculturalism: A Critical Reader.* On ethnic identities see K. Anthony Appiah and Henry Lewis Gates, Jr., *Identities.*

On black authenticity, see Ralph Ellison's *Invisible Man*; Richard Wright, *Black Power: A Record of Reactions in a Land of Pathos,* and Wright's *The Outsider; The Autobiography of Malcolm X,* as told to Alex Haley; C. V. Willie, *Oreo: Race and Marginal Men and Women.* On black identity and social and philosophical issues, see Lucius T. Outlaw, *On Race and Philosophy*; Leonard Harris, ed. *Philosophy Born of Struggle: Anthology of Afro-American Philosophy from 1917*; and Barbara Hall, "The Libertarian Role Model and the Burden of Uplifting the Race."

For a comparison of black and Jewish identity, see Laurence Mordekhai Thomas, *Vessels of Evil.* On problems with Jewish identity, see Laurie Shrage, "Ethnic Transgressions: Confessions of an Assimilated Jew," in Naomi Zack, ed., *American Mixed Race.* On mixed black-and-Jewish identity, see James McBride, *The Color of Water: A Black Man's Tribute to His White Mother,* and Naomi Zack, "On Being and Not-Being Black and Jewish," in Maria P. P. Root, ed., *The Multiracial Experience.* See also David Theo Goldberg and Michael Krausz, eds., *Jewish Identity,* and Lisa Tessman and Bat-Ami Bar On, eds., *Jewish Locations.*

The importance of skin color in black identity is examined in Kathy Russell, Midge Wilson, and Ronald Hall, *The Color Complex: The Politics of Skin Color Among African Americans;* Judy Scales-Trent, *Notes of a White Black Woman;* Caroline A. Streeter, "Ambiguous Bodies: Locating Black/White Women in Cultural Representations," in Root, ed., *The Multiracial Experience;* Brunetta Wolfman, "Color Fades over Time," in Naomi Zack, ed., *American Mixed Race.*

On Hispanic identity, see Gloria Anzuldúa, *Borderlands/La Frontera: The New Mestiza,* Anzuldúa, ed., *Making Face, Making Soul;* Ofelia Schutte, *Cultural Identity and Social Liberation in Latin American Thought;* Richard Rodriguez, *Hunger of Memory*; Linda Alcoff and Eduardo Mendieta, *Identities: Race, Class, Gender, and Nationality.*

On Native American identity, see Alexandra Harmon, "When Is an Indian Not an Indian? 'Friends of the Indian' and the Problem of Indian Identity," in *Journal of Ethnic Studies,* and M. Annette Jaimes, "Some Kind of Indian," in Zack, ed., *American Mixed Race.* For biographical sources, see Arnold Krupat, *Native American Autobiography: An Anthology.*

On Asian American identity, see Maxine Hong Kingston's *The Woman Warrior* for issues of Chinese American identity. See also Connie K. Kang, *Home Was the Land of Morning Calm: A Saga of a Korean American Family.*

CHAPTER 9

RACE AND GENDER

Imagine that your race changes—to white if you are black, to black if you are white, or to white or black if you are Asian, Native American, or multiracial. If you are not Hispanic, assume no change in ethnicity, but if you are Hispanic, assume that you become non-Hispanic. How do you think this change would affect you as a man or a woman? If you are LGBT (lesbian, gay, bisexual, transsexual), consider the racial or ethnic change from that perspective.

INTRODUCTION

In ordinary language, when people refer to sexual difference, they often do not distinguish between biological differences and social roles. However, many academic writers attempt to draw this line with the distinction between *sex* and **gender.** The term *sex* refers to the inherited biological characteristics of being male or female. The term *gender* refers to temperament and behavior within each sex, which includes sexual preferences, sexual roles, family roles, and broader roles in society, as well as aptitudes and mental and emotional dispositions. Most people develop a gender that is considered appropriate to their sex within their social context. But most psychologists and others who study gender now believe that gender roles are learned.

Differences in biological sex have an empirical foundation on a chromosomal level, and except for a small number of individuals, human beings appear to be either male or female. However, some feminist critics insist that our two-sex system simplifies a more complicated biological reality. Some infants are born *intersexed:* they may have the internal genitalia of one sex and the external genitalia of the other; their genitalia may be of a different sex than their chromosomes; or they may lack pronounced characteristics of either sex. When physicians resolve these situations by suppressing some sexual characteristics and enhancing others, a sexually *ambiguous* or *androgynous* reality is suppressed. Strictly speaking, the reality of sexual difference that includes intersexuals is what is natural, and the exclusive male or female system imposed on it is "manmade."

Although biological sex appears to be more fundamental than gender, other critics insist that this is true only of Western European cultures and only since the eighteenth century. In non–Western European cultural contexts, for example among some American Indian tribes, *berdache* are male-bodied individuals who assume the social roles of women, and are accepted as women because they choose women's roles. Another example of how gender can be more fundamental than sex appears in reports of *transsexuals* who claim to have known from an early age that despite the sex assigned to them at birth they are in fact the "opposite" sex. If we accept the validity of the introspections and longings of those whose gender is at odds with their assigned sex, then biological sex is not always foundational for sexual identity.

Before the seventeenth century in Europe, gender was more stable than biological sex as a source of identity. For example, respected medical authorities believed that women who exercised too strenuously would raise their body temperature, which was normally lower than that of men. As a result, female genitalia, which were believed to be inverted male genitalia, could "pop out" and such women would become men—a phenomenon that several learned doctors claimed to have directly observed. During the sixteenth and seventeenth centuries, women who assumed male social roles—for example, Queen Elizabeth I and the poet Aphra Behn—asserted that they had "masculine parts" that made such roles possible for them. (Queen Elizabeth insisted that she had the "heart and stomach of a king.")

After the early eighteenth century in Western culture, male and female sexual difference became closely associated with male and female gender difference. It has generally been assumed that men have the dominant social roles they do because of their biological sexual traits. For instance, male hormones are supposed to result in more aggressive behavior than female hormones. But men differ in their gender styles and in their degrees of masculinity, and women differ in their gender styles and degrees of femininity.

People differ in sexual preferences for partners, of opposite sex, same sex, or both opposite and same sex. To complicate matters even more, the gender of the sexual roles people enact may be different from their genders in nonsexual areas. For example, although aggression is associated with male gender and nonassertiveness with female gender, some heterosexual men are sexually nonassertive, and some heterosexual women are sexually aggressive.

Among all their variations, sex, gender, and sexuality are fundamental bases of identity and identification. In American life, race is also a very important, if not fundamental, basis of identity and identification; ethnicity often is as well. The two double categories of race/ethnicity and sex/gender may intersect in ways that result in differences in gender among people of the same sex with different racial and ethnic identities. In this chapter, we will focus on aspects of the *intersection* of gender and race. Historical aspects of black and white male gender are discussed in Section A, and black and white female gender in Section B. Section C is an introduction to some of the issues feminists have raised about racial differences among women.

A. BLACK AND WHITE MALE GENDER

In American history, black male gender was disadvantaged in comparison with white. During slavery, black men had none of the civil rights white men did, and from the end of slavery until the 1960s, they were denied access to the education, employment, and civic status available to white men. Insofar as adult male gender is the result of achievement in education and work that is recognized through civic status, black men were deprived of the opportunities to construct male gender routinely available to white men. In a society where men were the main economic providers for their nuclear families, black men were often unable to fulfill that role, as a result of discrimination in education, training, and employment. Black men therefore were unable to participate fully in the *patriarchal system,* in which men have been dominant over women personally, economically, professionally, intellectually, and politically.

The social and family roles associated with patriarchy gave white men control over the lives of their wives, daughters, and sisters, as well as the authority to protect them. Such roles were not available to black men in relation to black women during slavery, and after slavery, they were difficult for black men to construct. As a result, white slave-owners and, after slavery, white men generally, were able to directly exert control over the lives of black women.

The widespread exclusion of black men from patriarchy did not prevent black men from aspiring to the power and authority more easily attained by white men, and some attained them. But, along with the oppressive conditions of black male gender, black men were stereotyped as lazy, irresponsible, lawless, lewd, and unintelligent. They were also assigned occupational roles that were oppressive or personally limiting: menial worker, criminal, preacher, substance abuser, Uncle Tom, athlete, entertainer, violent black man, and so on. Missing from the range of normally attainable options were roles such as doctor, college professor, scientist, chief executive of a large institution, self-made millionaire, and well-to-do family man. Black men who attained and excelled at nonstereotypical roles tended to be categorized as exceptional black men. The implication of the adjective *exceptional* was that because the kind of achievements taken for granted by white men were not accessible to most black men, the black men who did attain them were odd and unusual. Thus the barriers to black male success were made to appear as traits of individuals rather than social restrictions.

The stereotypical gender roles assigned to black men tended to become self-fulfilling prophecies for two reasons. First, it is human nature to aspire to what others define as normal and customary, especially when stepping outside those norms may result in punishment from members of more powerful groups in society. Second, in Western culture, manhood is something to be achieved by young men, rather than an automatic conclusion to boyhood. Adult male personal identity and self-esteem depend on having done what is necessary to become a man. The behavior and accomplishments that certify manhood are observed by a young man's male peers and elders who already know him. Male roles that fall outside or beyond the range anointed by peers and elders may be useless for proving manhood in a young man's social context. If these peers and elders base their own manhood on racial stereotypes, then the stereotypical roles become the most viable options through which manhood can be achieved.

The ways in which men are recognized and publicly honored for high achievement by other men and women and children form a second important dimension of masculinity in American culture. Historically, white men were recognized by people of both sexes, all ages, and all races as eligible for public honor in a society in which men are publicly honored more than women. Black men were not equally eligible for public honor. Government officials and the public took a much longer time to honor black men of high achievement for the same deeds that immediately bestowed honor on white men. For example, American black men have fought in every war since the Revolutionary War, but their contributions as soldiers were not fully acclaimed until recently. In January 1997, black soldiers who deserved the Medal of Honor for bravery during World War II were finally decorated, some posthumously.

Blacks achieved full civil rights at about the time the second wave of feminism began in the 1960s. Women are now able to support themselves financially and to defer or reject traditional roles of dependence on men. Many women now occupy prestigious occupational roles previously reserved for white men and receive traditional male honors as well: there are two women on the Supreme Court; women have held the offices of U.S. attorney general, secretary of state, and national security adviser; women have been in military combat; and there are now women college presidents, professors, lawyers, doctors, and scientists. In a complementary fashion, many men now participate fully in the nurturing aspects of family life, and most men today realize that it is important for them to be aware of their own and others' emotions—a kind of sensitivity traditionally restricted to women. Generally speaking, the increase in female participation in workplaces has been accompanied by scholarly and popular criticism of patriarchy, or traditional white male gender dominance.

Compared to both white and black women, black men continue to be underrepresented in the gender roles retained by white men. Although Colin Powell was appointed secretary of state, black men have higher mortality and incarceration rates than white men. Fewer black men than black women graduate from college. Black men are also subject to criticism for some of the ways in which some of them have expressed their masculinity: harsh treatment of black women, sexual aggression toward all women, irresponsibility as fathers, criminal violence. Feminists criticize black male gender as part of patriarchy in the general sense, and some white conservatives typically view black male gender as dangerously deviant.

B. BLACK AND WHITE FEMALE GENDER

Before the 1970s, most middle- and upper-class American white women did not have economic or productive responsibilities outside the homes of their nuclear families. They were subordinate to men in the family and protected by men in situations outside the home. In contrast, after the Civil War black women were caregivers in extended families and worked outside their homes, as laborers and servants for whites, to support themselves and family members on the most basic levels of food, clothing, and housing. In the absence of black male patriarchs, they were often heads of households and single parents, long before the problems of single parents began to receive wide attention. Black women were not given the same physical and sexual protection that white men gave white women, and throughout much of American history, black men were unable to protect them. The result of these historical differences in circumstance is a less "feminine" and more self-reliant form of gender for black women than for white.

Some of the feminine roles denied black women were rejected by many white women after the 1970s. Nonetheless, the ways in which female gender was less feminine for black women did not amount to a more liberated situation. The employment available to black women was often exploitative and demeaning. Also, black women were often perceived, by men and women of both races, to fall short of ideals of female beauty and gender attractiveness.

American white normativity (see Chapter 7, Section B) applied Western European ideals of female attractiveness and moral goodness to women of all races. Those ideals derived from middle-class patterns of production that restricted women to the household. Before the 1600s, the majority of European households were extended social units of family members, servants, kin, and friends, who produced their own wealth, necessities for survival, and amenities by craft or agriculture. Everyone worked cooperatively within such households. After the 1600s, men worked in public places outside the home. European middle-class women were expected to take care of their homes and families and to support the employment, civic, and social activities of their husbands. If their husbands and fathers had enough money, drudgery could be assigned to women less well sponsored, and minor skills in the arts and music could be cultivated.

The female ideal, set by affluent families, was a physically weak but graceful creature, pleasant, tactful, intellectually superficial, and refined in manners and taste. Her sexuality was muted and she was expected to be spiritually uplifting to men. She ideally had pale skin, flowing, fine-textured hair, and delicate facial features. These ideals of white female virtue and beauty were unattainable by American black women, and other women of color, as a result of economic and social circumstances as well as physical differences. It is easy to imagine that if black or Asian women had been the members of the dominant social class, beauty ideals would have been based on their hereditary physical traits. The fact that rich white men were willing to subsidize white women of their class as decorative objects is probably the main reason for beauty ideals having been centered on white physical types. Most poor white women who could not become "ladies" in this way were aesthetically devalued. This exclusion of poor white women from the category of most desired white women further emphasizes the importance of social class in creating ideals of female beauty.

The aesthetic result of white middle- and upper-class dominance was a devaluation of black female attractiveness and beauty, by both whites and blacks. Black women held up as models of female beauty tended to resemble white European ideals, often because they were multiracial. This further burdened black women who did not resemble white ideals of beauty. In black culture, as well as white, beauty is an important part of female self-esteem. If some women are precluded from being beautiful within their own culture, as well as within white culture, then their self-esteem as women is potentially diminished. Of course, in any culture not all women are considered beautiful. But it is particularly cruel when some women are denied consideration solely on what are perceived to be racial grounds when these grounds have nothing to do with other standards of beauty, such as health, grace, symmetry, and personality and character.

The liabilities of the intersection of female sex and black race for black women were also evident in the kinds of occupational roles to which they were restricted. Stereotyped as nurturing, scheming, lewd, and unintelligent, they were typically assigned personally limiting occupational roles: servant, laborer, mammy, prostitute, church lady, matriarch. Although these roles often required near-heroic virtues of endurance, optimism, self-reliance, and altruism, they were all service roles. Black women who became professionals, entrepreneurs, or even successful entertainers were often viewed as "strong" black women or else perceived to be emotionally cold, selfish, and aggressive in unwomanly ways. Missing from the traditional occupational roles for black women was wide-scale recognition of their intellectual competence. In the early twenty-first century, there are a few acclaimed black female novelists but very few black female public intellectuals; black female nurses but fewer doctors; primary school teachers but fewer high school and college teachers; meter maids, postal employees, and police but not as many lawyers, prosecutors, and judges. The historical conditions that limited both male and female gender for African Americans have changed. When they live on through inertia or institutional racism, they become barriers to overcome through personal empowerment and group activism.

C. WOMEN OF COLOR AND FEMINISM

After the late 1970s, Indian, Asian, Chicana, Latina, African American, and multi- and biracial women activists and scholars constructed theories and descriptions of the lives of women of color in the United States. Some of their work has been developed as a criticism of earlier writing by white middle-class women in feminism and women's studies. Other strains of nonwhite feminism and women's studies have focused directly on goals and strategies for empowering American women of color.

The main criticism from feminist women of color about white feminism was that white feminists were preoccupied with themselves and their own middle-class problems. Feminists of color claimed that white feminists held a false essentialism of female gender that they mistakenly assumed was true for all women, regardless of race, ethnicity, or social class. Many white feminist theorists accepted this criticism and struggled with questions of whether a unified, universal type of feminism is possible. They abandoned a universal definition of women that was based on biology or culture, and they vowed not to speak for women of color. Feminists of color largely speak for themselves. This kind of ***difference feminism*** sometimes isolates feminists within their own racial or ethnic groups.

Feminists of different races have disagreed about whether racial liberation ought to take precedence over women's liberation, a question that has a long history in American political activism. Before the Civil War, there were strong alliances between women's rights advocates and abolitionists. Abolitionists, of course, wanted to end slavery, and nineteenth-century feminists were concerned to secure both voting and property rights for women. After the Civil War, many of the former male abolitionists broke with the cause of women's rights and secured voting rights for black men. This infuriated the *suffragists,* some of whom ignominiously tried to block passage of the Sixteenth Amendment. During Reconstruction and throughout the years of segregation, women's rights groups excluded black women. Black women formed their own networks of clubs, charities, and educational organizations that provided financial assistance and cultural encouragement within black communities.

After American women secured the vote in 1920, it became respectable for young middle-class white women to work before getting married, although career women were expected to remain single. During World War II, many American women participated in the defense industry and in support divisions of the military. After World War II, an economic boom was accompanied by a return to traditional nuclear family roles and values for white middle-class women. A contraction of the economy beginning in the early 1970s was accompanied by widespread acceptance of the goals of *women's liberation* movements that had formed during the 1960s. Today, the large majority of American women, irrespective of race or ethnicity, now expect that they and their daughters will need to work outside the home to contribute to family support, or that they will have to support themselves. They also expect that biological sex will not be a barrier to a fulfilling occupation. Law and public policy have supported those expectations, for instance, in greater access to higher education for women.

However, even in this generally liberatory climate for women, feminists of color perceive a need to define their problems within *parameters* of specific race and ethnicity. This is partly a reaction to ongoing perceptions of white racism throughout American society. It is also due to the facts that, in comparison with white women, women of color generally are more likely to be single heads of household, have less educational certification, make less money, be employed in lower-level, nonprofessional jobs, and experience unemployment. Asian women have educational levels and professional occupations comparable to those of white women. Single status and marital disruption have been higher for black and Puerto Rican women than for any other group, although all groups among women of color have experienced some increase in being heads of household during recent decades. Women heads of household disproportionately make up a new class of the poor, populated by women and children.

Some black feminists, out of concern for problems caused by racism against black males, have deferred addressing the oppression of black women by black men. These writers believe that for nonwhite women generally, racial oppression is more serious than gender oppression; they tend to think that white women are not as oppressed due to gender as all nonwhites are due to race. Some Native American feminists have emphasized the *matriarchal* political structures of traditional Indian cultures as well as indigenist beliefs that male and female genders ought to have equal power in human society. These writers have insisted that traditional Native American women already were liberated before the European invasion. The task of contemporary Indian feminists is therefore Indian liberation generally, through a return to traditional tribal cultural structures. Other feminists of color demand immediate liberatory measures and recognition for themselves as black women, Latinas, Chicanas, Asian women, Indian women, mixed-race women, and so forth.

Some of the demands for recognition and empowerment of nonwhite women have been forcefully made by feminists of color who describe and criticize contemporary society from the standpoint of *lesbian* experience. As lesbians, they are able to place the lives and perspectives of women at the center of human experience.

Some black women who have found inspiration as well as practical examples in the lives of their mothers and grandmothers have identified themselves as *womanists* since the 1980s. Many womanists are activists who emphasize the spiritual and social role of churches in black liberation. White feminists, by contrast, have often dismissed church activities on the grounds that organized religion is merely another oppressive dimension of patriarchy.

Many feminists of color feel that the particularly difficult intersections of race and gender that they experience make it necessary for them to create their knowledge based on their own experience. That is, they deliberately construct themselves as the only intellectuals who are qualified to analyze and change their own experience. Some believe that this intellectual authority can be used to liberate white women, men of color, and even some white men. If solutions to problems of people in the most difficult situations with the most marginalized identities can be found, then those solutions might apply to others who, in terms of intersection at least, are less oppressed. That is, the reasoning would be, "If *I* could do it, anyone could do it."

However, the importance of what women have in common should still be emphasized. Women are those human beings who identify with or are assigned to the category of biological females, or mothers, or heterosexual choices of men. Not all women are female from birth or mothers or men's sexual choices. But it is these identities that have made *feminism,* as advocacy for the well-being of women, necessary. Women of different racial and ethnic groups can better help each other if they recognize what women do have in common.

D. Discussion Questions

1. Discuss some instances in which people confuse social role differences between men and women with biological differences.

2. Is the disproportionate number of black males in the criminal justice system related to differences in black male gender in your opinion? Explain what you mean by *gender* in this answer.

3. Have you or has anyone you know experienced the limitations of a gender role assigned on the grounds of race or ethnicity?

4. Can you think of any aspects of male or female gender that have nothing to do with race? Be as specific as possible.

5. Do you think that a black female presidential candidate should be concerned more about barriers due to race or due to gender?

E. RECOMMENDED READING

For analyses of gender before the eighteenth century, see Merry E. Wiesner, *Women and Gender in Early Modern Europe,* and Naomi Zack, *Bachelors of Science: Seventeenth Century Identity, Then and Now,* chapters 4 and 12.

For discussions of black male gender, see Leonard Harris, "Honor: Emasculation and Empowerment," in Larry May and Robert A. Strikwerda, eds., *Rethinking Masculinity: Philosophical Explorations in Light of Feminism;* Waldo E. Martin, Jr., *The Mind of Frederick Douglass;* John P. Pittman, "Malcolm X: Masculinist Practice and Queer Theory," in Naomi Zack, ed., *RACE/SEX.* On occupational stereotypes and gender and race, see Judith Bradford and Crispin Sartwell, "Voiced Bodies/Embodied Voices," also in *RACE/SEX.*

For feminist psychological treatments of gender relative to race, see L. S. Brown and Maria P. P. Root, eds., *Diversity and Complexity in Feminist Therapy.* See also Ruben Martinez and Richard L. Dukes, "Ethnic and Gender Differences in Self Esteem," in *Youth and Society,* and Richard L. Dukes and Ruben Martinez, "The Impact of Ethgender Among Adolescents," in *Adolescence.* On feminist issues of essentialism, see Judith Butler, *Gender Trouble: Feminism and the Subversion of Identity,* and Nancy Holmstrom, "Do Women Have a Distinct Nature?" in Marjorie Pearsall, ed., *Women and Values: Readings in Recent Feminist Philosophy.*

For an account of the history of black and white feminism as political movements, see Eleanor Flexner, *A Century of Struggle.* See also the 2004 HBO movie *Iron-Jawed Angels.* Issues involved in the intersection of blackness and female gender are analyzed by Kimberle Crenshaw in "Demarginalizing the Intersection of Race and Sex: A Black Feminist Critique of Antidiscrimination Doctrine, Feminist Theory, and Antiracist Politics," in Alison Jagger, ed., *Living with Contradictions: Controversies in Feminist Social Ethics.* This intersection is explored in reference to Asian women by Karen Hossfeld in "Hiring Immigrant Women: Silicon Valley's 'Simple Formula,'" in Maxine Baca Zinn and Bonnie Thornton Dill, eds., *Women of Color in U.S. Society.*

A comprehensive source for black women's studies is Darlene Clark Hine, *Black Women in America: An Historical Encyclopedia,* 2 vols. Contemporary black feminist issues are discussed in the following sources: Patricia Hill Collins, "Learning to Think for Ourselves: Malcolm X's Black Nationalism Reconsidered," in Joe Wood, ed., *Malcolm X: In Our Own Image,* and Collins, *Black Feminist Thought;* Shirley M. Geiger, "African-American Single Mothers: Public Perceptions and Public Policies," in Kim Marie Vaz, ed., *Black Women in America;* Paula Giddings, *When and Where I Enter: The Impact of Black Women on Race and Sex in America;* B. A. Greene, "What Has Gone Before: The Legacy of Racism and Sexism in the Lives of Black Mothers and Daughters," in L. S. Brown and Maria P. P. Root, eds., *Diversity and Complexity in Feminist Therapy;* bell hooks, *Ain't I A Woman: Black Women and Feminism* and *Feminist Theory: From Margin to Center,* as well as "Sisterhood: Political Solidarity Between Women," in Janet Kourany, James Sterba, and Rosemarie Tong, eds., *Feminist Philosophies;* Gloria T. Hull et al., eds., *All the Women Are White, All the Blacks Are Men, but Some of Us Are Brave: Black Women's Studies;* Audre Lorde, *Sister Outsider;* Peggy McIntosh, "White Privilege and Male Privilege: A Personal Account of Coming to See Correspondences Through Work in Women's Studies," in Anne Minas, ed., *Gender Basics.*

A historical presentation of different ideals of white womanhood, written before the current wave of feminism, is Emily James Putnam's *The Lady: Studies of Certain Significant Phases of Her History.* See also Cheryl Herr, "The Erotics of Irishness."

For a nonfeminist black perspective on concerns shared by black Americans, see Nathan and Julia Hare, *The Endangered Black Family.* On womanism, see Alice Walker's *In Search of Our Mothers' Gardens.* On women and poverty, see Ruth Sidel, *Women and Children Last: The Plight of Poor Women in Affluent America.*

For feminist consideration of the situations of Indian and Asian Americans, see Paula Gunn Allen, *The Sacred Hoop: Recovering the Feminine in American Indian Traditions;* C. K. Bradshaw, "Beauty and the Beast: On Racial Ambiguity," in Maria P. P. Root, ed., *Racially Mixed People in America;* Bonnie Thornton Dill, "Fictive Kin, Paper Sons, and *Compadrazgo:* Women of Color and the Struggle for Family Survival," in Zinn and Dill, eds., *Women of Color in U.S. Society;* Amy Ling, *Between Worlds: Women Writers of Chinese Ancestry;* Evelyn P. Stevens, "Marianismo: The Other Face of Machismo in Latin America," in Anne Minas, ed., *Gender Basics.* See also Yoko Arisaka, "Asian Women: Invisibility, Locations, and Claims to Philosophy." On issues of how women are different and what they have in common, see Elizabeth V. Spelman, *Inessential Woman: Problems of Exclusion in Feminist Thought,* and Naomi Zack, *Inclusive Feminism: A Third Wave Theory of Women's Commonality.* See also Lisa Heldeke and Peg O'Connor, eds., *Oppression, Priviledge and Resistance.*

CHAPTER 10

RACE, ROMANCE, AND SEXUALITY

S uppose that you choose a romantic partner of a different race. How do you think your family and friends would react, and what would be the effects of this on your romantic relationship? If you cannot imagine making such a choice, explain why.

INTRODUCTION

There is a broad *folk model* of human sexuality in American culture that looks something like this: Human sexuality is a natural drive or set of desires that propels individuals toward sexual experiences with the opposite sex. These experiences are intensely pleasurable, and the primary sexual experience is intercourse. The *naturalness* of this sex drive is obvious because it is necessary for the reproduction of our species and can be observed throughout the biological kingdom, even in plants. *Notice that this model equates sex with heterosexuality and that it leaves love out of the picture.*

But there is a broad folk model for love as well: Falling in love is an exciting, almost hypnotic experience that is usually connected with strong sexual desire for the love object. If the bond of love is mutual and the pair have enough in common, and they are able to do so, then they should get married, have children, talk about their problems, raise their children, grow old together, and remain sexually faithful to one another throughout their lives. *Notice that this model associates heterosexuality with romantic love and that it leaves money out of the picture.*

There is no broad model for homosexual love, but there is a model for the importance of money: money is important but not as important as the well-being of one's family. Therefore, couples should work hard, save their money so they can buy a house, make more money, buy everything they need for the family, and set aside enough money so their children can go to college and duplicate the same lifestyle or, better yet, exceed it.

All three models work together as a simplified picture of what is normal and comes naturally, and as banal as these models appear, they have a powerful grip on the American psyche. As unifying ideals, there is nothing wrong with these models; but as descriptions of how human beings are, they omit the socially constructed aspects of both sexuality and romantic love, and they fail to take the social constructions of racial difference into account. The impact of racial difference on love and sex may make the combination of all three models more difficult to attain for members of some groups than for others.

The way that adults present themselves sexually and develop and express their sexual desires is a complex result of social, individual, and biological processes that begin in childhood: physical and psychological development, personal inclination, family influence, peer interaction, education, media images, advertising, and income. Sexuality may *seem* natural, but it is in fact highly influenced, if not structured, by changing cultural circumstances.

Even if there were a universal *sex drive* in human beings, that drive is never evident in what could be called a pure form. Sexual practices, sexual morality, and sexual choices vary widely from one culture to the next and over time within the same culture. Many external physical and social circumstances of human life, as well as individual desire and choice, determine the ways in which sexuality is experienced and expressed. It is therefore not surprising that race should intersect with sexuality as it does with gender. One obvious aspect of the intersection of sexuality and race is that the vast majority of Americans choose sexual partners who are of the same race as they. Related to that pervasive fact is the existence of myths about nonwhite sexuality and sexual stereotypes of nonwhites.

The purpose of this chapter is to examine some of the myths and stereotypes of nonwhite love and sexuality that have been created and re-created in popular culture. Section A is an analysis of the methodology of contemporary cultural criticism that uses novels, movies, and other pop cultural products as evidence for deep beliefs within the culture. Section B is a comparative discussion of romantic and sexual stereotypes of white and nonwhite men in the movies. Section C is a comparative discussion of romantic and sexual stereotypes of white and nonwhite women in the movies.

There are, of course, many other cultural sources and expressions of such stereotypes besides movies, such as print media, television, literature, theater, visual arts, popular fiction and nonfiction, advertising, and music. The advantage of focusing on movies is that they are accessible to both audiences and critics. Their popular consumption means that they gratify and influence large numbers of people. As material objects, movies are cultural documents that can be repeatedly experienced, which means that they can be studied systematically. Also, insofar as racial identification depends largely on visual appearance, movies literally show everyone what members of different races and ethnicities look like. Sections B and C will be severely dated soon after this edition is published. Readers are encouraged to contribute their own examples.

A. ANALYSIS OF A CRITICAL METHOD

Contemporary cultural critics who interpret media, novels, and big news stories seem to share a common method in showing how people are *stereotyped* and describing the *myths* about how stereotyped people behave and fare in life. The method is to describe how types of people and events are depicted in the example of the medium in question. This description is then generalized as a statement of how the filmmaker and audience, or novelist and reader, or journalist and readers, and so on, perceive all members of the type to which the character belongs. And the generalization is then critically examined for bias, that is, racism, sexism, and classism. For example, suppose a black woman in a movie plays the role of a sexually provocative maid who is raped and then commits suicide. A critic using this method might claim that the movie presents an image of black women as irrational menial workers who can be victimized and who will react self-destructively to such victimization. As a generalization about black women, the movie depiction and events could be interpreted as racist, sexist, and classist.

There seem to be several assumptions behind this critical method. First, the critic assumes that the creators of every artistic product think that their product will be viewed, heard, or read as a universal description of social reality. If the creators did not intend for their work to be accepted as universal, then they could not be held socially responsible for how they present characters who are members of specific groups. A second assumption behind such criticism is that the audience is willing to accept what the creators intend to portray as universally true. For example, they observe the plight of the maid as though she were an ***archetype*** rather than a representation of a unique individual. If the audience didn't believe that what they saw or read had this kind of general truth, the critical method based on generalization would be pointless. However, members of audiences are used to reacting to the real people they meet and interact with, as unique individuals, so why shouldn't they be expected to regard movie characters as particular individuals in the same way?

A response to this criticism of the critical method is that claims based on descriptions of events in popular cultural products need to have a wide empirical base in order to be valid. One movie in which a black woman is victimized is not sufficient to make a case about popular stereotypes about black women. Also, given the increase in independent filmmaking, critics of culture have a wide choice of subject matter. But if over a period of time, all or most black female roles in movies that do well at the box office depict menials who are victimized, then the critical generalizations about stereotype and myth would have some foundation. If the novel *Gone with the Wind* had a small cult following, not much about American nostalgia for the antebellum South could be asserted. But at the end of the twentieth century, this novel was still outselling the Bible, there was a well-attended theme park built around a "reproduction" of Scarlett O'Hara's ancestral plantation, Tara, in Georgia, and deluxe collectible editions of videos of the movie *Gone with the Wind* sold well. This would be an example of a strong basis for cultural criticism based on media analysis.

The critical method of examining stereotypes and myths through popular art further assumes that people look to film and other media to see what they already believe and to have those beliefs further articulated and strengthened. It is through the further articulation and strengthening process that the media may keep stereotypes and myths alive, teach them to upcoming generations, and bring large audiences up-to-date in a rapidly changing society. That is, as the media continually reach out to give the public what it wants, and the public reaches out to its media to find out what it wants, they form a partnership of creating and re creating stereotypes and myths. Although this process may not affect independent thinkers who are always vigilant and reluctant to suspend their disbelief, it does create a shared consensus about what other people think. For example, if there is a popular myth that young black males are predatory criminals, a white-on-white crime victim who wants sympathy but does not want to reveal the identity of the perpetrator may tell authorities that a black man did it.

B. Romantic and Sexual Movie Stereotypes of Men, by Race

The romantic and sexual desirability of northern European males is not a traditional basis for primary typing as it is, for example, with "Latin lovers." Therefore, strictly speaking, there are no white male romantic and sexual stereotypes. Rather, white males are portrayed as having nonromantic and nonsexual qualities that women find attractive, such as good looks, physical and psychological strength, heroism, decisiveness, courage, talent, power, and wealth. The psychological transformations toward desirability undergone by Bill Murray's character in *Groundhog Day* (1993) and Richard Gere's in *Pretty Woman* (1990) show that white males are not automatically attractive sexual objects. There are two ways to interpret this. The first is that white males have reserved normal masculine humanity for themselves, in a culture in which they dominate. The second is that white males as a group are romantically and sexually repressed.

The theory of white male repression is connected to a causal theory of the exaggerated eroticism of nonwhite males. As the result of a work ethic and moral traditions that do not consider love and sex important compared to money, knowledge, and power, white males project the erotic side of their psyches onto males of nonwhite racial groups. The nonwhite males, once mythologized as exaggeratedly erotic, are envied, feared, and hated by white males. At the same time, their exaggerated eroticism handicaps nonwhite males from depicting major roles connected to the serious concerns of life, such as business, science, political leadership, and military might.

In movies, racial divisions have been drawn so that the privileges of white masculinity are conferred mainly on northern Europeans. As the men get more southern in European geography, they tend to be portrayed as more interested in romance and sex. Another way of putting this is that masculine sexuality is cinematically depicted on a quantitative continuum from white to black skin. Thus, masculine sexuality increases as masculine gender power decreases. To a lesser extent, it also works the other way: masculine sexuality decreases as masculine gender power increases. Insofar as masculine sexuality is associated with heterosexuality, the "whiter" the man is, the more subject to portrayal as a "lightweight" who is diffident and passive—for example, some of the characters played by Hugh Grant. Similarly, the "blacker" the man is, the more is he subject to portrayal as a sexual predator, as in the stereotype of the black rapist.

The sexual and romantic stereotypes of black males were until recently based on attributes of large physical size, romantic infidelity, expertise in lovemaking, and emotional and physical abuse of female sexual objects of all races. It was rare for a serious love relationship between a man and a woman to be depicted with a black male protagonist or hero. Beyond sex, black men were stereotyped as romantically irresponsible or comical. The dutiful and supportive black husband was either a cardboard figure in popular entertainment, or a comedian. Such hyper-heterosexual stereotypes reinforce what some critics have identified as **homophobia** in African American communities. Black gay and bisexual men who conceal their sexuality on the "down low" are depicted in the (stage) musical *Not a Day Goes By*, and the 2003 HBO movie *Angels in America* has a black gay man as a central character.

Although Hispanics are officially classified as an ethnicity rather than a race, their romantic and sexual portrayals differ from white male stereotypes. Hispanic men tend to be stereotyped as "ladies' men," men who are very knowledgeable about the sensibilities and needs of women. They are frequently depicted in movies as fickle and unfaithful, emotionally superficial, and often financially as well as emotionally exploitative of women. Such characters are often very charming and engaging, however, such as Antonio Banderas's role in *Miami Rhapsody* (1995) or Johnny Depp's in *Don Juan De Marco* (1995). But the stereotype is not monolithic, because Mexican men are often depicted as stalwart family men, for example, in *Tortilla Soup* (2001) and *Walk on the Clouds* (1995).

Italians are white in American culture, but they are depicted with more intense interest in romance and sex than northern European men. The lead character in the HBO series *The Sopranos* always has more than one love interest, for example. Jewish men, by contrast, are not given roles as romantically serious as those assigned to other white ethnicities; instead, a strong humorous dimension seems to be consistently added to their sexuality. The positive aspect of such comedy is that it allows for wit, which is rare in movie depictions of romance today. The great success of Woody Allen's characters must in part be due to their intelligence.

Although Asian men frequently star in martial arts movies, they are rarely cast as sexual and romantic figures. When they do appear in such roles, they are likely to be portrayed as perverse or degenerate if young or middle-aged. As elders, they are often visible as ancient patriarchs, benign and wise grandfathers well removed from the erotic fray.

American Indian men, though stereotyped as either impossibly noble and heroic or violently out of control, are rarely portrayed in romantic contexts. It's not immediately clear why this is so except that current popular images of Indians generally run to the ethereal and near-extinct. Older images of Indians in westerns depicted them as "bloodthirsty savages," cruel scalpers and rapists whose actions on screen were meant to justify their massacre by white soldiers and cowboys. Men who are racially mixed in appearance tend to be romantically and sexually typed in the direction of the race that they most closely resemble, for example, Keanu Reeves's opposite Sandra Bullock in *Speed* (1994).

There is a sharp color line in cinematic depictions of sex and romance. Black men can be paired with black, Asian, mixed-black, Native American, East Indian, and dark-skinned Hispanic women without it being perceived necessary to present the racial difference as a problem. Black men are still not paired with white women unless the racial difference is one of the subjects of the movie. Such black-white pairings, which were historically taboo and resulted in violence against black men, do not result in the cinematic pair living happily ever after, for instance Spike Lee's *Jungle Fever* (1991).

C. ROMANTIC AND SEXUAL MOVIE STEREOTYPES OF WOMEN, BY RACE

First, unlike white males, white women are erotically stereotyped in American movies, and not every kind of white woman can be depicted in a sexual role. White women have to be within childbearing years and relatively thin in order to be cast in romantic and sexual roles that will attract large audiences. The romantic and sexual behavior of women in movies follows from their social or occupational roles. Thus, if a woman is someone's wife, her sexuality is likely to be subdued on screen—unless she is committing adultery, which takes her out of her wifely role. Mothers are rarely depicted in sexually exciting situations unless they are unfit mothers or unusually attractive. If a woman has a service job such as waitress, nurse, or secretary, she is likely to be portrayed as supportive and nurturing of the man with whom she is romantically or sexually involved. Professional or artistic women are less predictable romantically and sexually; although they are allowed to have intense and selfish romantic and sexual interests, their male partners are often harmed by them, suggesting that independent women are dangerous to men. Prostitutes are portrayed as the most sexual of working women but also the most unsuitable romantically from masculine points of view. Lesbians have become cinematic characters in recent years, but to be of interest to broad audiences, they have to look as though they would be sexually and romantically interesting to heterosexual men, that is, be nubile and thin, for example, Hilary Swank in *Boys Don't Cry* (1999) or all of the female leads in *High Art* (1998).

Generally, all women in romantic and sexual roles, regardless of race or ethnicity, are portrayed in movies from the perspective of male heterosexual viewers. Even in movies made for predominantly female audiences, female romantic and sexual characters are presented as sexually attractive to men. Male romantic leads, by contrast, do not have to be presented as sexually attractive to women by virtue of any special traits such as youth or thinness. They are presumed to be of romantic and sexual interest to women simply by being placed in romantic and sexual contexts. This suggests that for a man to be a romantic and sexual character it is enough if other men can identify with him, whereas the ability of women to have other women identify with them is not enough to certify their desirability. Thus in movies, women are still the *sexual objects,* in the sense of chosen recipients, rather than the *sexual subjects,* in the sense of those who do the choosing.

Although women are the chosen romantic and sexual objects in movies, there are still limitations on who may choose them. White women may be chosen by white men only. Nonwhite women may be chosen by men of any race, especially for casual sexual liaisons. In serious relationships on screen, especially marriage, non-white women are most likely to be chosen by men of the same race.

There are increasing roles for nonwhite women in the same range of occupations that are available to white women, but as romantic and sexual objects nonwhite women tend to be wives, girlfriends, entertainers, seductresses, and prostitutes. Although television shows and movies abound with black female judges in short courtroom scenes, and one does see nonwhite female doctors and lawyers with increasing frequency, the combination of these professional occupations with romantic and sexual appeal is less frequent. This suggests a general stereotype of either low socioeconomic class or a lack of intellectual talent in nonwhite women. However, the older stereotype of the (white) "dumb blonde" of working-class origins suggests that a more general image of female gender may be at work here. Exceptions are also increasingly frequent. In *Real Women Have Curves* (2002), America Ferrera's character rebels against her Chicana mother's shame over not conforming to Anglo ideals of thinness, and she further breaks away by leaving her home in Los Angeles to attend Columbia University.

Like men in romantic and sexual roles, Jewish and Italian women are presented as more sexual types than are northern European women. For example, Meryl Streep in *The Bridges of Madison County* (1995) is convincing as the Iowa farmwife lover of Clint Eastwood, in part because she is depicted as an Italian woman. However, as with Jewish men, the general sexual and romantic sensibility of Jewish women is often portrayed in ways that cast doubt on their conformity to traditional ideals of white female gender. Thus, Jewish women in romantic leads are stereotyped as overly talkative, critical, and generally not submissive to men, for example, Barbra Streisand in *The Way We Were* (1973).

Similar to portrayals of masculine sexuality, there is a cinematic color line from white to black skin, along which the intensity of female sexuality varies. If this is due to a suppression of sexuality in northern European women, to match the repression of sexuality in northern European men, it allows for a sublimation of sexuality into romance for northern European women.

The more intense sexualization of darker-skinned women is not a neutral fact. As sexual rather than romantic objects, these women are portrayed on screen as being unusually attractive to men. They can be viewed either as outlets for repressed sexuality or, in conjunction with their cinematic moral vices, as symbols of what has in European Christian culture been constructed as the dark, sinful side of the human psyche. Thus, parallel to the male white-black continuum with an English dandy on one end and a black rapist on the other, the female white-black continuum runs from frigid northern European women (including nuns) to oversexed black women (including prostitutes and other sinners). However, as with other generalizations, counter-examples are robust. In *How Stella Got Her Groove Back* (1998), Angela Bassett plays a forty-year-old stockbroker who is reluctant to yield to her attraction to a younger man. And in *Monster's Ball* (2001), Halle Berry's character enters a romance with the former prison guard who oversaw her husband's execution, for complex reasons that go beyond sexuality. Furthermore, Whoopi Goldberg in all of her movies has played black women who are humorous, intelligent, and far from being defined by myths about black female sexuality.

D. DISCUSSION QUESTIONS

1. Describe, in as much detail as you can, a sexual stereotype attached to a man or woman of a particular nonwhite race.

2. Describe a sexual stereotype attached to a man or woman of mixed race.

3. Describe in detail how a movie or TV show that you are familiar with reinforces a racial sexual stereotype. Also, describe one that breaks a stereotype.

4. Do you think people acquire racial sexual stereotypes from the movies? If so, what would the psychological process be?

5. What racial sexual stereotypes do nonwhites have about whites?

E. RECOMMENDED SOURCES

Film

Older portrayals of white men as nonsexual but nonetheless sexually attractive types are ubiquitous. See, for example, *Unforgiven, The American President, Mr. Holland's Opus,* and *Sabrina,* not to mention any one of thousands of action movies.

In the early days of American theater, in the genre of **minstrelsy,** blacks did not appear onstage, and their parts were played by whites in "blackface." In 2000, with *Bamboozled,* Spike Lee made fun of minstrelsy with black actors, at the expense of both black and white audiences. Until the late 1960s, serious black characters were rare on screen. But this is changing on an individual basis. See John Lahr, "Escaping the Matrix: The Making of Laurence Fishburne." The figure of the tragic mulatto can be traced through *Showboat, Imitation of Life,* and more recently, *Devil in a Blue Dress* (1995). Mixed-race men are also depicted as alienated tragic figures. See *Invitation to a Gunfight* (1964) and *Map of the Human Heart* (1993).

Even superficial interracial romantic relationships were generally doomed in plays and movies. When the man was black and the woman white, often lurid tragedy resulted, as in *Native Son* (1950, 1986). The sinister side of interracial sex in American life has been the lynching and castration of black men believed to have white female partners and the sexual exploitation and rape of black women by white men. The overt racism that swirls around these situations is depicted in the movies *Rosewood* (1997) and *A Time to Kill* (1996).

Such portrayals of interracial sex draw on broader myths about the sexuality of black men and women. Black men tend to be portrayed as romantically and sexually irresponsible, as, for instance, the black heroines of *Waiting to Exhale* (1995) lament. Black women are supposed to be highly interested in sex but even more interested in money, as the same movie attests. In contrast, the white heroines of *First Wives Club* (1996) are more interested in self-fulfillment. Other portrayals of black women emphasize their tribulations and sorrows, with success and happiness small blips at the end if the heroine overcomes adversity, as in *What's Love Got to*

Do with It? (1993). Sometimes, real-life tragedy converges with art, as in *Lady Day: The Many Faces of Billie Holliday* (1991).

There have been sensitive cinematic portrayals of love problems resulting from cultural conflicts. See Frederic Mitterand's 1995 version of *Madame Butterfly* for a depiction of Asian female passivity. In the 1992 movie *The Last of His Tribe,* the genocide of the Washo Indians in central California is dramatized by the alienation and enforced sexual loneliness of their last survivor in 1911.

Media Events and Sex and Race

At the end of the twentieth century, the American public weathered at least three major media storms concerning the alleged dangerous sexuality of black men: Mike Tyson's rape trial, Clarence Thomas's Supreme Court nomination hearings, and the O. J. Simpson trial. Most Americans believe that Mike Tyson was guilty of rape, Clarence Thomas of sexual harassment, and O. J. Simpson of murder. Whether these judgments are correct or not, they reinforce negative stereotypes and myths. In 2004, there was a similar media circus about Kobe Bryant's alleged rape of a white woman.

Marlon Riggs discusses portrayals of black male sexuality on television in "Sexuality, Television, and Death: A Black Gay Dialogue on Malcolm X," in Joe Wood, ed., *Malcolm X: In Our Own Image.* Bridget A. Freydberg chronicles roles played by black and Hispanic women in older movies, in "Sapphires, Spitfires, Sluts and Superbitches: Aframericans and Latinas in Contemporary American Film," in Kim Marie Vaz, ed., *Black Women in America.*

There have been no recent media events featuring black women that have compared to the scandals involving black men, with the exception of the vilification of Anita Hill, who testified against Clarence Thomas. See Toni Morrison, ed., *Racing Justice, En-gendering Power: Essays on Anita Hill, Clarence Thomas and the Construction of Social Reality,* and Jane Flax, *The American Dream in Black and White*. It may be, however, that the public outcry following the televised exposure of Janet Jackson's breast on Super Bowl Sunday in 2004 is comparable to attention paid to the sexual misconduct of black men.

Readings on interracial sexual relations include Beth Day, *Sexual Life Between Blacks and Whites: The Roots of Racism;* L. R. Tenzer, *A Completely New Look at Interracial Sexuality: Public Opinion and Select Commentaries;* I. Stuart and L. Abt, eds., *Interracial Marriage: Expectations and Realities.* (There is also a 1996 film, *Mr. and Mrs. Loving,* about the couple who brought the lawsuit that resulted in the U.S. Supreme Court striking down existing anti-miscegenation laws in 1967.) See also Calvin Hernton, *Sex and Racism in America.*

Thomas Laquer presents a historical analysis of the relationship between sex and gender in *Making Sex: Body and Gender from the Greeks to Freud.* Lawrence Stone offers a historical account of early modern sexuality in *The Family, Sex and Marriage in England, 1500–1800.*

Toni Morrison's novel *The Bluest Eye* explores the effects on black women of ideals of white female sexuality. Laurie Shrage examines the fact that the majority of working prostitutes worldwide are nonwhite in *Moral Dilemmas of Feminism: Prostitution, Adultery and Abortion,* chapter 6.

For philosophical analyses of social constructions of nonwhite sexuality, see the following, all in Naomi Zack, ed., *RACE/SEX:* Lewis R. Gordon, "Race, Sex and Matrices of Desire in an Antiblack World"; Kevin Thomas Miles, "Body Badges: Race and Sex"; Naomi Zack, "The American Sexualization of Race." See also L. Jones, *Bulletproof Diva: Tales of Race, Sex, and Hair.*

For international analyses of nonwhite homosexuality, see Anne McClintock, Jose Esteban Muñoz, and Trish Rosen, eds., *Race and Queer Sexuality.* See also Gina Marchetti, *Romance and 'The Yellow Peril': Race, Sex and Discursive Strategies in Hollywood Fiction;* Russell Leong, *Asian American Sexualities: Dimensions of the Gay and Lesbian Experience;* Curtis Chin, Witness Aloud: Lesbian, Gay, and Bisexual Asian/Pacific American Writing. See also Åsebrit Sundquist, *Pocahontas & Co.: The Fictional American Indian Woman in Nineteenth-Century Literature: A Study of Method;* Ward Churchill, *Fantasies of the Master Race.*

CHAPTER 11

RACE AND CLASS

S uppose that someone makes a false assumption, based on your race or ethnicity, about your family income and whether your parents went to college. You set the record straight, and the other person is clearly embarrassed. What are the reasons for his or her embarrassment?

INTRODUCTION

A classless, egalitarian society has long been an American ideal, especially in the western states. The ideal is that everyone, regardless of origins, is equal in the eyes of the law and has the same opportunities to strive for material success and the same rights to respect and privacy. Throughout the nineteenth century, it was popularly believed that privilege and snobbery were symptoms of European decadence and corruption and that Americans were all equal because of their constitutional rights as individuals, their spirit of independence, and their shared sense of being part of a young, dynamic civilization. A system of *social caste,* with unchanging hereditary membership at each level of a hierarchy of social status and economic and political power, was deeply repugnant to the majority of Americans. This idealistic aversion to class and caste has been reinforced in practice by the continuously changing nature of American culture. Americans have never had a strong, broad sense of the importance of history. The past is something vaguely behind us that we constantly shed, even as we nostalgically reinvent selected parts of it.

Detailed knowledge of the past, and attachment to *tradition* simply because it is tradition, are important components of class and caste systems. Therefore, the lack of a strong sense of history is part of the American aversion to class and caste. Nonetheless, this aversion is not the same as an actual absence of class and caste. Since colonial days, there have been inherited divisions between rich and poor, powerful and disenfranchised. Although Americans do not make rigid personal or moral judgments about preferred family backgrounds and *breeding,* education and income are still great social dividers.

Men from established, prestigious families who are also graduates of a handful of exclusive preparatory schools and universities have occupied the highest political, business, and institutional positions in the United States since the nineteenth century. In parallel ways, their mothers, sisters, and wives have been occupied in charities, formal social events, and support for the arts. This ruling elite marries within its own ranks and is the unacknowledged American upper class. Members of the vast middle class (or classes) below it range from affluent professionals to skilled blue-collar workers and small-business proprietors. Below the middle class are the poor: employed unskilled workers and the occasionally unemployed. At the bottom is an underclass: clients of welfare, the homeless, seasonal workers, the chronically unemployed, petty criminals who work the streets, and indigent criminals in prison, awaiting trial, or on probation. Successful, affluent criminals are upwardly mobile in the class system.

The different socioeconomic levels are generally acknowledged, but most Americans hesitate to call them a class system, for two reasons. First, it is believed that opportunity exists at every level for those who are hardworking and enterprising. Second, many groups and individuals have moved up socioeconomically. Although a smaller number have moved down and there are always individuals moving down due to unemployment, these cases are not considered typical. The hope of upward mobility for oneself and one's family is a potent source of optimism about the future.

It should be remembered that despite upward mobility, adults at every socioeconomic level have children who automatically start out as members of the class to which their parents belong. Also, as the socioeconomic levels get lower, so do the moral appraisals attached to them. Poverty itself is shameful in the United States. Between 35 million and 42 million Americans are poor, but they are not visible in the ways members of other disadvantaged groups are. The very words *up* and *down* and *upper, middle,* and *lower* suggest that something more than variety is at stake with class difference.

In the United States, the mere possession of money has always conferred security and respect for just about anyone. Historically, upward mobility through the unacknowledged class system has usually accompanied financial success. The archetypal immigrant success story begins with a first generation that works hard at whatever employment it can get. Parents in the first generation assist the second generation financially and encourage success in the educational system. The second generation sees the third generation achieve solid business or professional status and full social acceptance as American by the larger society.

The popular model of an American classless and casteless society breaks down against the limiting facts of poverty within the white group and the ongoing conditions of racial segregation and discrimination within each class. Just as race intersects with gender and sexuality, it also intersects with socioeconomic class. The issues involved in that intersection form the topics of this chapter. Section A is a discussion of traditional *liberation theory* generally and *class theory* in particular. Section B is a discussion of the relevance of socioeconomic and racial difference to childhood experience. Section C focuses directly on how social class intersects with race at this time in the United States.

A. LIBERATION THEORY AND CLASS THEORY

An *ideology* is a critical description and analysis of social reality that is motivated by a commitment to change some aspects of that reality. Unlike religion or theology, ideology has purely secular concerns and is usually formulated around the conditions and goals of a particular historical group. Communism, socialism, and capitalism are ideologies, as are feminism and black liberation. Over time, the scholarly development of ideologies results in *critical theories.* The ongoing gap between the ideological goals and reality is analyzed in terms of existing social structures that are not fully understood by their participants. The absence of justice and equality may be explained in terms of the interests of dominant groups that have unfair advantages, such as white men, white racists, profit-motivated business people, or power-motivated politicians. However, unless members of subordinate groups such as women, nonwhites, consumers, and citizens become aware of their positions as members of subordinate groups, liberatory social change is unlikely. Critical theorists usually offer their analyses in the service of such liberatory change.

There is a long tradition in Western culture of political ideologies based on theories of social classes. The ancient Greeks viewed social classes as political reflections of natural classes among human beings. They believed there was a *natural aristocracy* of morally and intellectually superior human beings. This natural aristocracy was assumed to consist of rich men of high social status who had a right to rule. The justification for this ancient *elitism* was, first, that it was believed right for the best to rule and, second, that everyone would benefit if the best ruled.

The European industrial revolution gave rise to a new middle class that invested for profit and accumulated material wealth as its reward. This capitalistic owning class had its own political theorists, who attacked the privileges of monarchs and nobles on the grounds that all men were equal. They argued that those men who had acquired material goods had a fundamental right to the enjoyment of their possessions and the freedom to acquire more, and that they were also entitled to political representation to protect their property rights. One part of the justification for capitalism and representative government was *natural law:* God had made men equal, decreed that they should work, and given them the power to construct social and legal systems that would protect their private property. The other part of the justification for capitalism and representative government was the claim that, in the long run, all members of society would be better off and prosper if there were freedom for the enterprising to acquire wealth and keep it. Surplus wealth would support science and the arts and provide charitable assistance to those who labored for subsistence without acquiring anything. Women were not originally part of the capitalistic system except as wives in the middle class and laborers among the working poor. Upper-class women had complex social duties, besides their domestic ones. The role of non-Europeans, especially those from parts of the world that were colonized to use their raw materials in capitalistic production, was politically and socially *marginalized.*

During the nineteenth century, the third phase in Western European political ideology centered on the working class. It was at this stage that Karl Marx gave the critical theory of social and economic class its most radical liberatory form. According to Marx, all human beings had to work and produce or process material things to survive. Every human society had characteristic and dominant means of production, which in the nineteenth century were industrial enterprises such as factories and mines. The social class that controlled the dominant nineteenth-century means of production, and that was, through representative government, the effective ruling class, was the *bourgeoisie.* The bourgeoisie lived and ruled on the basis of the difference in the value of the goods produced by the workers, or *proletariat,* and what it paid the proletariat in wages. This difference was the *profit* that motivated capitalists. The European proletariat was exploited because it was not paid enough to securely sustain life or develop personally in leisure time. Therefore, according to *Marxist ideology,* the proletariat ought to take over and run the means of production through which it already produced everything. Common ownership of the means of production by the workers through their government, or *communism,* was justified on the grounds that it was morally right and that all classes in society would live more fulfilling lives as a result.

Within Western political ideology, the class posited as potentially liberatory for all thus shifted from the aristocracy in ancient times, to the middle class during the early modern period, to the working class in the late modern period. Of course, this shift marks the chronology of influential theories rather than popular belief. In the United States, for example, communism was never widely accepted as a political ideology, and bourgeois ideology, or the ideology of capitalism, remains dominant.

As critical theories, both feminism and racial liberation also operate on the premises that the liberation of women and nonwhites is just, and that once these groups are liberated, everyone else will benefit. However, they are not so much class theories as they are theories about dominance and participation. Many feminists believe that full equality for women will also entail full equality and more enriching lives for all men. Many black liberationists believe that full social equality for black people will also set white people free. In both cases, universal liberation is projected because situations of oppression are believed to waste energy and repress love, creativity, and personal freedom among oppressors and oppressed alike.

It is not merely the goods that accrue to individuals due to their social class, gender, or race that are important for human happiness and fulfillment according to these theories. Rather, the nature of the work each group contributes is the focus. If people labor at boring, repetitive, and arduous tasks for low pay, or if they are not paid for their work or its value is unrecognized, they lack full status as human beings in their culture. Although the solution to poverty in a technologically complex society might be more money through higher wages, this solution does not address nonmaterial satisfactions.

Some Native American critical theorists have rejected Marxist analyses as irrelevant to Indian liberatory struggles because they do not think that redistribution of wealth and employment would result in the human goods that they value. Within Indian cultures, natural environments themselves are believed to be more important than the consumer items produced from resources extracted from these environments. Therefore, both capitalism and communism are considered parts of the same unbalanced and unnatural cultural process. Indian identity and loyalty are expressed in relation to particular Indian nations (that non-Indians used to call tribes), which, if not externally interfered with by Euro-Americans, would continue in ways of living that are mutually beneficial to human beings and nature.

In contrast to those Native American critical theorists who believe that social class oppression is irrelevant to their fundamental concerns, some African American critical theorists have argued that high unemployment and poverty, rather than racism, is the fundamental cause of African American problems. These theorists contend that the civil rights legislation of the 1960s made it possible only for blacks who were already advantaged to rise socioeconomically. Since the mid-1960s, remedies for racism such as affirmative action programs have not improved conditions for the non-middle-class blacks, who remain poor and educationally disadvantaged. If anything, the gains afforded advantaged blacks have divided the black community, especially after the new black middle class left the inner cities. Therefore, these critics propose that the way to solve the problems of the black urban poor is to create employment and educational opportunities directly for them or encourage them to do so themselves.

B. CHILDHOOD, CLASS, AND RACE

The more complicated adult life is, the longer the period of childhood. Childhood is a variable chunk of human life without adult responsibility or obligation. In contemporary Western middle-class culture, childhood is supposed to be nurturing and enjoyable for children. Adults are supposed to take care of children, and the work of childhood is learning and play. This concept of childhood is not universal, either across cultures or historically. During the Middle Ages, eight was held to be the age of reason, and children were expected to be gainfully employed unless they belonged to leisured groups in which adults did not work either. Child labor among the poor did not officially end in Western society until the early twentieth century, and many children throughout the world are still expected to earn their keep and contribute to family income.

There are varied theories about the influence of events in childhood on later life. The application of such theories to middle-class child rearing began in the late 1600s. It then became accepted among educated, progressive-minded parents in England and France that children ought to be taught through play and motivated by parental praise and blame rather than physical punishment. Thought was given to the practical content of educational curricula, to teach the sons of the bourgeoisie how to carry on the productive economic and civic responsibilities of their fathers.

Most middle-class parents today believe that they have an obligation to protect their children from the harsh realities of human life, indulge their desire for play, and, above all, not harm them. They also agree that the serious business of parenting includes preparing children to become productive members of the middle class when they grow up.

Not only the virtues of child rearing but the virtues of children themselves have their base in middle-class values in the United States. Since the middle class is predominantly white, nonwhite and non-middle-class groups have different values to impart to children and they reinforce different virtues of childhood. Parents who do not have college educations or the financial and social resources—that is, the *leisure*—to teach their children how to behave like middle-class children are unlikely to *reproduce* middle-class values in the course of child rearing. Children of the poor are therefore likely to grow up with different values, different ideas of what is important in life, from middle-class children. If their parents have to deal with racism, children will learn antiracist strategies from those examples. Such defenses against racism may include a deliberate rejection of the activities at which only white people seem to excel, such as success in school. Neighborhood violence might cause fears about physical survival in childhood and make it seem as though having weapons and being prepared to fight are the best tactics for remaining alive. Without resources for play, alcohol, drugs, and other high-risk indulgences may appear to be acceptable forms of recreation.

The children of migrant agricultural workers, who have to labor and grow up without a stable sense of place, also fail to experience the structures of childhood that are considered normal in the middle class, perhaps more so than any other group. If they are further denied access to public services, such as education and health care, their chances of living more advantaged lives than their parents are further reduced.

C. CLASS AND RACE

Most people grow up to belong to the same social class as their parents (although, as noted, Americans do not like to identify by class). It has already been noted in Chapter 6 that nonwhite race is a barrier to full access to middle- and upper-class advantages. This has resulted in nonwhites disproportionately remaining in the working class over generations.

Although white members of the working class have been exploited by white managers and entrepreneurs, the white working class has not always made strong demands for liberation on the grounds of working-class identity. It has been suggested that one reason for this is that white identity has been an implicit part of white working-class wages. The American union movement was successful in securing higher wages, health insurance, unemployment benefits, and the curtailment of child labor, but labor unions have traditionally had white majorities. To this day, many Hispanic workers in agriculture, and Asian workers in low-tech assembly jobs, are not unionized. Union workers tend to be skilled workers who consider themselves middle-class. Racial disparity in union membership and the lack of a strong working-class identity across racial difference have had a "whitening" effect on the successful segment of the American working class.

The middle class can be defined as the group that is able to attain and maintain the economic and social goals of home ownership, steady employment, college education, and more or less stable nuclear family life. Personal fulfillment and job satisfaction are most likely to be found in middle-class employment. Traditionally in American history, the middle class has been white, although it does have nonwhite members. Generally, black members of the middle class consistently do not do as well as their white counterparts: they make less money, own less property, and send fewer children to college; their health statistics are also not as favorable as those of whites. Asians and Jews are generally well established in the economic aspects of middle-class life. Hispanics do not generally have a strong presence in the middle class, and Native Americans are barely visible there.

There are very few nonwhite members of the American upper class. Within the Asian American and black communities, there are socioeconomic class structures that in themselves have been based on racial or ethnic difference. For example, Vietnamese refugees occupy the lowest socioeconomic levels among Asians; newly arrived immigrants from China and Korea who did not have high socioeconomic status in their countries of origin do not have it in the United States when they start out in the workforce.

The African American community has contained socioeconomic division since colonial days. There were free blacks in the North and even in slave-owning states all through the period of slavery. Some were *freedmen* and their descendants, whereas others had never been enslaved. This group was never accepted as equals by whites, but its members could own property and acquire literacy. Among enslaved blacks, those who were overseers, had domestic authority, or were owned by wealthy men were better off materially and had higher social status. The black members of the American middle class, especially those who have family traditions of college education and membership in the professions, have been an upper class within the black community.

Until the ***Harlem Renaissance*** of the 1930s, when African Americans generally began to unite as a racial group, there was an American ***mulatto elite,*** mixed race in ancestry and appearance, that had family histories of advanced education and professional employment within the black community. Recognition of the white ancestry of this class contributed to its elevated social status, and its members were frequently selected by white leaders to be leaders of projects concerning blacks overall. This historical association of privilege and whiteness at times made the mulatto elite exceptionally unpopular with poor blacks and their spokespersons. Although the mulatto elite no longer exists, blacks who are successful in mainstream white society are still often resented by poor, undereducated, and underemployed blacks, as well as by whites who are less successful. Within the black community this resentment carries the accusation of not being an authentic member of "the race."

In both urban and rural areas, black race has intersected with disadvantaged socioeconomic class to create a ***black underclass*** of hard-core unemployed and their children. The plight of the urban section of this class is viewed partly as the result of black middle-class flight from black urban neighborhoods to suburbs. The plight of the rural section is viewed partly as a general migration to cities by enterprising young people from depressed rural areas. More broadly, the existence of a black underclass is viewed as the most unfortunate result of institutionalized antiblack racism in the United States. Members of this class are disproportionately incarcerated within a prison system that between 1970 and 2000 increased from 400,000 to 1.3 million. Still, the demographic and racist background causes of this class do not prevent it from being feared and hated by other socioeconomic and racial groups in the culture. It is believed that the disproportionate number of black men who are involved in the criminal justice system are "bred" in female-headed households within the black urban underclass, and that the black urban underclass is the main "grassroots" support for illegal drug use and distribution in the United States today. Nonetheless, the increase in American prisons from 592 in 1974 to 1,023 in 2000 was in many counties motivated by anticipated profits from prison construction, income from employment of staff, and more federal funds for public services insofar as inmates are counted as residents of the counties in which they are imprisoned. Finally, it should be noted that because working-class Americans view themselves as middle-class, and under-class Americans are not part of any traditional class system, classic theories of social class as a locus for liberatory identities are often now inadequate. Indeed, much of this book has used ideas of race and racial identity as more insightful tools for understanding social injustice.

D. DISCUSSION QUESTIONS

1. How would you describe your social class or the social class of a close friend?

2. If sex and race are the first things Americans notice about strangers, at what stage in interaction do you think social class is noticed, and what are the *codes* for it?

3. Describe the social class structure of a racial group different from your own.

4. What conclusions can be drawn about the importance of race in determining social class in the United States?

5. Do you think that white racism varies according to social class in the United States—that is, that blue-collar, middle-class, and upper-class whites typically have different forms of racism? Describe how.

E. RECOMMENDED READING

The classic sources in Western political theory for the ideas that some groups will liberate all are (for the aristocracy) Plato, *The Republic,* and Aristotle, *Politics,* and *Nicomachean Ethics;* (for the middle class or bourgeoisie) John Locke, *Two Treatises of Government,* II, and Adam Smith, *The Wealth of Nations;* in interpretation of Locke, see C. B. MacPherson's *The Political Theory of Possessive Individualism,* and on natural law theory, see Edward S. Corwin, *The "Higher Law" Background of American Constitutional Law;* (for the working class) Karl Marx and Frederick Engels, "The Communist Manifesto," in Lawrence H. Simon, ed., *Karl Marx, Selected Writings;* for interpretations and further applications of Marx, see Nancy Holmstrom, "Race, Gender and Human Nature," in Naomi Zack, ed., *RACE/SEX,* and Sidney Hook, *From Hegel to Marx.* An activist application of Marxian ideology to undereducated workers is Paulo Freire's *Pedagogy of the Oppressed.* On the importance of race and class in childhood, see C. E. Sleeter, ed., *Empowerment Through Multicultural Education;* Jennifer Clancy, "Multiracial Identity Assertion in the Sociopolitical Context of Primary Education," in Naomi Zack, ed., *American*

Mixed Race; Helena Jia Hershel, "The Influence of Gender and Race Status on Self-Esteem During Childhood and Adolescence," in Naomi Zack, ed., *RACE/SEX.* On Native American rejection of Marxist ideology, see Ward Churchill, ed., *Marxism and Native Americans.*

On the historical study of childhood, see Philippe Ariès's analysis of ideas and practices of childhood in *Centuries of Childhood.* John Locke presents the modern model for middle-class child rearing in "Some Thoughts Concerning Education," in James A. Axtell, ed., *The Educational Writings of John Locke;* an interpretation of Locke's ideas is in Naomi Zack, *Bachelors of Science: Seventeenth Century Identity, Then and Now,* chapter 10. Nancy Chodorow in *The Reproduction of Mothering* explains how gender roles are reproduced in families. Cultural variations in forms of the family are discussed by Linda Nicholson in *Gender and History* and Naomi Zack in "'The Family' and Radical Family Theory," in Hilde Lindemann Nelson, ed., *Feminism and Families.*

On the effects of socioeconomic conditions on migrant childhood experience, see Robert Coles, *Uprooted Children.* See also Michelle Moody-Adams, "Race, Class and the Social Construction of Self-Respect," in John P. Pittman, ed., *African-American Perspectives and Philosophical Traditions.*

For socioeconomic statistics on American racial and ethnic groups, see *The Statistical Record of Black Americans; The Statistical Record of Asian Americans; The Statistical Record of Native North Americans,* and so on. For up-to-date information on disadvantaged groups, consult the National Urban League online at www.nul.org. Historical sources about free blacks during the period of slavery include Ira Berlin, *Slaves Without Masters: The Free Negro in the Antebellum South;* David W. Cohen and Jack P. Greene, eds., *Neither Slave nor Free: The Freedmen of African Descent in the Slave Societies of the New World.* On differences in social class within the black group, see W. E. Cross, *Shades of Black: Diversity in African-American Identity.* For a study of how differences in social science research findings about blacks vary with the race of the investigators, see Wade W. Nobles and Goddard L. Lawford, *Understanding the Black Family.*

For further reading on the intersection of race and social class, see Robert and Jane Hollowell Coles, *Women of Crisis;* Angela Y. Davis, *Women, Race and Class;* Carl N. Degler, *Neither Black Nor White: Slavery and Race Relations in Brazil and the U.S.;* Gerald Horne, "On the Criminalization of a Race," in *Political Affairs;* Bill E. Lawson, ed., *The Underclass Question;* Thomas Sowell, *The Economics and Politics of Race: An International Perspective;* William Julius Wilson, *The Truly Disadvantaged.* On American poverty generally, see David K. Shipler, *The Working Poor: Invisible in America.* See also Walter Benn Michaels, "Diversity's False Solace." On race and class inequalities in education, see Jonathan Kozol, *Savage Inequalities: Children in American Schools.*

CONCLUSION

You go to group therapy once a week to work on a very specific personal problem that you share with other members of the group. The group is diverse in race, ethnicity, gender, and sexual preference, but in over two years, no one has ever mentioned race. You think that the group's concerns are deeper than race, but lately you've noticed that people seem to go out of their way to avoid mentioning race. Do you think the group would have to talk about race in order to make important progress on the main subject of concern, even though that subject has nothing to do with race?

INTRODUCTION

The chapter headings in this book by no means exhaust the topics under which race has been studied and experienced in American life, or how we can think about it. And any reader who has supplemented the text with more specific external readings is aware of the extent to which the ideas presented here are general and inconclusive. This is partly due to the *toolbox* intention behind the book. Tools for thinking about race do not determine what you will think about or your conclusions. Also, race itself, as an idea or complex of ideas, is general and inconclusive. Therefore, to bring some closure to the discussions begun here, it might be helpful to consider two things: (A) Racial thinking in real life requires an awareness of boundaries, and (B) Americans might be ready for a new paradigm of race.

A. BOUNDARIES AND RACE

The notion of *boundaries,* and drawing and respecting boundaries, can be borrowed from contemporary clinical and self-help psychology. When a person, *P,* sets boundaries in an interaction with another person, *Q, P* communicates to *Q* that certain areas of *P*'s life, person, and experience are "off-limits" to *Q*. This usually means that in order to remain in *P*'s good graces, *Q* must refrain from evaluating, attempting to control, taking possession of, or even acquiring information about whatever is on *P*'s side of the boundary. This concept of boundaries rests on an assumption that no two people can or should be all things to one another, that different degrees of intimacy are appropriate in different relationships, that people will respect the needs of other people to maintain different kinds of distance from them, and that everyone lives his or her own life. Boundaries support respect itself.

People have strong emotional responses in matters of race, not because of arbitrary whim or temperament but because they have directly learned, been taught, or made generalizations resulting in important factual and moral beliefs. The varied ways in which beliefs about race are connected to emotions are in themselves reasons to approach racial matters with respect for the boundaries of others and to let it be known what one's own boundaries are. This is not to say that racial issues ought not to be rationally discussed, criticized, and negotiated whenever problems arise. But it is to say that boundaries need to be respected in such discussions so that everyone has the space to take responsibility for what he or she brings to the discussion. We need to assume that our interlocutors are capable of the same reflection and careful thought that we are. And we need to be sensitive to cues that our speech and behavior may be considered inappropriate.

If it seems paradoxical to speak of boundaries in the context of a discussion about race in a society that, as noted in this book's introduction, is divided or splintered by race, we need to remember some basics about human rights. Many human rights are negative. *Negative rights* concern what others may not do to us. Each individual has rights not to be harmed. The worst violations of human rights that have been committed on the grounds of race, such as assault, mutilation, murder, theft, rape, kidnapping, degradation, and persecution, have involved transgressions of the boundaries of others in ways that impact on survival. Boundaries are limitations not necessarily on where people may go physically but on what they may do in the range of actions that affect the rights of others. In this sense, forced segregation by race is a violation of the boundaries of those segregated because it limits their freedom of action. Voluntary segregation by race may be an exercise of boundary rights, an expression of other racial problems, or both.

A respect for boundaries in the relatively gentle arenas of public discussion, identity, and individual life choices ought to be easier to secure than were the fundamental rights to life and liberty that are the foundation for setting boundaries. The right to freedom of speech includes a right to try to change the mind of another person. However, one does not have a right to change someone's mind if that person does not want to engage in discussion or refuses to discuss the topic in question. And one does not have a right to impose moral judgments about what other people ought to think and do, so long as their actions do not harm others.

In American society, freedom includes individual *autonomy,* which literally means "self-rule." Individuals develop their capacity to make decisions, and they have the power to act on their decisions. Racial identity, however, is connected with membership in groups and loyalties to the decisions made by other group members and leaders. Therefore, racial autonomy has traditionally meant the self-rule of groups rather than individuals. The combination of individual and group autonomy may require individuals to draw boundaries within racial groups.

Finally, boundaries concern what people do, their spheres of free decision and action, rather than what they are, or their identities. In order to define and protect their identities, people draw *borders.* On a biological level, individuals must maintain borders between themselves and the external environment in order to survive. On a social level, in which some identities are important for status and success, the need for borders may result in aversion to those who represent low status and failure. For example, those who are white, young, or male may have social borders between themselves and those who are nonwhite, old, or female. But those who are nonwhite, old, or female may also have borders of their own to protect their identities.

B. A NEW PARADIGM OF RACE?

A *cultural paradigm* is a set of assumptions about an area of human life, or the world, that has been shared by a sufficiently large and influential number of people so that the set of assumptions is part of common sense. The paradigm functions as a theory that explains past and present experiences, and it generates predictions and expectations about future experience.

The current paradigm of race divides people into races as a matter of biological fact and attaches different expectations regarding culture and behavior to those racial groups. A new paradigm of race might begin with knowledge that there is no biological foundation for the different racial groups. As a result, what was previously thought of as race might be thought of as ethnicity. Because ethnicity is already accepted as a fluid, changeable, interlocking system of human categories and lifestyle choices, racial identity and racial membership could as well be viewed as a fluid, changeable, interlocking system of human categories and lifestyle choices. Mixed-race realities support this reconfiguration of race as ethnicity, and so does consideration of the ways in which ideas of race have changed over time and across cultures.

When people attach strong differences to what they think of as racial difference, these attachments could be viewed as beliefs that individuals are entitled to, much as they are entitled to varied religious beliefs. When the practice of these beliefs is a source of fulfillment and self-expression, they would merit the same respect as the practice of other beliefs that derive from cultural traditions. When the beliefs about racial difference result in harm to other human beings, they would be viewed as moral defects, or sadistic and criminal delusions, and treated accordingly; when such beliefs are self-destructive, they would require both psychological and social treatment.

A new paradigm of race might have built into it some detachment from race that would allow for the possibility that racial categorization, identity, and struggle will pass out of history. From this detached perspective, race would be no more than an idea about human beings that was useful for organizing society in the past but is increasingly without use or benefit as time goes on.

C. Discussion Questions

1. Suppose that students who belong to racial minorities sit together in a classroom that is predominantly white. What kinds of boundaries or borders might they be drawing?

2. Name some acceptable boundaries and borders concerning race that in your opinion are worthy of respect. Name some that are not worthy of respect.

3. Do you think Americans are ready for a new paradigm of race? How do you think such a paradigm might be different from the old paradigm?

4. If people who are attached to the present paradigm are offended by the new paradigm, what rights do they have in the matter?

D. Recommended Reading

In considering discussion question 1, see Beverly Daniel Tatum, *"Why Are All the Black Kids Sitting Together in the Cafeteria?" And Other Conversations About Race.*

For ideas about boundaries as applicable to race, see the following: Laurence Thomas, "Moral Deference," in John P. Pittman, ed., *African-American Perspectives and Philosophical Traditions;* Audre Lorde, "The Uses of Anger: Women Responding to Racism," in Anne Minas, ed., *Gender Basics;* Glenn C. Loury, "Self-Censorship in Public Discourse," in Glenn C. Loury, ed., *One by One from the Inside Out.* On borders and aversion, see Iris Marion Young, *Justice and the Politics of Difference,* chapter 5. For a psychological analysis of boundaries presented in terms of "image management," see Erving Goffman, *The Presentation of Self in Everyday Life.* A comprehensive philosophical discussion of rights is Judith Jarvis Thomson's *The Realm of Rights.* The classic liberal source for freedom of thought, speech, and lifestyle is John Stuart Mill's essay *On Liberty.*

The canonical source for the current concept of a paradigm is Thomas S. Kuhn, *The Structure of Scientific Revolutions.* Laurie Shrage presents a playful view of racial identity as changing choices in "Passing beyond the Other Race or Sex," in Naomi Zack, ed., *RACE/SEX.* A new paradigm of race is presented in Naomi Zack, *Philosophy of Science and Race,* chapter 7. On identities independent of race, see Jason Hill, *Becoming a Cosmopolitan: What it Means to be a Human Being in the New Millenium.*

GLOSSARY

Note: Words are defined as they are used in the context of this book and related sources.

abstract Pertaining to parts of things that are identified as members of a group; the process of identifying those parts.

affirm To recognize in a positive or benevolent way.

affirmative action Strategy of increasing educational and employment opportunities for disadvantaged groups, especially women and members of racial minorities, by requiring their admission to situations where they were previously excluded or are not present in numbers proportional to their presence in a wider population.

African American American of African descent; black.

ambiguous Unable to be determined. A sexually ambiguous person is someone who does not appear to be definitely male or female.

American Jewish identity The meaning of being Jewish to Jews who are Americans.

anachronism An opinion, belief, or action that would be more characteristic of a different time in history than the one in which it occurs or to which it is applied.

analyze To break down into the simplest conceptual parts.

androgynous Having neither male nor female sexual traits; appearing to have neither male nor female sexual traits.

appropriation Takeover of something without the right to do so.

aracial Without any racial identity; without specific racial identity.

archetype A generalized image of a kind or type of person, which is shared within a culture.

Asian Racial designation for descendants of people originating in areas west of the Pacific Ocean and east of the Caspian Sea.

assimilation Process of becoming part of a dominant culture by taking on its most important characteristics in place of one's own subordinate group characteristics.

atheist Person who does not believe in God on the grounds that God does not exist.

authentic appearance Looking and behaving as members of one's racial or ethnic group are expected to appear and behave.

authentic provenance   Having and being known to have the ancestry of the group that one belongs to.

authentic solidarity   Loyalty and helpfulness to members of one's racial or ethnic group, simply because they are members of one's own group.

authenticity   Genuineness or realness as the member of a racial or ethnic group.

authority   Recognized power that is vested in an individual, group, or organization.

autonomy   Individual self-rule; the freedom of individuals to choose their actions and develop as persons.

aversive   Avoiding; disliking; rejecting.

basic rules of logic   The assumptions behind systematic thought, such as the rule of noncontradiction: a statement cannot be both true and false at the same time.

berdache   Social role characteristics of people in non-Western cultures who are accepted as members of the opposite sex within their communities.

bigotry   Devotion to one's own beliefs or group to the point of intolerance of difference or hatred of others.

biologism   Belief that important social aspects of human life and behavior can be explained by the science of biology.

biracial   Descended from two races.

black   Appearing to belong to the Negro race or having an ancestor of Negro descent; Black (with capital *B*) usually refers to the ethnicity of black people.

Black Power   The ability of black people to affirm and liberate themselves, an idea and term formulated during activist movements in the 1960s and 1970s.

black underclass   Poor, usually urban, inadequately educated part of black population with high rates of unemployment and involvement in the criminal justice system as defendants.

blood quantum   Percentage of Native American ancestry required for recognized membership in some tribes or for designation as Indian by the U.S. federal government.

borders   Ways of preserving personal identity or what an individual believes the self to be.

boundaries   The limits an individual wants to set on the behavior of others with regard to that individual, usually within the fundamental rights and liberties of that individual.

bourgeoisie   Middle class; property-owners or owners of means of production in society.

breed   In biological terms, a type within a species, having common inherited traits that are usually visible.

breeding   In social class terms, a combination of preferred or believed-to-be superior ancestry and upbringing.

capitalism   Competitive economic system of private ownership of property and the means of production in which goods are produced for motives of monetary profit and workers are employed for wages or salaries.

Chicano/a   Preferred term for Mexican Americans.

citizenship rights   The entitlements of individuals who are recognized by the government to be fully participating members of a political body, such as the right to vote and the right to full protection under the laws.

civil rights   Basic freedom and entitlements of citizenship of members of a society that others may not violate without legal punishment.

Civil Rights movement   Social activism that resulted in racial integration and voting rights for black Americans by the mid-1960s.

class theory   Set of hypotheses about groups in society that explain how they have developed and now interact as social classes.

classic racism   Dislike or hatred of members of other racial groups, usually non-whites, often with intention to harm them.

client   Recipient of a social service.

code   When one thing is a sign for another, sometimes used as a verb, e.g., her clothes *code* black.

cognitive   Pertaining to intellectual processes and activities, in contrast to emotional ones, for example.

collateral kin   Relative(s) having common ancestor(s) but not common parents, e.g., cousins.

collective responsibility   When all members of a group, individually or as a group, are responsible for the actions of some members.

color-blind   Lacking in discrimination when race is assumed to be mainly a matter of skin color.

colored   Term for Negro in the United States before 1960s, now considered racist; term for mixed race in South Africa.

colorism   Social and personal ranking of people based on skin hue, especially within a nonwhite racial group, with lighter hues preferred.

communism   Economic and political system in which major means of production are owned by the government in the name of the people.

compensation   Benefit conferred on account of harm suffered or disadvantage experienced, to give recipient(s) better opportunities to succeed in life.

concept   The meaning of a word.

concrete egalitarianism   Position that people of all races and ethnicities are equal as members of their distinct groups, not as individuals.

consensus   Broad agreement on an issue or sameness in opinion or belief, often developed through open discussion.

consequentialism   Moral theory in which the goodness or badness of actions is assessed according to their consequences.

conservatism   Set of beliefs and practices that in cultural and political contexts imply a resistance to change.

covert racism   Hidden racism, often deliberately concealed.

creed   System of beliefs that people are born into or choose; to say that something is a matter of creed avoids pronouncing on its truth or falsity.

criteria   Requirements, conditions, or standards that have to be met before something can be granted; characteristics or traits that have to be present for something to be judged to be of a certain kind or type.

critical race theory   Analysis of the role of the U.S. legal system and capitalist economy in maintaining injustice based on race, may be developed through narratives from personal experience.

critical theory   Analysis of the power relations and dominant-subordinate behavior in a society, which are unjust and not always recognized for what they are by participants.

cultural authenticity   Displaying knowledge of the history and tradition of one's racial or ethnic group, which display is expected by others.

culture   System of practices and beliefs that persist within a group of people over time, including everyday social, intimate, familial, economic, and political behavior as well as art, music, dress, food, and ceremonies.

cultural paradigm   A set of beliefs about a certain area of human life, or the world, that is widely shared within a culture. Experience is described and explained in terms of the paradigm, and predictions and expectations are based on it.

cultural genocide   The deliberate destruction of a group's cultural practices so that they die out as a tradition that can be taught to succeeding generations.

customary   That which is normal or usual, frequently done, observed, believed, etc.

de facto   In existence or in fact; term used to refer to segregation that is not legislated.

de jure   By law; term used to refer to legalized segregation.

descriptive   The nonevaluative nature of a verbal account that is meant to relate how things are in fact.

diaspora   All the members of a racial or ethnic group in different geographical locations when, due to historical circumstances, they are not presently located in the same geographical area.

difference feminism   Idea that feminism must be conceptualized and practiced differently by women of different races and social classes.

discrimination   Actions or choices in favor of members of one group as opposed to another, based on their racial or ethnic classification.

diversity   Noticeable difference(s) in gender, race, or ethnicity that have consequences in society; the presence together of people with such difference.

Ebonics   Variation of English used by American ethnic blacks, composed of traditional black cultural speech and current slang.

egalitarianism   Position that all human beings are equal, as individuals, regardless of race or ethnicity.

eliminative   That which does away with a concept or idea in use because it is self-contradictory or has no factual basis.

eliminativism   Getting rid of a term and what it means.

elitism   Affirmation of the privileged position of a social group with natural or cultural advantages.

emancipation   Freedom, usually following a situation of oppression.

emancipatory tradition   Intellectual and political practices that are intended to further or result in emancipation for a particular group.

empiricism   Commitment that statements about reality be based on observation and investigation.

entitlements   Special rights to social or material goods that are conferred on some groups.

environmental racism   Harm or destruction of environment that affects people unequally as racial groups.

ethical   Pertaining to right and wrong; a person who does the right thing is an ethical person.

ethnically neutral   Having no preferences pertaining to the ethnicity of others, or having no evident ethnic identity oneself.

ethnicity   Human cultural traits as learned behavior; the combination of learned cultural behavior with a specific ancestry and physical appearance.

feminism   Contemporary interdisciplinary scholarly thought, personal ideology, and social and political activism that affirms the rights and value of women and analyzes the contemporary and historical conditions of their exclusion and oppression.

fighting words   Words that directly incite others to violent action.

folk   People who share beliefs in a culture; the lay public or mass of citizens, rather than educated elites or public officials.

folk model   Description of ideas or behavior that laypeople share within a culture.

fractional   Divided into numbers of less than one, as in a type of mixed-race identity that specifies the different parts of racial ancestry in numerical fractions.

freedmen   Former African American slaves who were freed.

full blood   A monoracial person, usually also displaying common notions of racial or ethnic authenticity; used especially in context of Native American identity.

fundamentalists   In a religious sense, people who believe in the literal truth of their religion as set down in a holy book.

gender   The behavioral and social role aspects of maleness or femaleness.

general   Pertaining to a large number or all of the individual things or people in a group, as wholes.

generic   Unspecified, as in *generic mixed-race identity*.

genocide   Deliberate destruction of an entire group of people or their culture.

good evidence   Factual reports that have been verified and are sufficient to support a claim, generalization, or conclusion.

grand theory   System of explanation and prediction that applies to all the subjects in an area of inquiry.

Harlem Renaissance   Period during the 1920s and 1930s when black arts and literature began to flourish on the basis of the pride of American blacks in their achievements and culture.

hate speech   Offensive speech that is intended to insult and harm others on account of their race, ethnicity, or gender.

Hispanic   An ethnic designation referring to a Spanish surname, descent from Spanish-speaking people, or residents of Portugal or Latin America, includes Latinos[/as] and Chicanos[as], although some members of the latter two groups have rejected Hispanic designation because they have no Spanish ancestry.

homogeneous   The same within, having similar members.

homophobic   Fearing or hating homosexuals and lesbians.

hyperdescent   System in which children of mixed parentage acquire the social and racial status of the parent whose social and racial status is higher.

hypodescent   System in which children of mixed parentage acquire the social and racial status of the parent whose social and racial status is lower.

identification   Categorization of a person by others in terms of race, ethnicity, or gender. (More broadly, other categories also apply, such as age and physical ableness.)

identify   To categorize another by race or ethnicity; to put oneself in the place of another or imagine oneself to be another specific individual or member of a racial or ethnic group different from one's own; to state one's race or ethnicity.

identity   Self-categorization of a person in terms of race, ethnicity, or gender (more broadly, other categories also apply, such as occupation); in the philosophical sense, that which makes a person the same person throughout changes; also, what a person is to himself or herself.

identity politics   Formal or informal political system in which people vote or otherwise exert influence as members of racial, gendered, ethnic, or other groups with interests and status unrecognized by the majority (for instance, homosexuals, lesbians, and the disabled).

ideology   System of beliefs about how the world ought to be, based on moral assumptions, economic interests, value judgments, or fundamental political beliefs.

inclusive   Capable of containing whole units instead of an addition of fractions to make one whole, as in *inclusive mixed-race identity* that encompasses all different aspects of a person's racial ancestry.

indigenism   Political and ideological liberation theory of contemporary Native Americans based on their ancestors being the original, or "native" inhabitants of North and South America.

institutionalized   Being part of an institution so that one's life is lived according to its rules; it applies, e.g., to prison inmates, lifelong social service clients.

institutional racism   Formal practices and traditions in social organizations, or customs, that harm some racial groups or deny them the same opportunities as other racial groups.

integration   Freedom of physical movement for people of nonwhite races that results in their presence among whites in political, economic, educational, and social life.

intellectual error   Mistake in opinion due to error in reasoning, ignorance, or incorrect judgment of evidence.

intellectual remedy   Correction of intellectual error by providing information or pointing out error in reasoning or judging evidence.

intent of the law   What the law is supposed to accomplish in its application.

internalization   Negative belief of others that one has adopted about oneself.

intersection   When two or more categories in which a person is classified and identified work in combination to create a category or form of experience different from that of any of the categories originally combined.

intersectionality   Combination of two or more identities that are objects of oppression or disadvantage.

intersexed   Having the primary biological traits of both males and females, or having neither.

justice   Fairness in civic and political life; characteristic of laws and legal practices that are in agreement with broad moral or ethical intuitions.

la raza   Concept and reality of people of Latin American countries as one race containing racial variation within itself.

Latino[/a]   The ethnic category of people descended from residents of Latin America.

leisure   Conditions necessary for recreation and self-care and development.

lesbian   A woman who prefers other women as sexual partners; in feminist contexts, the centering of women's experience.

liberation   Freedom after oppression; actions undertaken to achieve freedom; the goal of freedom for an oppressed group.

liberation theory   Hypothesis, plan, description, ideology, or analysis of current cultural conditions that is intended to achieve freedom for a particular group(s).

liberatory   Supportive of, or tending toward greater freedom or less oppression.

line   Relations connecting direct ancestors or direct descendants; pre-eighteenth-century concept of race.

logic   Formal system of rules of thought.

logical contradictories   Two statements that cannot both be true and cannot both be false, e.g., "No S is P" and "Some S is P."

mainstream   Dominant part of American society including the upper class, professionals, and all those active in civic, social, corporate, educational, and political life; "the system."

marginalize   Keep outside the center or exclude from full participation and empowerment.

Marxist ideology   Marxism; ideology based on the writings of Karl Marx and Frederick Engels.

matriarchal   Ruled by women.

melting pot   Model of the United States as a place in which individuals from different cultures would contribute to one new culture through work, civic life, and social life, and would lose their original ethnicities through intermarriage and assimilation.

meritocracy   System in which individuals are rewarded on the basis of their demonstrated aptitudes, skills, and achievements.

microdiversity   Racial diversity on an individual level, as is present in individuals of mixed racial ancestry.

minstrelsy   Late-nineteenth- and early-twentieth-century theatrical genre in which white men wore "blackface" to imitate both black men and women in stereotypical roles.

miscegenation   Racial mixture in human reproduction.

mixed race   Having ancestry of more than one race.

monoethnic   Having ancestry of all one ethnicity.

monoracial   Having ancestry of all one race.

moral   Ethical; having to do with right or wrong, usually in instances involving important harm or benefit to people.

moral status   Standing of a person as a moral agent and as someone who is the object of moral or immoral behavior by others.

mulatto   Person with one black and one white parent; after 1920, the term came to mean a person with any degree of mixed black-and-white ancestry.

mulatto elite   Before 1920, part of black population that was mixed race and had advantages of interactions with whites as well as middle-class education, employment, and cultural experience.

multiculturalism   Program that includes people from different cultures as well as their distinctive intellectual, literary, and artistic products.

multiethnic   Having ancestry from two or more ethnic groups.

multiracial   Having ancestry from more than two different races; sometimes used as a synonym for *mixed race* to include biracial.

myth   Shared beliefs about events or people that serve a social purpose but have little or no basis in reality.

narrative   An account of experiences and events that focuses on the particulars of what takes place, rather than a generalization about types of experiences or events; a story.

Native American   Member of the group of descendants of people who inhabited the Americas before European colonialism, or a member of a group that identifies with such descendants.

nativism   Late-nineteenth and early-twentieth-century belief that Americans born in the United States were culturally and morally superior to immigrants.

natural aristocracy   Group of people believed to be superior to others solely due to traits they are born with (not originally a racial concept).

natural law   Laws believed to be given to men by God, believed by Christians to be a foundation for democratic constitutional government with safeguards for individual rights, especially the right to own private property.

naturalness   Quality of being present by nature or in nature, without human intervention or cultural influence.

negative right   A right not to have certain actions taken with regard to oneself, for instance, the right to be left alone so long as one is obeying the laws.

neoconservative   Since 1970, characteristic of political programs and individuals who reject extreme social changes, support American capitalism, and favor minimal government spending and intervention in the lives of private citizens.

nonethnic   Having no evident ethnic identity.

nonmaterialistic   Not primarily concerned with physical objects of monetary value or with money.

nonobservant   Characteristic of some Jews whereby they do not follow the religious practices of Judaism.

normative   The nature of a proposal or persuasive account of how things ought to be, based on assumptions about values and moral goodness.

octoroon   Person who has seven white great-grandparents and one black great-grandparent.

offensive   Shocking; disgusting; emotionally or morally upsetting.

one-drop rule   American social and legal custom of classifying anyone with one black ancestor, regardless of how far back, as black.

"other"   Category to be checked on official forms when the standard racial alternatives of black, white, Asian, or Indian are not checked.

outcome   Numbers of women and members of racial minority groups who gain access in a hiring, admissions, or promotion process.

overgeneralization   A conclusion or generalization based on insufficient evidence or experience.

overt racism   Racism that is deliberate and explicit.

paradigm   Set of shared beliefs through which an area of reality is interpreted.

parameters   Conceptual boundaries, foundations, or restrictions.

pass   To present oneself as different from what one is, especially used in reference to people with black ancestry who present themselves as white.

patriarchy   Social system in which men dominate in all important areas of life, usually associated with their roles as fathers and husbands but extending to public life as well.

person   A being with legal rights and recognized social and moral importance.

personal authenticity   Courage to express one's beliefs and opinions or display how one is when others disagree or disapprove.

personal identity   Philosophical concept of the sameness of persons, which is usually determined by what cannot be changed if the person is to be judged the same person; how a person seems to be to his or her self.

perspective   Point of view or position from which one understands and interprets areas of knowledge and reality.

pluralism   Combination of distinct ethnic or racial groups in public life.

pluralistic society   A public whole composed of different racial or ethnic groups that are treated equally and valued by their members and members of other groups for their distinct identities.

population(s)   Current scientific concept of a group of people who share some of the physical similarities that previously were attributed to race.

positive right   An entitlement to something fundamental to citizenship, for example, the right to vote.

pragmatic   Practical, a form of calculation or evaluation that places a strong emphasis on results, consequences, and material benefits.

preferential treatment   Form of affirmative action in which qualified women or nonwhites are preferred over white males to whom they are equal in qualifications.

principles   Rules for behavior, especially moral rules.

profit   In production, the monetary difference between the material, labor, and capital costs of production and the price received for the products.

proletariat   Marxist term for nineteenth- and twentieth-century laborers; generally, the working class.

provenance   The history of something whereby its initial circumstances and changes in circumstances are traced in time; usually applied to art objects, but also ironically applicable to people in terms of identities.

proving a negative   Convincing or persuading others that something is not the case or does not exist. Usually the burden of proof is on the person who asserts that something *is* the case or that something *does* exist.

psychologies of race   The ways in which beliefs about race motivate people on individual levels.

public policy   Set of rules for official action, intended to bring about an end desired by citizens or mandated by law.

quadroon   Person who has three white grandparents and one black grandparent.

quotas   In affirmative action contexts, specific numbers of members of racial minorities, or women, that are required to be hired or admitted even if their qualifications do not fully merit it.

race   Idea of a distinct biological type of human being; term referring generally to racial difference and racial relations.

race relations   Literally the interactions of people who belong to different races, figuratively a U.S. euphemism for issues of racial difference and racism.

racial determinism   Belief that racial membership alone causes other, nonracial human characteristics.

racial essences   Idea of important general traits that all members of a distinct race are assumed to share, causing them to be members of that race, now recognized not to have a scientific basis.

racialist   Person who believes in the existence of races as a biological reality.

racism   Beliefs and practices that harm members of some races and not others.

racist   Racialist who harbors ill will or intent to do harm against others due to their racial membership; adjective describing the beliefs or actions of racists.

radical   Extreme, literally means connected to the roots of something.

rationalize   Give reasons for something that justify it, which are not the real reasons or motives.

received opinion   Belief(s) widely accepted and not normally questioned.

reconfigure   To change the way in which something is defined without changing it completely; to shift a perspective on an area of human experience.

reduces   Translates into something else that is conceptually more precise.

reparation   Compensation that includes recognition that harm has been injustly inflicted.

reproduction   Continual creation of social structures, as well as oppressive categories, within a culture; biological production of next generation.

reverse discrimination   When a group that previously practiced discrimination becomes the object of discrimination.

rhizomatic   Pertaining to the horizontal root structure of plants that grow along the ground and do not have main taproots; used as a metaphor for mixed-race identity that can spring up in one generation.

role-model argument   Argument in favor of affirmative action on the basis of its putting members from previously excluded groups in new social and professional roles.

rooted   Deriving nourishment from soil through roots, especially a main taproot; used as a metaphor for monoracial identity traced back in time through ancestry.

segregation   Policy of keeping people physically separate in employment, education, housing, social activities, etc., on the basis of race, especially when nonwhite racial membership results in exclusion from goods of society monopolized by the white majority.

Semite   Member of a Caucasian race that now consists of Jews and Arabs.

separatism   Movement or belief that members of a distinct racial, ethnic, or gender group ought to withdraw from other groups in society, socially, economically, politically, and geographically (if possible).

sex   Biological difference based on reproductive function and chromosomal markers.

sex drive   A strong desire to engage in sexual activity, assumed to be universally present in human beings.

sexual objects   Persons or things who, without regard for their own feelings, are sexually sought after by others.

sexual subjects   Persons who actively desire others, usually with the power to actualize their desires.

social caste   Inherited social class.

social class   Group in society that has a distinctive status and experience, economically, politically and socially; according to Marxism, the social class of a group is determined by its relationship to the most important means of production.

social entity   A group of people who interact with one another based on a shared perception of their membership in that group.

social group   A number of people identified as a collectivity, may or may not be a social entity.

social reality   The beliefs and practices that individuals have to take into account in interacting with others; the things that most members of a society believe exist.

socially constructed   Not present in nature but created and maintained in culture and often thought to be "natural."

socially intelligible   Clear or understandable to others in the same society.

stereotype   Fixed, often derogatory, idea about members of a group that is applied to all members, regardless of individual difference; may be true of some members of the group or of no members of the group.

stigma   A mark or sign of something undesirable.

strategy   A type of action that is a means to an end.

strict scrutiny   Standard applied by the U.S. Supreme Court to see whether a race-based policy is justified, because there are no alternatives to achieve the same end and its benefits outweigh its harms.

suffragists   Late-nineteenth- and early-twentieth-century women activists who organized, wrote, spoke, and demonstrated to secure the right of women to vote.

tactics   Goal-directed actions, usually more specific than strategy.

taxonomy   System of types or categories in an area of knowledge or reality.

thinking critically   Looking at the problems or falseness in a belief or opinion; investigating the basis of beliefs and analyzing them; following rules of logic and good evidence; thinking for oneself as opposed to accepting beliefs and opinions of others.

token   An individual who is meant to represent his or her entire race.

traditional   Pertaining to how things were done in the past.

traditional nonwhite identities   Identities that conform to official categories of black, Asian, and Indian.

traditional values   Aspects of social and private life that are sought after or retained because they are thought to be morally good and based on past custom.

transsexual   The gender characteristics of an individual whose gender does not match the biological sex he or she was characterized by at birth (also used as a noun).

unintentional racism   Speech or action that harms members of some racial group(s), though not done for that reason.

universalism   Position that all human beings are or should be the same in certain ways, regardless of race, ethnicity, nationality, gender, or any other form of difference.

utility   Something that is of benefit to human beings.

valorize   Honor, idealize.

WASP   Acronym for White Anglo-Saxon Protestant.

white   Racial designation referring to European ancestry and appearance or, more formally, to the absence of nonwhite ancestry.

white flight   Deliberate movement of whites out of a neighborhood when people of color begin to live there.

white purity   White racial identity that rests on both the absence of and an aversion to nonwhites.

white-race traitor   A white person who does not side with other whites in matters of race, especially when he or she judges the positions of other whites on these matters to be racist.

white-race treason   Repudiation of the privileges of whiteness by white people who think that these privileges are morally unjustified and racist against nonwhites.

white supremacy Belief that whites are superior to nonwhites in important human traits and that they ought to dominate nonwhites in society.

white trash Derogatory popular name for the white group that is poor or culturally backward, now sometimes used affirmatively.

whiteness studies Scholarly writings about the cultural aspects of white racial identity and identification.

womanism Contemporary form of feminism developed by black women writers and scholars that emphasizes their experience and knowledge, as well as their sources of spiritual inspiration in religion and the lives of other black women.

women's liberation Term for the movement and ideology of women's emancipation, or for feminism, that was in use during the 1960s and 1970s.

word Sound or mark that symbolizes something other than itself.

Yiddish High German dialect written in Hebrew letters, used by European Jews.

Zionism Jewish religious and political beliefs and actions that hold Israel, as the original Jewish homeland, to be of central importance to Jews throughout the Jewish diaspora.

BIBLIOGRAPHY

Note: Complete citations of anthologies are listed under editors' last names when the anthologies are cited more than once.

Court Cases

Brown v. Board of Education, 347 U.S. 483 (1954).
Gratz v. Bollinger, 123 S.Ct. 2411 (2003).
Grutter v. Bollinger, 123 S.Ct. 2325 (2003).
Loving v. Virginia, 338 U.S. 1 (1968).
Regents of the University of California v. Bakke, 438 U.S. 265 (1978).

Web Data

National Urban League, New York Urban League. www.nul.org; www.nyul.org
www.census.gov

PBS Documentaries (viewing and video information at www.pbs.org)

Race: The Power of an Illusion, California Newsreel. 3 parts, 3 hrs. (2003).
The New Americans, Independent Lens. 6 hrs. (2004).
My Journey Home, WETA, Washington, DC, 3 hrs. (2004).
Searching for Asian America, NAATA (National Asian American Telecommunications Association). 90 min. (2004).

Books and Articles

Alcoff, Linda, "Mestizo Identity." In Zack, *American Mixed Race,* 257–278.
Alcoff, Linda, and Eduardo Mendieta. *Identities: Race, Class, Gender, and Nationality.* Malden, MA: Blackwell, 2003.

Allen, Anita L. "The Role Model Argument and Faculty Diversity." In Pittman, *African-American Perspectives and Philosophical Traditions,* 267–281.

———. "Interracial Marriage: Folk Ethics in Contemporary Philosophy." In Zack, *Women of Color and Philosophy,* pp. 182–206.

Allen, James Paul, and Eugene James Turner. *We the People: An Atlas of America's Ethnic Diversity.* New York: Macmillan, 1988.

Allen, Paula Gunn. *The Sacred Hoop: Recovering the Feminine in American Indian Traditions.* Boston: Beacon Press, 1986.

Allison, Dorothy. *Bastard out of Carolina.* New York: Dutton, 1992.

Alonso, William, and Paul Starr, eds. *The Politics of Numbers.* New York: Russell Sage Foundation, 1987.

Alvarez, Julia. *How the Garcia Girls Lost Their Accents.* Chapel Hill, NC: Algonquin Books, 1991.

Anderson, Benedict. *Imagined Communities.* London: Verso Books, 1983.

Angier, Natalie. "Do Races Really Matter?" *New York Times*, August 22, 2000, pp. F1, F5.

Anzuldúa, Gloria. *Borderlands/La Frontera: The New Mestiza.* San Francisco: Sisters/ Aunt Lute Book Company, 1987.

———. *Making Face, Making Soul.* San Francisco: Aunt Lute, 1990.

Appiah, K. Anthony. "Racisms." In Goldberg, *Anatomy of Racism,* 3–17.

———. *In My Father's House.* Oxford: Oxford University Press, 1992.

———. "'But Would That Still be Me?': Notes on Gender, 'Race' Ethnicity as Sources of Identity." In Zack, *RACE/SEX,* 75–82.

———. "Race, Culture, Identity." In *Color Conscious: The Political Morality of Race,* ed. K. Anthony Appiah and Amy Gutman, 3–75. Princeton, NJ: Princeton University Press, 1996.

Appiah, K. Anthony, and Henry Louis Gates, Jr. *Identities.* Chicago: University of Chicago Press, 1995.

Ariès, Philippe. *Centuries of Childhood.* Trans. Robert Baldick. New York: Alfred A. Knopf, 1962.

Arisaka, Yoko. "Asian Women: Invisibility, Locations, and Claims to Philosophy." In Zack, *Women of Color and Philosophy,* pp. 209–234.

Aristotle. *The Politics.* Trans. T. A. Sinclair. Ed. Trevor J. Saunders. New York: Penguin, 1981.

———. *Nicomachean Ethics.* Trans. Terence Irwin. Indianapolis: Hackett, 1985.

Augenbraum, Harold, and Ilan Stavans, eds. *Growing Up Latino.* Boston: Houghton Mifflin, 1993.

Azoulay, Karya Gibel. *Black, Jewish, and Interracial.* Durham, NC: Duke University Press, 1997.

Baca Zinn, Maxine, and Bonnie Thornton Dill, eds. *Women of Color in U.S. Society.* Philadelphia: Temple University Press, 1994.

Bell, Derrick. *And We Are Not Saved: The Elusive Quest for Racial Justice.* New York: Basic Books, 1987.

Bell, Linda, and David Blumenfeld, eds. *Overcoming Sexism and Racism.* Lanham, MD: Rowman and Littlefield, 1994.

Belliotti, Raymond A. *Seeking Identity.* Lawrence: University Press of Kansas, 1995.

Berlin, Ira. *Slaves Without Masters: The Free Negro in the Antebellum South.* New York: Pantheon Books, 1975.

Bernal, Martin. *Black Athena: Vol. I, The Fabrication of Ancient Greece, 1785–1985.* New Brunswick, NJ: Rutgers University Press, 1987.

Berry, Bernita C. "'I Just See People': Exercises in Learning the Effects of Racism and Sexism." In Bell and Blumenfeld, *Overcoming Sexism and Racism,* 45–51.

Bhabha, Homi. *The Location of Culture.* New York: Routledge, 1994.

Bilgrami, Akeel. "What Is a Muslim? Fundamental Commitment and Cultural Identity." In Appiah and Gates, *Identities,* pp. 198–219.

Blackburn, Daniel G. "Why Race Is Not a Biological Concept." In Lang, *Race and Racism,* pp. 3–26.

Boas, Franz. *The Mind of Primitive Man.* New York: Macmillan, 1938.

———. *Race, Language and Culture.* New York: Macmillan, 1940.

Boxill, Bernard. "The Morality of Reparation." *Social Theory and Practice* 2, no. 1 (1972): 113–122.

Boxill, Bernard, ed. *Race and Racism.* Oxford: Oxford University Press, 2001.

Boyarin, Daniel, and Jonathan Boyarin. "Diaspora: Generation and the Ground of Jewish Identity." In Appiah and Gates, *Identities,* pp. 305–337.

Bradford, Judith, and Crispin Sartwell. "Voiced Bodies/Embodied Voices." In Zack, *RACE/SEX,* 191–204.

Bradshaw, C. K. "Beauty and the Beast: On Racial Ambiguity." In Root, *Racially Mixed People in America,* 77–89.

Brown, L. S., and Maria P. P. Root, eds. *Diversity and Complexity in Feminist Therapy.* New York: Haworth Press, 1990.

Butler, Judith. *Gender Trouble: Feminism and the Subversion of Identity.* New York: Routledge, 1990.

Butler, Robert Olen. *A Good Scent from a Strange Mountain: Stories.* New York: Henry Holt, 1992.

Callicott, Baird J. *In Defense of the Land Ethic.* Albany: State University of New York Press, 1989.

Card, Claudia. "Race, Racism, and Ethnicity." In Bell and Blumenfeld, *Overcoming Sexism and Racism,* 141–152.

Charles, Camille Zubrinsky. "Neighborhood Racial-Composition Preferences: Evidenced from a Multiethnic Metropolis." *Social Problems* 47, no. 3 (2000): 379–407.

Chavez, Linda. *Out of the Barrio: Toward a New Politics of Hispanic Assimilation.* New York: Basic Books, 1991.

Chin, Curtis. *Witness Aloud: Lesbian, Gay and Bisexual Asian/Pacific American Writing.* New York: Asian American Writers' Workshop, 1993.

Chodorow, Nancy. *The Reproduction of Mothering.* Berkeley: University of California Press, 1978.

Churchill, Ward. *Fantasies of the Master Race.* Ed. M. Annette Jaimes. Monroe, ME: Common Courage Press, 1992.

———. *Struggle for the Land.* Monroe, ME: Common Courage Press, 1992.

———. *Indians Are Us?* Monroe, ME: Common Courage Press, 1994.

Churchill, Ward, ed. *From a Native Son: Selected Essays on Indigenism, 1985–1995.* Boston: South End Press, 1996.

———. *Marxism and Native Americans.* Boston: South End Press, 1993.

Civil Rights Project at Harvard University, The. "Reaffirming Diversity: A Legal Analysis of the University of Michigan Affirmative Action Cases." A Joint Statement of Constitutional Law Scholars (Erwin Hemerinsky, Drew Days III, Richard Fallon, Pamela S. Karlan, Kenneth L. Karst, Frank Michelman, Eric Schnapper, Laurence H. Tribe, Mark Tushnet, and of the Civil Rights Project, Harvard University, Angelo N. Ancheta, Christopher F. Edley, Jr.). Cambridge, MA: Civil Rights Project at Harvard University, 2003. At http://www.civilrightsproject.harvard.edu.

Clancy, Jennifer. "Multiracial Identity Assertion in the Sociopolitical Context of Primary Education." In Zack, *American Mixed Race,* 211–220.

Clements, Susan. "Five Arrows." In Zack, *American Mixed Race,* 3–12.

Cohen, Carl, and James P. Sterba. *Affirmative Action and Racial Preference: A Debate (Point/Counterpoint).* New York: Oxford University Press, 2003.

Cohen, David W., and Jack P. Greene, eds. *Neither Slave nor Free: The Freedmen of African Descent in the Slave Societies of the New World.* Baltimore: Johns Hopkins University Press, 1972.

Coles, Robert. *Uprooted Children.* Pittsburgh: University of Pittsburgh Press, 1970.

Coles, Robert, and Jane Hollowell Coles. *Women of Crisis.* New York: Delacorte Press/Seymour Lawrence, 1978.

Collins, Patricia Hill. *Black Feminist Thought.* London: Harper Collins Academic Press, 1990.

———. "Learning to Think for Ourselves: Malcolm X's Black Nationalism Reconsidered." In *Malcolm X: In Our Own Image,* ed. Joe Wood, 75–87. New York: Doubleday, 1992.

Copi, Irving M. *Introduction to Logic.* New York: Macmillan, 1961.

Cordova, V. F. "Exploring the Sources of Western Thought." In Zack, *Women of Color and Philosophy,* pp. 69–90.

Corlett, Angelo J. "Parallels of Ethnicity and Gender." In Zack, *RACE/SEX,* 83–94.

———. *Race, Racism and Reparations.* Ithaca: Cornell University Press, 2003.

Corwin, Edward S. *The "Higher Law" Background of American Constitutional Law.* Ithaca, NY: Cornell University Press, 1986.

Cox, Oliver C. *Caste, Class and Race.* New York: Doubleday, 1948.

Crenshaw, Kimberle. "Demarginalizing the Intersection of Race and Sex: A Black Feminist Critique of Antidiscrimination Doctrine, Feminist Theory, and Antiracist Politics." In Jagger, *Living with Contradictions,* 39–52.

Cross, W. E. *Shades of Black: Diversity in African-American Identity.* Philadelphia: Temple University Press, 1991.

Davis, Angela Y. *Women, Race and Class.* New York: Random House, 1983.

Davis, F. James. *Who Is Black?* University Park: Pennsylvania State University Press, 1991.

———. "The Hawaiian Alternative to the One-Drop Rule." In Zack, *American Mixed Race,* 115–132.

Davis, Marilyn P. *Mexican Voices/American Dreams.* New York: Henry Holt, 1990.

Davy, Kate. "Outing Whiteness: A Feminist/Lesbian Project." *Theatre Journal* 47, no. 2 (May 1995): 189–205.

Day, Beth. *Sexual Life Between Blacks and Whites: The Roots of Racism.* New York: World Publishing, Times Mirror, 1972.

Degler, Carl N. *Neither Black nor White: Slavery and Race Relations in Brazil and the U.S.* New York: Macmillan, 1971.

Delgado, Richard. *Critical Race Theory: The Cutting Edge.* Philadelphia: Temple University Press, 1995.

Devine, Philip E. *Human Diversity and the Culture Wars: A Philosophical Perspective on Contemporary Cultural Conflict.* Westport, CT: Praeger, 1996.

Dill, Bonnie Thornton. "Fictive Kin, Paper Sons, and *Compadrazgo:* Women of Color and the Struggle for Family Survival." In Zinn and Dill, *Women of Color in U.S. Society,* 149–179.

Dinnerstein, Leonard, Roger L. Nichols, and David M. Reimers, eds. *Natives and Strangers: A Multicultural History of Americans.* Rev. ed. Oxford: Oxford University Press, 1996.

Domínguez, Virginia. *White by Definition: Social Classification in Creole Louisiana.* New Brunswick, NJ: Rutgers University Press, 1986.

Dooling, D. M., and Paul Jordan-Smith, eds. *I Become Part of It: Sacred Dimensions in Native American Life.* New York: Parabola Books, 1989.

D'Souza, Dinesh. *The End of Racism.* New York: Free Press, 1995.

Du Bois, W. E. B. *The Souls of Black Folk.* 1903. Reprint, New York: Penguin Books, 1989.

Dukes, Richard L., and Ruben Martinez. "The Impact of Ethgender Among Adolescents." *Adolescence* 29, no. 113 (Spring 1994): 105–115.

Ellison, Ralph. *Invisible Man.* New York: Random House, 1952.

Erdrich, Louise. *Love Medicine.* New York: HarperCollins, 1993.

Erikson, Erik. *Identity and the Life Cycle.* New York: W. W. Norton, 1980.

Espiritu, Yen Le. *Asian American Panethnicity: Bridging Institutions and Identities.* Philadelphia: Temple University Press, 1992.

Eze, Emmanuel Chukwudi, ed. *Race and the Enlightenment: A Reader.* Malden, MA: Blackwell, 1997.

Ezorsky, Gertrude. *Racism and Justice.* Ithaca, NY: Cornell University Press, 1991.

Fanon, Franz. *Black Skin, White Masks.* New York: Grove Press, 1967.

Farrakhan, Louis. "Interview in *National Alliance* Newspaper." In *Independent Black Leadership in America,* ed. William Pleasant, 7–53. New York: Castillo International Publications, 1990.

Fernández, Carlos A. "La Raza and the Melting Pot." In Root, *Racially Mixed People in America.* pp. 126–143.

———. "Testimony of the Association of MultiEthnic Americans." In Zack, *American Mixed Race,* 191–210.

Finley, M. I. *Ancient Slavery and Modern Ideology.* New York: Pelican, 1983.

Fish, Stanley. "There's No Such Thing as Free Speech and It's a Good Thing." In *Today's Moral Issues: Classic and Contemporary Perspectives,* ed. Daniel Bonevac. Mountainview, CA: Mayfield, 1996, 126–134.

Flax, Jane. *The American Dream in Black and White: The Clarence Thomas Hearings.* Ithaca: Cornell University Press, 1998.

Flexner, Eleanor. *A Century of Struggle.* New York: Atheneum, 1974.

Fogelin, Robert J. *Understanding Arguments.* New York: Harcourt Brace Jovanovich, 1978.

Forbes, Jack D. *Black Africans and Native Americans: Color, Race and Caste in the Evolution of Red-Black Peoples.* London: Blackwell, 1988.

———. "Blood Quantum: A Relic of Racism and Termination." At http://www. Yvwiiusdinvnohii.net/Articles2000/JDForbes 001126.Blood.htm.

Foxworthy, Jeff. *Red Ain't Dead.* Atlanta: Longstreet Press, 1991.

Frankenberg, Ruth. *Displacing Whiteness: Essays in Social and Cultural Criticism.* Durham, NC: Duke University Press, 1997.

Frazier, Gregory W. *Urban Indians: Drums from the Cities.* Denver: Arrowstar, 1993.

Freedle, Roy O. "Correcting the SAT's Ethnic and Social-Class Bias: A Method for Reestimating SAT Scores." *Harvard Educational Review* 73, no. 1 (Spring 2003): 1–43.

Freire, Paulo. *Pedagogy of the Oppressed.* Trans. Myra Bergman Ramos. New York: Continuum, 1990.

Freydberg, Bridget A. "Sapphires, Spitfires, Sluts and Superbitches: Aframericans and Latinas in Contemporary American Film." In Vaz, *Black Women in America,* 206–221.

Frye, Marilyn. "White Woman Feminist." In Bell and Blumenfeld, *Overcoming Sexism and Racism,* 113–134.

Fugita, Stephen, and Marilyn Fernandez. *Altered Lives, Enduring Community: Japanese Americans Remember Their World War II Incarceration.* Seattle: University of Washington Press, 2004.

Funderburg, L. *Black, White, Other: Biracial Americans Talk About Race and Identity.* New York: William Morrow, 1994.

Garcia, J. L. A. "Racism as a Model for Understanding Sexism." In Zack, *RACE/SEX,* 45–60.

Gatewood, Willard B. *Aristocrats of Color: The Black Elite, 1880–1920.* Bloomington: Indiana University Press, 1990.

Geiger, Shirley M. "African-American Single Mothers: Public Perceptions and Public Policies." In Vaz, *Black Women in America,* 244–260.

Giddings, Paula. *When and Where I Enter: The Impact of Black Women on Race and Sex in America.* New York: Bantam, 1984.

Gilman, Sander L. *Difference and Pathology: Stereotypes of Sexuality, Race and Madness.* Ithaca, NY: Cornell University Press, 1985.

Gilroy, Paul. *The Black Atlantic: Modernity and Double Consciousness.* Cambridge, MA: Harvard University Press, 1993.

Glazer, Nathan. "Individual Rights Against Group Rights." In Kymlicka, *The Rights of Minority Cultures,* 123–138.

Goffman, Erving. *The Presentation of Self in Everyday Life.* New York: Doubleday, 1959.

Goldberg, David Theo. *Racist Culture: Philosophy and the Politics of Meaning.* Cambridge, MA: Blackwell, 1993.

———. "Made in the USA." In Zack, *American Mixed Race,* 237–256.

Goldberg, David Theo, ed. *Anatomy of Racism.* Minneapolis: University of Minnesota Press, 1990.

———. *Multiculturalism: A Critical Reader.* Oxford: Blackwell, 1994.

Goldberg, David, and Michael Krausz, eds. *Jewish Identity.* Philadelphia: Temple University Press, 1993.

Gordon, Lewis R. *Bad Faith and Antiblack Racism.* Atlantic Highlands, NJ: Humanities Press, 1995.

———. *Fanon and the Crisis of European Man: An Essay on Philosophy and the Human Sciences.* New York: Routledge, 1995.

———. "Race, Sex and Matrices of Desire in an Antiblack World." In Zack, *RACE/SEX,* 117–132.

Gordon, Lewis R., ed. *Existence in Black: An Anthology of Existentialist Black Philosophy.* New York: Routledge, 1997.

Gordon, Milton M. *Assimilation in American Life.* New York: Oxford University Press, 1964.

Gould, Stephen Jay. *The Mismeasure of Man.* New York: W. W. Norton, 1981.

Graham, Richard, ed. *The Idea of Race in Latin America, 1870–1940.* Austin: University of Texas Press, 1990.

Graham, Susan R. "Grassroots Advocacy." In Zack, *American Mixed Race,* 185–190.

Grant, Joanne. *Black Protest: History, Documents and Analyses, 1619–Present.* New York: Ballantine Books, 1968.

Graves, Joseph L. *The Emperor's New Clothes: Biological Theories of Race at the Millennium.* New Brunswick, NJ: Rutgers University Press, 2001.

Greene, B. A. "What Has Gone Before: The Legacy of Racism and Sexism in the Lives of Black Mothers and Daughters." In *Diversity and Complexity in Feminist Therapy,* ed. L. S. Brown and M. P. P. Root. New York: Haworth, 1990.

Gwaltney, John Langston. *Drylongso: A Self-Portrait of Black America.* New York: Vintage Books, 1980.

Hacker, Andrew. "Goodbye to Affirmative Action?" *New York Review of Books,* July 11, 1996, 21–26.

Hall, Barbara. "The Libertarian Role Model and the Burden of Uplifting the Race." In Zack, *Women of Color and Philosophy,* 168–181.

Hare, Nathan, and Julia Hare. *The Endangered Black Family.* San Francisco: Black Think Tank, 1984.

Hamilton, Cynthia. "Women, Home and Community: The Struggle in an Urban Environment." In Jagger, *Living with Contradictions,* 676–679.

Harmon, Alexandra. "When Is an Indian Not an Indian? 'Friends of the Indian' and the Problem of Indian Identity." *Journal of Ethnic Studies* 18, no. 2 (1991): 95–123.

Harris, Leonard. "Honor: Emasculation and Empowerment." In *Rethinking Masculinity: Philosophical Explorations in Light of Feminism,* ed. Larry May and Robert A. Strikwerda, 191–208. Lanham, MD: Rowman and Littlefield, 1992.

Harris, Leonard, ed. *Philosophy Born of Struggle: Anthology of Afro-American Philosophy from 1917.* Dubuque: Kendall/Hunt, 1983.

———. *The Philosophy of Alain Locke.* Philadelphia: Temple University Press, 1989.

Harris, Nigel. *The New Untouchables: Immigration and the New World Worker.* New York: I. B.Tauris, 1995.

Harris, Virginia R. "Prison of Color." In *Racism in the Lives of Women,* ed. Jeanne Adleman and Gloria Enguídanos, 75–84. New York: Haworth, 1995.

Hawley, John C., ed. *Cross-Addressing: Resistance Literature and Cultural Borders.* Albany: State University of New York Press, 1997.

Heldke, Lisa, and Peg O'Connor, eds. *Oppression, Privilege and Resistance: Theoretical Perspectives on Racism, Sexism, and Heterosexism.* New York: McGraw-Hill, 2003.

Herbst, Philip H. *The Color of Words: An Encyclopaedic Dictionary of Ethnic Bias in the United States.* Yarmouth, ME: Intercultural Press, 1997.

Hernton, Calvin. *Sex and Racism in America.* New York: Grove Press, 1965.

Herr, Cheryl. "The Erotics of Irishness." In Appiah and Gates, *Identities,* 271–304.

Hershel, Helena Jia. "Therapeutic Perspectives on Biracial Formation and Internalized Oppression." In Zack, *American Mixed Race,* 169–184.

———. "The Influence of Gender and Race Status on Self-Esteem During Childhood and Adolescence." In Zack, *RACE/SEX,* 109–116.

Hill, Jason, D. *Becoming a Cosmopolitan: What It Means to be a Human Being in the New Millennium.* Lanham, MD: Rowman and Littlefield, 2000.

Hine, Darlene Clark. *Black Women in America: An Historical Encyclopedia.* 2 vols. Brooklyn, NY: Carlson, 1993.

Hines, P., and L. Berg-Cross. "Racial Differences in Global Self-Esteem." *Journal of Social Psychology* 113 (1981): 271–281.

Hollinger, David A. "Amalgamation and Hypodescent: The Question of Ethnoracial Mixture in the History of the United States." *American Historical Review,* 108:5 (December 2003): 1363–1390.

Holmstrom, Nancy. "Do Women Have a Distinct Nature?" In *Women and Values: Readings in Recent Feminist Philosophy,* ed. Marjorie Pearsall. Belmont, CA: Wadsworth, 1986. [Reprinted from *Philosophical Forum* 14, no. 1 (Fall 1982): 25–42.]

———. "Race, Gender and Human Nature." In Zack, *RACE/SEX,* 95–108.

Hong, Maria. *Growing Up Asian American: An Anthology.* New York: William Morrow, 1993.

Hook, Sidney. *From Hegel to Marx.* Ann Arbor: University of Michigan Press, 1962.

hooks, bell. *Ain't I a Woman: Black Women and Feminism.* Boston: South End Press, 1981.

———. *Feminist Theory: From Margin to Center.* Boston: South End Press, 1984.

———. "Sisterhood: Political Solidarity Between Women." In *Feminist Philosophies,* ed. Janet Kourany, James Sterba, and Rosemarie Tong. Englewood Cliffs, NJ: Prentice-Hall, 1992.

Horne, Gerald. "On the Criminalization of a Race." *Political Affairs* 73, no. 2 (February 1994): 26–30.

Horsman, Reginald. *Race and Manifest Destiny.* Cambridge, MA: Harvard University Press, 1981.

Hossfeld, Karen. "Hiring Immigrant Women: Silicon Valley's 'Simple Formula.'" In Zinn and Dill, *Women of Color in U.S. Society,* 65–94.

Hull, Gloria T., et al., eds. *All the Women Are White, All the Blacks Are Men, but Some of Us Are Brave: Black Women's Studies.* New York: Feminist Press, 1982.

Hurley, Patrick J., and Joseph P. DeMarco, *Learning Fallacies and Arguments: A Multimedia Approach,* 7th ed. Belmont, CA: Wadsworth, 2001.

———. *A Concise Introduction to Logic with InfoTrace® and CD-Rom,* 8th ed. Belmont, CA: Wadsworth, 2003.

Ifekwunigwe, Jayne O. *"Mixed Race" Studies: A Reader.* New York: Routledge, 2004.

Ignatiev, Noel. *How the Irish Became White: Irish-Americans and African-Americans in 19th Century Philadelphia.* New York: Verso, 1995.

Ignatiev, Noel, and John Garvey, eds. *Race Traitor.* New York: Routledge, 1996.

Illinois Advisory Committee to the United States Commission on Civil Rights. *Civil Rights Issues Facing Asian Americans in Metropolitan Chicago.* Chicago: U.S. Commission on Civil Rights, 1995.

International Human Genome Sequencing Consortium. "Initial Sequencing and Analysis of the Human Genome." *Nature,* February 15, 2001, 860–892.

Jablonski, Nina, and George Chaplin. "The Evolution of Human Skin Coloration." *Journal of Human Evolution* 39 no. 1. In July (2000): 57–106.

Jagger, Alison M., ed. *Living with Contradictions: Controversies in Feminist Social Ethics.* Boulder, CO: Westview Press, 1994.

Jaimes, M. Annette. "Some Kind of Indian." In Zack, *American Mixed Race,* 133–154.

Jaimes, M. Annette, ed. *The State of Native America.* Boston: South End Press, 1992.

Jaynes, Gerald D. *Immigration and Race: New Challenges for American Democracy.* New Haven, CT: Yale University Press, 2000.

Johnson, Allen G. *Privilege, Power and Difference.* New York: McGraw-Hill, 2001.

Johnson, Kevin R. *How Did You Get to Be Mexican: A White/Brown Man's Search for Identity.* Philadelphia: Temple University Press, 1999.

Johnson, Kevin R., ed. *Mixed Race America and the Law: A Reader.* New York: New York University Press, 2003.

Jones, L. *Bulletproof Diva: Tales of Race, Sex, and Hair.* New York: Doubleday, 1994.

Jones, Maldwyn Allen. *American Immigration.* Chicago: University of Chicago Press, 1960.

Kang, Connie K. *Home Was the Land of Morning Calm: A Saga of a Korean American Family.* Reading, MA: Addison-Wesley, 1995.

Kellough, J. Edward. "Affirmative Action in Government Employment." *The Annals* 523 (September 1992): 117–130.

Kerner Report on Civil Disorders, Supplemental Studies for the National Advisory Commission on Civil Disorders. New York: Praeger, 1968. (See also Assembly on the Kerner Report Revisited, Monticello, IL, 1970; *The Kerner Report Revisited.* Urbana, IL: Institute of Government and Public Affairs, University of Illinois, 1970.)

Kibria, Nazli. "Migration and Vietnamese American Women: Remaking Ethnicity." In Zinn and Dill, *Women of Color in U.S. Society,* 247–264.

———. *Becoming Asian American: Second Generation Chinese and Korean American Identities.* Baltimore: Johns Hopkins University Press, 2003.

Kingston, Maxine Hong. *The Woman Warrior.* New York: Vintage, 1989.

Kovel, Joel. *White Racism: A Psychohistory.* London: Free Association, 1988.

Kozol, Jonathan. *Savage Inequalities: Children in American Schools*. New York: Crown, 1991.

Krupat, Arnold, ed. *Native American Autobiography: An Anthology*. Madison: University of Wisconsin Press, 1994.

Kuhl, Stefan. *The Nazi Connection: Eugenics, American Racism, and German National Socialism*. New York: Oxford University Press, 1994.

Kuhn, Thomas S. *The Structure of Scientific Revolutions*. Chicago: University of Chicago Press, 1970.

Kuper, Leo, ed. *Race, Science and Society*. New York: Columbia University Press, 1965.

Kymlicka, Will, ed. *The Rights of Minority Cultures*. Oxford: Oxford University Press, 1995.

Lahr, John. "Escaping the Matrix: The Making of Laurence Fishburne." *The New Yorker,* April 5, 2004, 46–57.

Lang, Berel. *Act and Idea in the Nazi Genocide*. Chicago: University of Chicago Press, 1990.

———. "Metaphysical Racism." In Zack, *RACE/SEX,* 17–28.

Lang, Berel, ed. *Race and Racism in Theory and Practice*. Lanham, MD: Rowman and Littlefield, 2000.

Laquer, Thomas. *Making Sex: Body and Gender from the Greeks to Freud*. Cambridge, MA: Harvard University Press, 1990.

Lawrence, Cecile Ann. "Racelessness." In Zack, *American Mixed Race,* 299–307.

Lawson, Bill E., ed. *The Underclass Question*. Philadelphia: Temple University Press, 1992.

Leong, Russell. *Asian American Sexualities: Dimensions of the Gay and Lesbian Experience*. New York: Routledge, 1996.

Lesley, Craig, ed. *Talking Leaves: Contemporary Native American Short Stories*. New York: Dell, 1991.

Levine, Lawrence W. *Highbrow/Lowbrow: The Emergence of Cultural Hierarchy in America*. Cambridge, MA: Harvard University Press, 1988.

Levine, Michael P., and Tamas Pataki, eds. *Racism in Mind*. Ithaca, NY: Cornell University Press, 2004.

Lewontin, Richard C., Steven Rose, and Leon J. Kamin. *Not in Our Genes*. New York: Pantheon Books, 1984.

Ling, Amy. *Between Worlds: Women Writers of Chinese Ancestry*. New York: Pergamon Press, 1990.

Locke, John. "Some Thoughts Concerning Education." In *The Educational Writings of John Locke,* ed. James A. Axtell. Cambridge, UK: Cambridge University Press, 1968.

———. *Two Treatises of Government,* ed. Peter Laslett. Cambridge, UK: Cambridge University Press, 1991.

Lopez, Ian F. Haney. *White by Law: The Legal Construction of Race*. New York: New York University Press, 1996.

Lorde, Audre. *Sister Outsider*. Trumansburg, NY: Crossing Press, 1984.

———. "The Uses of Anger: Women Responding to Racism." In Minas, *Gender Basics,* 39–44.

Lott, Tommy L. *The Invention of Race: Black Culture and the Politics of Representation*. Malden, MA: Blackwell, 1999.

Lott, Tommy L., ed. *Subjugation and Bondage: Critical Essays on Slavery and Social Philosophy.* Lanham, MD: Rowman and Littlefield, 1998.

Loury, Glenn C. "Self-Censorship in Public Discourse." In *One by One from the Inside Out,* ed. Glenn Loury. New York: Free Press, 1995.

———. *The Anatomy of Racial Inequality.* Cambridge, MA: Harvard University Press, 2002.

Lyden, Fremont J., and Lyman H. Legters, eds. *Native Americans and Public Policy.* Pittsburgh: University of Pittsburgh Press, 1992.

Ma, Sheng-Mei. *The Deathly Embrace: Orientalism and Asian American Identity.* Minneapolis: University of Minnesota Press, 2000.

Macdonald, Andrew. *The Turner Diaries.* Hillsboro, VA: National Vanguard Books, 1978.

MacPherson, C. B. *The Political Theory of Possessive Individualism.* Oxford: Oxford University Press, 1970.

Malcolm X. *The Autobiography of Malcolm X* (as told to Alex Haley). New York: Ballantine, 1973.

Marchetti, Gina. *Romance and 'The Yellow Peril': Race, Sex and Discursive Strategies in Hollywood Fiction.* Chicago: University of Chicago Press, 1993.

Martin, Waldo E., Jr. *The Mind of Frederick Douglass.* Chapel Hill, NC: University of North Carolina Press, 1984.

Martinez, Ruben, and Richard L. Dukes. "Ethnic and Gender Differences in Self Esteem." *Youth and Society* 22, no. 3 (March 1991): 318–338.

Marx, Karl, and Frederick Engels. "The Communist Manifesto." In *Karl Marx, Selected Writings,* ed. Lawrence H. Simon. Indianapolis: Hackett, 1994.

Mathews, Jay. "The Bias Question." *Atlantic Monthly,* November 2003, 131–139.

Matsuda, Mari, Charles R. Lawrence, and Kimberle Williams Crenshaw. *Words That Wound: Critical Race Theory, Assaultive Speech, and the First Amendment.* Boulder, CO: Westview Press, 1993.

Matthiessen, Peter. *Indian Country.* New York: Viking, 1992.

McBride, James. *The Color of Water: A Black Man's Tribute to His White Mother.* New York: Riverhead Books, 1996.

McClintock, Anne, Jose Esteban Muñoz, and Trish Rosen, eds. *Race and Queer Sexuality.* Durham: Duke University Press. 3–4 (1997).

McCord, David, and William Cleveland. *Black and Red: The Historical Meeting of Africans and Native Americans.* Atlanta: Dreamkeeper Press, 1990.

McGary, Howard. "Alienation and the African-American Experience." In Pittman, *African-American Perspectives and Philosophical Traditions,* 282–296.

———. *Race and Social Justice.* London: Blackwell, 1999.

McIntosh, Peggy. "White Privilege and Male Privilege: A Personal Account of Coming to See Correspondences Through Work in Women's Studies." In Minas, *Gender Basics*, 30–38.

Means, Russell. "Same Old Song." In Churchill, *Marxism and Native Americans,* 19–33.

Mencke, John G. *Mulattoes and Race Mixture: American Attitudes and Images, 1865–1918.* Ann Arbor: University Microfilms Inc. Research Press, 1979.

Mendieta, Eduardo, ed. *Latin American Philosophy: Currents, Issues, Debates.* Bloomington: Indiana University Press, 2003.

Michaels, Walter Benn. *Our America: Nativism, Modernism, and Pluralism.* Durham, NC: Duke University Press, 1995.

———. "Race into Culture: A Critical Genealogy of Cultural Identity." In Appiah and Gates, *Identities,* 32–62.

———. "Diversity's False Solace." *New York Times Magazine,* April 11, 2004.

Miles, Kevin Thomas. "Body Badges: Race and Sex." In Zack, *RACE/SEX,* 133–144.

Mill, John Stuart. *On Liberty.* Indianapolis: Hackett, 1978.

Mills, Charles. *The Racial Contract.* Ithaca, NY: Cornell University Press, 1997.

Minas, Anne, ed. *Gender Basics.* Belmont, CA: Wadsworth, 1993.

Momaday, N. Scott. *House of Dawn.* New York: Harper and Row, 1968.

Montagu, Ashley. *Man's Most Dangerous Myth: The Fallacy of Race.* Cleveland: World, 1964.

———. *The Concept of Race.* London: Collier Books, 1969.

Moody-Adams, Michelle. "Race, Class, and the Social Construction of Self-Respect." In Pittman, *African-American Perspectives and Philosophical Traditions,* 251–266.

Morrison, Toni. *The Bluest Eye.* New York: Washington Square, 1970.

Morrison, Toni, ed. *Race-ing Justice, En-gendering Power: Essays on Anita Hill, Clarence Thomas and the Construction of Social Reality.* New York: Pantheon Books, 1992.

Nabokov, Peter, ed. *Native American Testimony: A Chronicle of Indian-White Relations from Prophecy to the Present.* New York: Penguin Books, 1991.

Nelson, Hilde Lindemann, ed. *Feminism and Families.* New York: Routledge, 1996.

Newton, Lisa H. "Reversed Discrimination as Unjustified." In Jagger, *Living with Contradictions,* 62–65.

Nicholson, Linda. *Gender and History.* New York: Columbia University Press, 1986.

———. "The Myth of the Traditional Family." In Nelson, *Feminism and Families,* 27–42.

Nobles, Wade W., and Goddard L. Lawford. *Understanding the Black Family.* Oakland, CA: Institute for the Advanced Study of Black Family Life and Culture, 1984.

Noonan, Harold W. *Personal Identity.* London: Routledge, 1989.

Novick, Michael. *White Lies, White Power: The Fight Against White Supremacy and Reactionary Violence.* Monroe, ME: Common Courage, 1995.

Omi, Michael, and Howard Winant. *Racial Formation in the United States: From the 1960s to the 1980s.* New York: Routledge & Kegan Paul, 1986.

Outlaw, Lucius T. *On Race and Philosophy.* New York: Routledge, 1996.

Pierpoint, Claudia Roth. "The Measure of America: How a Rebel Anthropologist Waged War on Racism." *The New Yorker,* March 8, 2004, 48–63.

Pittman, John P. "Malcolm X: Masculinist Practice and Queer Theory." In Zack, *RACE/SEX,* 205–217.

Pittman, John P., ed. *African-American Perspectives and Philosophical Traditions.* New York: Routledge, 1996.

Plato. *The Republic.* Trans. Desmond Lee. New York: Penguin, 1987.

Putnam, Emily James. *The Lady: Studies of Certain Significant Phases of Her History.* Chicago: University of Chicago Press, 1970.

Rauch, Jonathan. "The Humanitarian Threat." In *Today's Moral Issues: Classic and Contemporary Perspectives,* ed. Daniel Bonevac, 135–148. Mountain View, CA: Mayfield, 1995.

Riccucci, Norma M. "Merit, Equity, and Test Validity." *Administration and Society* 23, no. 1 (May 1991): 74–93.

Ridgeway, James. *Blood in the Face.* New York: Thundermouth Press, 1990.

Riggs, Marlon. "Sexuality, Television, and Death: A Black Gay Dialogue on Malcolm X." In *Malcolm X: In Our Own Image,* ed. Joe Wood. New York: Doubleday, 1992.

Roberts, Rodney C., ed. *Injustice and Rectification.* New York: Peter Lang, 2002.

Rodriguez, Richard. *Hunger of Memory: The Education of Richard Rodriguez.* Boston: David R. Godine, 1981.

Roediger, David R. *The Wages of Whiteness: Race and the Making of the American Working Class.* London: Verso, 1992.

Root, Maria P. P. "A Bill of Rights for Racially Mixed People." In Root, *The Multiracial Experience,* 3–14.

———. "The Multiracial Contribution to the Psychological Browning of America." In Zack, *American Mixed Race,* 231–236.

Root, Maria P. P., ed. *Racially Mixed People in America.* Newbury Park, CA: Sage, 1993.

———. *The Multiracial Experience: Racial Borders as the New Frontier.* Thousand Oaks, CA: Sage, 1996.

Roth, Henry. *Call It Sleep.* New York: Cooper Square, 1970.

Rothenberg, Paula S., ed. *White Privilege: Essential Readings on the Other Side of Racism.* New York: Worth, 2002.

Russell, Kathy, Midge Wilson, and Ronald Hall. *The Color Complex: The Politics of Skin Color Among African Americans.* New York: Harcourt Brace Jovanovich, 1992.

Said, Edward. *Orientalism.* New York: Random House, 1978.

Sartre, Jean-Paul. *Anti-Semite and Jew.* New York: Schocken Books, 1948.

Sartwell, Crispin. *Act Like You Know: African-American Autobiography and White Identity.* Chicago: University of Chicago Press, 1998.

Scales-Trent, Judy. *Notes of a White Black Woman.* University Park: Pennsylvania State University Press, 1995.

Scheik, William J. *The Half-Blood: A Cultural Symbol in 19th-Century American Fiction.* Lexington: University Press of Kentucky, 1979.

Schusky, Ernest L. *The Right to Be Indian.* San Francisco: American Indian Educational Publishers, 1970.

Schutte, Ofelia. *Cultural Identity and Social Liberation in Latin American Thought.* Albany: State University of New York Press, 1993.

Shipler, David K. *The Working Poor: Invisible in America.* New York: Alfred E. Knopf, 2004.

Shrage, Laurie. *Moral Dilemmas of Feminism: Prostitution, Adultery, and Abortion.* New York: Routledge, 1994.

———. "Ethnic Transgressions: Confessions of an Assimilated Jew." In Zack, *American Mixed Race,* 287–296.

———. "Passing Beyond the Other Race or Sex." In Zack, *RACE/SEX,* 183–190.

Sidel, Ruth. *Women and Children Last: The Plight of Poor Women in Affluent America.* New York: Penguin Books, 1992.

Singer, L. "Ethnogenesis and Negro-Americans Today." *Social Research* 29, no. 4 (Winter 1962): 419–432.

Sleeter, C. E., ed. *Empowerment Through Multicultural Education.* Albany: State University of New York Press, 1991.

Smith, Adam. *Wealth of Nations: An Inquiry into the Nature and Causes of the Wealth of Nations.* 2 vols. Ed. H. H. Cambell, A. S. Skinner, and W. B. Todd. Oxford: Clarendon Press, 1976.

Sollors, Werner, ed. *Theories of Ethnicity: A Classical Reader.* New York: New York University Press, 1996.

Sowell, Thomas. *The Economics and Politics of Race: An International Perspective.* New York: William Morrow, 1983.

———. *Civil Rights: Rhetoric or Reality?* New York: William Morrow, 1984.

Spelman, Elizabeth V. *Inessential Woman: Problems of Exclusion in Feminist Thought.* Boston: Beacon Press, 1988.

Spencer, Rainier. *Spurious Issues: Race and Multiracial Identity Politics in the United States.* Boulder, CO: Westview Press, 1999.

Spickard, Paul R. *Mixed Blood: Intermarriage and Ethnic Identity in Twentieth Century America.* Madison: University of Wisconsin Press, 1989.

Spickard, Paul R., and W. Jeffrey Burroughs, eds. *We Are a People: Narrative and Multiplicity in Constructing Ethnic Identity (Asian American History and Culture).* Philadelphia: Temple University Press, 2000.

Squire-Hakey, Mariella. "Yankee Imperialism and Imperialist Nostalgia." In Zack, *American Mixed Race,* 221–229.

Stanton, William. *The Leopard's Spots: Scientific Attitudes Toward Race in America, 1819–59.* Chicago: University of Chicago Press, 1960.

Statistical Record of Asian Americans. Detroit, MI: Gale Research, 1993.

Statistical Record of Black Americans. Detroit, MI: Gale Research, 1990.

Statistical Record of Native North Americans. Detroit, MI: Gale Research, 1993.

Steinberg, Steven. *The Ethnic Myth.* Boston: Beacon Press, 1989.

Stepan, Nancy Leys. *The Idea of Race in Science: Great Britain, 1800–1950.* London: Archon Books, 1982.

———. "Race and Gender: The Role of Analogy in Science." In Goldberg, *Anatomy of Racism,* 38–57.

Sterba, James P. *Contemporary Social and Political Philosophy.* Belmont, CA: Wadsworth, 1995.

———. "Racism and Sexism: The Common Ground." In Zack, *RACE/SEX,* 61–74.

Stevens, Evelyn P. "Marianismo: The Other Face of Machismo in Latin America." In Minas, *Gender Basics,* 483–490.

Stone, Lawrence. *The Family, Sex and Marriage in England, 1500–1800.* New York: Harper and Row, 1979.

Stowe, David. "*Un*colored People: The Rise of Whiteness Studies." *Lingua Franca* (September/October 1996): 68–77.

Streeter, Caroline A. "Ambiguous Bodies: Locating Black/White Women in Cultural Representations." In Root, *The Multiracial Experience,* 305–322.

Stuart, I., and L. Abt, eds. *Interracial Marriage: Expectations and Realities.* New York: Grossman, 1973.

Sundquist, Åsebrit. *Pocahontas & Co.: The Fictional American Indian Woman in Nineteenth-Century Literature: A Study of Method.* Atlantic Highlands, NJ: Humanities Press International, 1987.

Takaki, Ronald. *Strangers from a Different Shore: A History of Asian Americans.* New York: Penguin Books, 1989.

Tatum, Beverly Daniel. *"Why Are All the Black Kids Sitting Together in the Cafeteria?" And Other Conversations About Race.* New York: Basic Books, 1997.

Tedlock, Dennis, and Barbara Tedlock, eds. *Teachings from the American Earth.* New York: Liveright, 1975.

Tenzer, L. R. *A Completely New Look at Interracial Sexuality: Public Opinion and Select Commentaries.* Manahawkin, NJ: Scholar's Publishing House, 1990.

Tessman, Lisa, and Bat-Ami Bar On, eds. *Jewish Locations.* Lanham, MD: Rowman and Littlefield, 2001.

Thernstrom, Stephen, ed. *Harvard Encyclopedia of American Ethnic Groups.* Cambridge, MA: Belknap Press of Harvard University Press, 1980.

Thomas, Laurence. "Sexism and Racism: Some Conceptual Differences." *Ethics* 90 (1980): 239–250.

———. "Moral Flourishing in an Unjust World." *Journal of Moral Education* 22, no. 2 (1993): 83–96.

———. "Moral Deference." In Pittman, *African-American Perspectives and Philosophical Traditions,* 233–250.

———. *Vessels of Evil.* Philadelphia: Temple University Press, 1993.

Thomson, Judith Jarvis. *The Realm of Rights.* Cambridge, MA: Harvard University Press, 1990.

Thornton, Russell. *American Indian Holocaust Survival: A Population History Since 1492.* Norman: University of Oklahoma Press, 1987.

Twain, Mark. *The Tragedy of Pudd'nhead Wilson.* New York: Norton, 1980.

United Nations Charter: The Universal Declaration of Human Rights, reprinted in *Vice and Virtue in Everyday Life,* ed. Christina Sommers and Fred Sommers, 203–209. Fort Worth, TX: Harcourt Brace, 1993.

U.S. Bureau of the Census. *Characteristics of the Population.* Vol. 1, Part 1, Sections 1 and 2. Washington, DC: Government Printing Office, 1970.

U.S. Bureau of the Census. *Census of Population: General Population Characteristics— United States.* Vol. 1990 CP-1-1. Washington, DC: Government Printing Office, 1990.

Vaz, Kim Marie, ed., *Black Women in America.* Thousand Oaks, CA: Sage, 1995.

Wacker, R. Fred. *Ethnicity, Pluralism and Race.* Westwood, CT: Greenwood, 1983.

Walker, Alice. *In Search of Our Mothers' Gardens.* New York: Harcourt Brace Jovanovich, 1983.

Walters, Anne Schulherr. "That Alchemical Bering Strait Theory! Or Introducing America's Indigenous Sovereign Nations' Worldviews to Informal Logic Courses." In Zack, *Women of Color and Philosophy,* 152–157.

———. *American Indian Thought: Philosophical Essays.* Malden, MA: Blackwell, 2003.

Walzer, Michael. "Pluralism: A Political Perspective." In Kymlicka, *The Rights of Minority Cultures,* 139–154.

Waters, Mary C. *Black Identities: West Indian Dreams and American Realities.* Cambridge, MA: Harvard University Press, 1999.

Wautischer, Helmut, ed. *Tribal Epistemologies: Essays in the Philosophy of Anthropology.* Brookfield, VT: Ashgate, 1998.

Webster, Yehudi O. *The Racialization of America.* New York: St. Martin's Press, 1992.

———. *Against the Multicultural Agenda: A Critical Thinking Alternative.* Westport, CT: Praeger, 1997.

West, Cornel. *Race Matters.* Boston: Beacon Press, 1993.

Westra, Laura, and Peter S. Wenz, eds. *Faces of Environmental Racism.* Lanham, MD: Rowman and Littlefield, 1995.

Wiesner, Merry E. *Women and Gender in Early Modern Europe.* Cambridge, UK: Cambridge University Press, 1993.

Williams, Patricia J. *The Alchemy of Race and Rights.* Cambridge, MA: Harvard University Press, 1991.

———. *The Rooster's Egg: On the Persistence of Prejudice.* Cambridge, MA: Harvard University Press, 1995.

Williamson, Joel. *New People.* New York: Free Press, 1980.

Willie, C. V. *Oreo: Race and Marginal Men and Women.* Wakefield, MA: Parameter Press, 1975.

Wilson, Robin. "A Kinder, Less Ambitious Professoriate," *Chronicle of Higher Education,* November 8, 2002, 10–11.

Wilson, Terry P. "Blood Quantum: Native American Mixed Bloods." In Root, *Racially Mixed People in America,* 108–125.

Wilson, William Julius. *The Truly Disadvantaged.* Chicago: University of Chicago Press, 1987.

———. "Studying Inner-City Social Dislocations: The Challenge of Public Agenda Research." *American Sociological Review* 56 (February 1991): 10.

Wolfman, Brunetta. "Color Fades over Time." In Zack, *American Mixed Race,* 13–24.

Wray, Matt, and Annalee Newitz, eds. *White Trash: Race and Class.* New York: Routledge, 1997.

Wright, Richard. *The Outsider.* New York: Harper and Row, 1953.

———. *Black Power: A Record of Reactions in a Land of Pathos.* New York: Harper and Brothers, 1954.

Young, Iris Marion. *Justice and the Politics of Difference.* Princeton, NJ: Princeton University Press, 1990.

Zack, Naomi. *Race and Mixed Race.* Philadelphia: Temple University Press, 1993.

———. "Life After Race." In *American Mixed Race,* 297 308.

———. "Mixed Black and White Race and Public Policy," *Hypatia* (Feminist Ethics and Social Policy, Part I), vol. 1, no. 1 (Winter 1995): 120–132.

———. *Bachelors of Science: Seventeenth Century Identity, Then and Now.* Philadelphia: Temple University Press, 1996.

———. "On Being and Not-Being Black and Jewish." In Root, *The Multiracial Experience,* 140–151.

———. " 'The Family' and Radical Family Theory." In Nelson, *Feminism and Families,* 43–53.

———. "The American Sexualization of Race." In Zack, *RACE/SEX,* 29–44.

———. "Race and Philosophic Meaning." In Zack, *RACE/SEX,* 145–156.

———. "Descartes' Awake-Asleep Distinction and Realism." In Zack, *Women of Color and Philosophy,* 280–302.

——. "American Mixed Race: Theoretical and Legal Issues," *Harvard BlackLetter Law Journal* 17 (Spring 2001): 33–46.

——. "Philosophical Aspects of the 1998 AAA [American Anthropological Association] Statement of Race." *Anthropological Theory* 1, no. 4 (2001): 445–465.

——. *Philosophy of Science and Race*. New York: Routledge, 2002.

——. "Race and Racial Discrimination." In *Oxford Handbook of Practical Ethics*, ed. Hugh Lafollette, 245–271. New York: Oxford University Press, 2002.

——. "Reparations and the Rectification of Race." *Journal of Ethics,* Special issue, *Race, Racism and Reparations* 3 (2003): 139–151.

——. *Inclusive Feminism: A Third Wave Theory of Women's Commonality*. Lanham, MD: Rowman and Littlefield, 2005.

Zack, Naomi, ed. *American Mixed Race: The Culture of Microdiversity*. Lanham, MD: Rowman and Littlefield, 1995.

——. *RACE/SEX: Their Sameness, Difference and Interplay*. New York: Routledge, 1997.

——. *Women of Color and Philosophy: A Critical Reader*. Malden, MA: Blackwell, 2000.

Zack, Naomi, Laurie Shrage, and Crispin Sartwell, eds. *Race, Class, Gender, and Sexuality: The Big Questions*. Malden, MA: Blackwell, 1998.

INDEX

Note: terms that are in boldface in text and defined in glossary are followed by **g.** Full citations of books listed here and in Recommended Reading sections are in the Bibliography.